PRAISE FOR SHARE YOUR JOURNEY

and

PAUL'S PERSONAL WRITING WORKSHOPS

From Professional Writers and Writing Teachers

"*Share Your Journey* is to good writing as *Joy of Cooking* is to good food. I wish all my students had this book before taking my writing classes; hell, I wish I had this book earlier in my career. It's smart, fun, and every page contains nuggets of essential advice."

–Gary Goshgarian, professor, Northeastern University;
As Gary Braver, bestselling and award-winning author of *Tunnel Vision*

"If I had to parachute only one book to a Robinson Crusoe-type stranded on a deserted island who wanted to write his personal story, I have no doubt it would be Paul Sochaczewski's *Share Your Journey: Mastering Personal Writing*. The tool kit Paul offers allows the person with a story and some raw talent to build a word castle that rises to the heavens."

–Christopher G. Moore, author of the Vincent Calvino novels and *Heart Talk*

"Before I became a journalist, Paul had shown me how to write a convincing personal travel piece, something that both tells a good story and connects well with the reader. This was a breakthrough for me; the resulting article, about a quirky Indonesian theater group, led to my first appearance in the major mainline press – the *Wall Street Journal*. His good advice helped place this piece, which in turn helped me land a foreign correspondent's position in Asia with a Dow Jones-owned newsweekly. I'm delighted that Paul's wisdom and sense of humor animate his new book, *Share Your Journey*. Many major writers have offered advice – think of John Steinbeck, William Safire, or George Orwell – but Paul's Ten Tips, buttressed by some great to-the-point examples, will stand among the best advice a nonfiction writer can ever hope to have."

–James Clad, former professor at Georgetown University and Johns Hopkins University;
former *Far Eastern Economic Review* bureau chief in Malaysia, India, and the Philippines;
former US assistant secretary of defense; author of *Behind the Myth: Business, Money and Power in Southeast Asia*

"I had just completed a new book and was pleased with it, until I read *Share Your Journey* and realized how I could make it better. Many writing guides turn what should be a liberating experience into drudgery and scolding rules. *Share Your Journey* is different; it helps you unleash an inner voice you may not have realized was inside you. It's also great fun. As a writer of fiction and biography infused with personal travel, I appreciate its originality and power. I wish many of the fellow writers I review would adapt its suggestions!"

—Nigel Barley, author of *Island of Dreams*, *White Rajah*, and *In the Footsteps of Stamford Raffles*

"Paul Sochaczewski learned his craft slowly and carefully over a period of decades and he now shares the secrets to why he's successful in a book. Based on his writing workshops, he offers ten simple and obvious but too often overlooked guidelines, then amply illustrates each with samples from his own works and a library full of other writers (many of them household names), demonstrating how easily it can be done."

—Jerry Hopkins, former editor of *Rolling Stone* and bestselling author of *No One Here Gets Out Alive*, *Bangkok Babylon*, *Elvis: The Biography*, and *Romancing the East*

"In *Share Your Journey* Paul Sochaczewski immediately seduces the reader to enter a land of exotic literary chocolates, emeralds, and hallucinatory dreams. In his professional wandering, teaching writing to the world, he has also amassed enough *mots* — both *bon* and *mal* — to create this enticing volume. Like all serious writers, Sochaczewski has no hesitation mixing the wit with the chaff. He notes the importance of zest and gusto in the great Ray Bradbury's writing "secret" … and he provides examples of published rubbish, real junk writing that has been published in *The New York Times* and other high-standard outlets, and points out why they fail and how they could have been done better. All these examples have a purpose, are wonderfully relevant, and provide the meat and potatoes for Sochaczewski's Ten Writing Tips. Want more? Searching for the Holy Grail (yes, he reminds us, you are on a hero's journey) of personal expression? Sochaczewski actually provides the single sentence that guarantees the writer will actually learn Writing. Like the *Theory of Natural Selection*, developed by his spiritual mentor Alfred Russel Wallace, the three-word instruction is blazingly obvious. This book is caviar for those who long to express themselves."

—Harry Rolnick, author of *The Chinese Gourmet*, *The Complete Book of Coffee*, and *Spice Chronicles: Exotic Tales of a Hungry Traveler*

"If you want to write, if you want to improve your writing, if you want your writing to leap off the page and click its heels in mid-air, read this book and follow its good advice. This is a lifetime's wisdom, offered by a pro."

–Thomas Bass, author of *The Spy Who Loved Us*, *Vietnamerica*, and *The Predictors*;
professor of English and journalism at State University of New York

"As publisher of Moon Publications for seventeen years, I worked with scores of writers to produce award-winning guidebooks to countries and regions around the world. *Share Your Journey* is an invaluable aid to all writers wishing to discover their voices and effectively connect to their readers."

–Bill Dalton, author of *Indonesia Handbook*

"Many writing-advice books *tell* you how to write but don't *show* you how to do it. This book fulfills the writing mantra, "show don't tell." It provides excellent examples of good as well as stilted writing. Sochaczewski does it with humour, cartoons, memorable visuals, and practical advice. The Ten Writing Tips are great signposts for anyone attempting to write a personal story. My particular favourite is *Cinema – Write like Steven Spielberg Directs*. I will recommend this book to my creative writing students."

–Josephine Chia, creative writing mentor in UK and Singapore;
author of *Frog Under a Coconut Shell* and *Kampong Spirit – Gotong Royong*

From Workshop Participants

"You are one of the most respectful, naturally honoring people I have ever met. When you teach you value every person and diminish no one. I have rarely seen such a dynamic, let alone the ability to sustain it over several days with a large number of people. Similarly, you can keep your own personality out of the way when need be; you actively stay engaged – even when the students' paragraphs could set snails to sleep. It is quite a rare gift to be a writing teacher and enhance the seeds of creativity and growth as you do and assist in the emergence of the writer's conscious expression. I found myself a witness to that extraordinary gift."

–*Lizee from Canada*

"With elegance, deep knowledge, and great generosity, Paul has taken me into story, catalyzing my own writing in a way I'd hoped for but was too scared really to expect. I'm thrilled I did this."

—Shelley from Australia

"Life changing event – I loved the layers and the learning that evolved."

—Virginia from Denmark

"Phenomenal! I learned so much, I was inspired. Very powerful and enjoyable. Paul was strict but supportive, and the participants soon got into the swing of helping each other achieve writing breakthroughs."

—Lynne from the UK

"A master teacher, combining information, humor, compassion, focus, and pushing people to stretch. The equivalent of two workshops in one."

—Philip from Indonesia

"The workshop was a marker moment for me, and thanks to your coaching I moved though a major writing barrier. I cannot thank you enough."

—George from Switzerland

"I was so pleased with the opportunity to work with you. You were professional, generous, and inspiring, and I got kicked back into action. You were so right; your key Ten Tips for good writing keep popping up everywhere. Your communication skills were superb, and I really respect your well thought out, yet flexible structure."

—Mary Jane from Singapore

"I very much appreciated all the valuable information, your patience, your empathy, your commitment, your critical thinking and sense of humor."

—David from the United States

"For twelve years I had intended to write about my experiences in Africa in the early 1990s, and so far I hadn't committed a single word to paper. Within days of attending Paul's workshop, I had written 2,500 words, was full of ideas, and couldn't wait to sit down at the keyboard and continue the story."

—Barry from Switzerland

"I both appreciated and enjoyed Paul's enlightened workshop, particularly his Ten Writing Tips. Being an engineer, my writing is typically dry and formal, far removed from personal travel writing. The course gave me priceless insights on how and where to start."

—*Colin from Thailand*

"An experience we will treasure for the rest of our lives – the warmth and dynamics were amazing. People left feeling incredibly good about themselves and each other and with the motivation to write – it was transformational, just as you said it should be."

—*Bronwen from New Zealand*

"Gave my creative muse a kick in the pants."

—*Dzeni from Singapore*

"It was as if it was predestined that I take this workshop. What I found a bit of a mind-blower was how much good stuff one can write in such short spaces of time. The workshop has given me confidence and unleashed a power and energy that tells me I can actually write."

—*Robin from Switzerland*

"Informative, useful, inspiring, and enjoyable, with many ideas for new ways to approach my writing."

—*Karin from Sweden*

"At first I was concerned because you were so strict and organized – you took care to set up the room beforehand, and got us to agree to put away our cell phones. You created a safe space and asked us to commit to respecting and supporting each other. And it worked – you promised us transformation and that's what happened. You didn't allow us to write bull. You combined the bad cop approach with a generosity of support and spirit that allowed me to flourish and find a writing voice I never knew I had."

—*Melanie from Ireland*

"'Too much psycho-babble in your head,' my husband said. Could writing become a reality for me? The advice in Paul's workshop was good for writing just about anything. His Ten Writing Tips worked; he shined a light on a path that dealt with my self-doubt and low self-esteem. A Cinderella slipper moment."

—*Jenny from the United States*

"Enjoyed it so much; well-planned and no letdown in the momentum. Plenty of 'movement.'"

—*Arunee from Thailand*

"Fantastic. My problem was that I didn't know how to start and you just fixed it. I loved the session of writing with music. I was so surprised that it could make my writing so much easier. Now I feel like I can write anything easily."

—*Ning from Thailand*

"Before I met Paul my only writing experience was the preparation of scientific research manuscripts. And with a profession that involves the editing of such manuscripts, I struggled to deviate from a cold, academic style. Paul has shown me how to tell my personal story and move from 'cold' to 'hot' while retaining my voice and factual content. Learning from him gave me the confidence to write my first article about my own personal journey, and later, to launch my own blog, which is something I never imagined I would have the courage to do."

—*Melissa from the UK*

"I enjoyed *Share Your Journey* so much – it was really refreshing to relearn the writing process and to get new knowledge/perspectives on writing through your Ten Writing Tips. I've started to write a story based on a recent event and am incorporating the scene elements and the cold-hot concept. I am one of those folks who is not comfortable using "I" in writing, and your book helped me overcome this blockage – so much more useful and fun than other nonfiction writing courses I've attended."

—*Mira from Indonesia*

"Paul has genuine warmth that shines out before the course even begins. He creates a relaxed and accepting atmosphere in which it's okay to experiment and have a very (very!) rough first draft. Paul was honest with us about our writing, but never in a way that bruised. Participants arrived from a variety of backgrounds and with a wide range of goals, but Paul worked to ensure we all got what we needed from the day."

—*Resli from the United States*

SHARE

YOUR

JOURNEY

SHARE YOUR JOURNEY

MASTERING PERSONAL WRITING

The (Surprisingly Easy) Techniques
Professional Writers Use to Write
Personal Memoirs and Travel Stories
That Connect with Editors and Readers

Paul Spencer Sochaczewski

EXPLORER'S EYE PRESS

GENEVA, SWITZERLAND

Published by
Explorer's Eye Press
Geneva, Switzerland
info@explorerseyepress.com

ISBN: 978-2-940573-16-5

Sincere thanks and respect to the many talented writers, artists, illustrators, cartoonists, and photographers who kindly gave permission to reprint their creations. These include: *New Yorker* (cartoons and texts); *The New York Times*/Pars International (texts and photo); Hearst Corporation (Beetle Bailey, Dennis the Menace); Universal Uclick (Doonesbury, Garfield, Calvin and Hobbes, Non-Sequitur, Peanuts); Ed Kashi/VII; James Morgan; Tom Gauld; Sony Music; Sarah Steenland; and Penguin Random House (Bill Bryson).

Every effort has been made to secure permissions to reprint excerpts, cartoons, and photographs included in this book. Any concerns should be reported to the publisher.

Cover photo: The Photo Fiend

Edited and designed by Stacey Aaronson
www.TheBookDoctorIsIn.com

Printed in the United States of America

To Monique, for being there.

∽

Dedicated to the magic that occurs
when the writer touches the reader.

∽

And a special thanks to friends who offered suggestions
on how to improve this book.

CONTENTS

∾

WRITING A PERSONAL STORY

Your family has been bugging you to write the story of how you quit medical school and found enlightenment in an Indian ashram. Or the story of how your spinster Aunt Edna became the world's first topless rodeo clown.

Perhaps you have an inner drive to tell folks about your trek in the Andes when you met the love of your life, or the time you contracted typhoid and were saved by a shaman in Vietnam.

Your quest might be big and life-changing, or small and silly. Doesn't matter. It's your journey and only you can tell it.

Congratulations. You're finally going to write your personal story. It might result in a blog. A year-end letter to the family. An article for the local newspaper. A family history. Regardless of the final format, the ideas in this book can help.

These tips are written primarily for writers creating personal essays, personal travel pieces, and family histories. These ideas will help you write what is commonly called creative nonfiction, or literary nonfiction; that is, a true story told in an interesting way (using the same techniques that the writer of a murder mystery uses to keep you up all night). Put another way, it's truth, well told, or as writer Lee Gutkind calls it, "the literature of reality." Some late twentieth-century proponents of creative nonfiction (although they didn't all use this term): Truman Capote, Tom Wolfe, Gay Talese, Norman Mailer, and Hunter S. Thompson.

While this book is oriented toward nonfiction, the Ten Writing Tips relate equally well to fiction.

Everyone has a personal story to tell.

Useful Advice from Someone Who Wrote Pretty Well

The article ["There Goes (Varoom! Varoom!) That Kandy-Kolored (Thphhhhhh!) Tangerine-Flake Streamline Baby (Rahghhh!) Around the Bend (Brummmmmmmmmmmmm)..."] was by no means like a short story, despite the use of scenes and dialogue ... It was a garage sale ... vignettes, odds and ends of scholarship, bits of memoir, short bursts of sociology, apostrophes, epithets, moans, cackles ... That was its virtue. It showed me the possibility of there being something "new" in journalism ... It was the discovery that it was possible in nonfiction, in journalism, to use any literary device, from the traditional dialogisms of the essay to stream-of-consciousness, and to use many different kinds simultaneously ... to excite the reader both intellectually and emotionally.

—Tom Wolfe and E.W. Johnson. *The New Journalism.* New York: Harper & Row, 1973.

_____

How to Use This Book

The suggestions in this book are based on my writing workshops. There is a structure, but you don't have to read this book sequentially. It's okay to pick an idea at random and run with it.

_____

The Basic Ground Rules

Writers who take my workshop confirm that these tips work. But that's all they are – suggestions. At the end of the day it's your name on the manuscript and you have to decide if my advice is right for you. All I ask is that if you find ideas that are intriguing, try them on, like a new pair of shoes. If they fit, take them home.

Recognizing these principles will change the way you write, read, watch TV. You'll be seeing Nancy Reagan conflicts, Little Red Riding Hood-influenced scenes, and Scheherazade-like teasers everywhere.

GETTING STARTED

The Power of Your Voice

You have one job as a writer:
Tell the story and get the reader to turn the page.

A COMMON LAMENT

"I've never written, I don't know how to start, nobody cares about what I say."

I hear it constantly, and my reply is generally:

There was a time in the life of every famous writer when she was inexperienced, uncertain, and in search of a meaningful voice. Writers do not magically emerge from a chrysalis in the form of a fully defined butterfly. Experienced and famous writers start off as beginners, pounding away at a keyboard, wondering if they will ever make a sale. Everybody starts out as a virgin. Then the fun begins.

Useful Advice from Someone Who Wrote Pretty Well

Yet if I were asked to name the most important items in a writer's make-up, the things that shape his material and rush him along the road to where he wants to go, I could only warn him to look to his zest, see to his gusto.

—Ray Bradbury

LOTS OF PEOPLE WANT TO WRITE, BUT DON'T

Let's say you want to record your family's history – how great-grandfather Ishmael skipped out of Lithuania hours before he was to be arrested for horse theft, or how Aunt Esmeralda defied her strict Mexico City parents and eloped with a gin-addled Colombian poet.

You (and each person you write about) are on a hero's journey.

As a result of your adventures you had an impact on people, and other people had an impact on you. Lives may have been changed, sometimes just a bit, sometimes dramatically.

People tell their personal stories all the time over a beer or holiday dinner table. Story *telling* comes naturally. So why then, should the act of *writing* a story be intimidating?

Worldwide it's the same. People aren't too sure how to start, what to say, how to focus, how to make it interesting for other people.

The basic problem is that these hesitant writers don't know how to begin. There's too much stuff in their heads. They become overwhelmed with options – paralysis by analysis. They're overwhelmed before they start because the perceived task is too big –

6

they convince themselves they have to write a book when all they really need to do is write a single scene.

HERE'S MY STORY

In one article very early in my career, I wrote about a trip to the Galapagos Islands in Ecuador. It was a straightforward chronological recounting of events, much like a series of journal entries. The article, published in *Silver Kris*, the in-flight magazine for Singapore Airlines, was flat. Same bland recipe for an article I wrote about a trip to Kashmir in northern India. I went here, I went there, I did this, I ate this. I spewed out text based on my journal notes. The article, in retrospect, lacked conflict, didn't have enough dialogue, was in need of a main theme, yet this story won a prize from the Pacific Asia Travel Association for reportage. Go figure.

At first we're all like kids in a candy store. We've had so many experiences, met so many interesting people, learned so much about ourselves and human nature, and are so infatuated by our own insights that we become overwhelmed by the choices available, so we tend to throw it all in.

So, what's a wannabe writer to do? To someone who's never written a personal story, asking him to write a book or article is a bit like telling a couch potato to go run a marathon. It ain't gonna happen. It's too daunting.

A beginner doesn't train to run a marathon by running a marathon. You train by running perhaps a kilometer a day for a few weeks, stretching, going to the gym, meeting other runners who have gone through the same thing, visualizing crossing the finish line.

HERE'S THE SECRET

In literary terms, the way through this Gordian Knot is to start with a manageable task. *Write a scene.* Just a single scene. A scene doesn't have to be long. It *does*, however, have to be important to you and to your story. Once you write the first scene, the rest is (relatively) straightforward.

**Useful Advice from Someone
Who Wrote Pretty Well**

If there is a magic in story writing, and I am convinced there is, no one has ever been able to reduce it to a recipe that can be passed from one person to another. The formula seems to lie solely in the aching urge of the writer to convey something he feels important to the reader ... You must perceive the excellence that makes a good story good or the errors that make a bad story. For a bad story is only an ineffective story.

—John Steinbeck

FIND YOUR VOICE

This book contains lots of recommended ingredients. But good writing, like good cooking or singing or lovemaking, goes beyond technique into the impossible-to-quantify realm of heart, imagination, passion, and experimentation.

This is another way of saying: Find Your Voice.

What is voice?

Voice refers to each person's unique style. It's usually used to describe a person's writing voice, but it also relates to physical and lifestyle attributes like the timbre of your speech; your posture, hairstyle, or clothes sense; whether you have bad breath or a good nose job; whether you are neat or tidy, gruff or polite. People have various voices, depending on the situation, but generally as a writer's career develops, a distinctive voice evolves, much like that of a composer or painter.

Without a distinctive voice your writing risks coming across as tone-deaf, the color of the ancient gray linoleum in your grandmother's kitchen.

Develop your voice, if you want to make contact with the reader.

The clearer a voice you have, the more some people will enjoy reading your work and say, "I don't know why, but I like the way she writes."

Shout. Whisper. Jitterbug. Caress. Intimidate. Philosophize. You've got plenty of voices, experiment to see which one works best. Write like a teenager. Take chances. Experiment until you find your comfort zone. As George Bernard Shaw said, "A life making mistakes is not only more honourable, but more useful than a life spent doing nothing at all."

∞

Here's a writer with a clear voice (which is eminently suitable for the publication):

> But it doesn't matter, because no one will be looking at him [the groom]. They'll be looking at the bride. It is far, far worse for her, because she has to wear "The Dress." The first bride to popularize white wedding dresses was Queen Victoria. She was a tiny, round, plain girl with a nose like a claw hammer and less chin than a terrapin. Charitably, the best thing you could say for her on her wedding day was that she looked like an ornamental toilet tissue cover. Before Victoria, brides wore what suited them ... Every bride is told repeatedly that she is breathtaking, but white is an unforgiving un-color unless you're a baby or a corpse ... Wedding dresses are a collective blind spot, an aesthetic dead zone. We are brainwashed to believe that a wedding dress is magic, that it has the ability to transform everyone into a raging, shaggable piece of hot, virginal, must-have, never-been-had gorgeousness. But, like all fairy spells, it only works for one day. In any other context, a wedding dress makes you look like a transvestite, which is presumably why the groom isn't allowed to see it before it's too late to change his mind.
>
> —A.A. Gill. "Can This Wedding Be Saved?" *Vanity Fair*. September 2012.

VOICE: A WARNING

Here's the big risk. *Not everyone will like your voice.* To some, your insights will be perceived as ill-informed, your jokes in poor taste (Hillary Clinton, Mother Teresa, and Marilyn Monroe walk into a bar ...), your style awkward, your observations of others simplistic, your opinion of yourself arrogant, your outlook on life naïve.

Take a writer like James Joyce, who had a voice so distinctive that it was impenetrable to the average reader.

Or consider Paul Theroux, arguably the most successful modern travel writer. Theroux writes true to his own voice and personality, and that's his strength. But not everyone loves him; a *New York Times* review of one of his books complained that "Theroux has never been overburdened by modesty. Although he has claimed that a prerequisite of traveling responsibly is avoiding arrogance, his previous travelogues have all been pungent with self-regard."

It's great to develop your own voice; but be aware that the more voice you have the easier it is for readers to either fall in love with you or stop reading. Connecting with the reader is part technique, part chemistry.

BE BRAVE WITH YOUR VOICE

Victorian naturalist Alfred Russel Wallace wrote a classic travel book that focused on his investigations into the biology and human societies of Southeast Asia. But he moved beyond cold scientific descriptions and took the chance to expose a bit of his own passion, a rather daring initiative for a man who wanted to be taken seriously as a serious scientist:

The beauty and brilliancy of this insect [a new species of bird-winged butterfly, more than 18 centimeters – seven inches – across the wings, which are velvety black and fiery orange] are indescribable, and none but a naturalist can understand the intense excitement I experienced when I at length captured it. On taking it out of my net and opening the glorious wings, my heart began to beat violently, the blood rushed to my head, and I felt much more like fainting than I have done when in apprehension of immediate death. I had a headache the rest of the day, so great was the excitement produced by what will appear to most people a very inadequate cause.

—Alfred Russel Wallace. *The Malay Archipelago*. London: MacMillan, 1859.

EXPLORE YOUR VOICE

An artist explores his voice constantly. Henri Matisse painted these three very different impressions of the Pont Saint-Michel using the same point of view (but different mental states) during a six-month period between 1900 and 1901.

Each artist has a unique voice. Explore yours.

HURT WOMAN, DONE THREE WAYS

How important is voice? Literature and music abound in stories of women done wrong. Listen to how different composers handled the theme of a hurt woman.

"Un Bel Dì"
Act II. *Madame Butterfly*. Music: Giacomo Puccini.
Libretto: Luigi Illica and Giuseppe Giacosa.

"Piece of My Heart"
First recorded by Erma Franklin, popularized by Big Brother and the Holding Company featuring Janis Joplin.
Written by Jerry Ragovoy and Bert Berns.

"I'm Gonna Wash That Man Right Outta My Hair"
South Pacific. Richard Rodgers and Oscar Hammerstein II.

Useful Advice from Someone Who Wrote Pretty Well

Rules, tips, and recommendations of famous writers are all fine. John Steinbeck wrote six guidelines, David Ogilvy ten, Elmore Leonard ten, Henry Miller eleven, Margaret Atwood ten, William Safire eighteen, Robert Heinlein five, and George Orwell six. But don't be afraid to ignore them and follow your own muse.

As Oscar Wilde said: "Consistency is the last refuge of the unimaginative."

Seek the *"wow."*

To Outline or Not to Outline?

Some writing coaches tell their students to outline their stories before they begin. This doesn't work for me – sometimes I don't know what my story is about until I begin to write it.

When I was in high school, I had a part-time job working as a stockboy in a combination drug store and liquor store. My job was to stock the shelves – cough syrup and Miller, vitamins and Canadian Club. On my first day at work, I went up and down the aisles compiling a list of what I needed to bring up from the storeroom in the basement. At the end of my two-hour stint, my boss asked me what I had accomplished. I showed him the list. "But the shelves are still empty," he said. "Don't confuse making a list with your real job, which is to replenish the stock."

Same thing with writing. Outlining (or making lists) can easily turn into procrastination. I suggest you just write the thing and see what evolves. You may have written a shaky story, but you will have written a story nevertheless. Then you can go back and rewrite it. For most people rewriting and editing are less intimidating activities than creating.

Creative Inspiration Isn't the Same as Creative Work

Creative Inspiration is figuring out the theme, finding your voice, determining who the main characters are, seeing if there are layers or messages. Creative Inspiration is writing the first draft, perhaps as quickly as you can, without worrying about the editor on your shoulder. Inspiration is figuring out what kind of building you want to design.

Creative Work is editing, revision, ax murder, rewriting, and eventually fine-tuning. Creative Work is seeing if your building design is functional, revising accordingly, and finally, choosing the curtains and table lamps.

You need to do both.

Your quest for Creative Inspiration might not be appreciated by those around you.

INVOKE HINDU GODS

Shiva   **Vishnu**

Put another way, Creative Inspiration is the personality of Shiva, who has the big ideas. Creative Work is the specialty of Vishnu, who makes sure the universe functions smoothly.

Hindu gods sometimes make goofy decisions. They are assertive and powerful, but exhibit human foibles. They make people beautiful yet they cause acne. They control the rhythm of life – when something seems to end, it's really just heralding the beginning of a new cycle.

And while you're at it, don't neglect Ganesha, the son of Shiva, who is the god of new ventures, literature, science, learning, and business. He opens doors and removes obstacles.

Ganesha

Sometimes Creative Work can be awfully difficult.

DON'T EVER DO THIS

DON'T BUY INTO THE "NO PAIN, NO GAIN" MINDSET

Most writing books tell the writer that she's engaged in a difficult, lonely, self-centered process. True, sometimes.

But I believe that we should also value writing that comes quickly, in a flow of energy. Gioachino Rossini claimed he wrote The Barber of Seville, today one of the world's most popular operas, in a twelve-day burst of creativity. Alfred Russel Wallace, who developed the Theory of Natural Selection, said, "I am a believer in inspiration. All my best ideas have come to me suddenly."

If you're not having fun writing this stuff, why should the reader have fun reading it? The energy you put in determines the energy the reader takes away. As Hemingway said: "When you stop doing things for fun, you might as well be dead."

Useful Advice from Someone Who Wrote Pretty Well

The secret of good cooking is, first, having a love of it ... If you're convinced that cooking is drudgery, you're never going to be good at it, and you might as well warm up something frozen.

—James Beard

The reader will sense the type of energy you put into a story.

Be magnanimous with your genius.

FIGURE OUT WHAT THE STORY'S ABOUT

A friend went to Ecuador on business and took a vacation in the Galapagos Islands. In just one paragraph of an email, he illuminated at least a half dozen ways to focus the story.

> Some of the interesting people I met and their intriguing stories – a German couple sailing around the world (they started their adventure sailing down the Danube into the Black sea), an Ecuadorian bed-and-breakfast owner who used to sing traditional songs in New York and San Francisco, a former deep-sea diver/charter boat owner/ pilot/skydiver and general raconteur, and a whole group of South Pacific islanders taking part in a year-long sailing adventure to popularize the need to conserve the oceans. In this last group, there were even a few Samoans who knew people I have dealt with in Apia (the world is getting quite small when I can meet people in the Galapagos with mutual colleagues in Samoa!).

> But he doesn't have a story yet – all he has are ideas, characters, and situations. So, what's his story about? Here are a few of the many directions my friend could take:

* Traveling broadens his world – he never would have met these folks if he had stayed in Geneva
* The joys of combining pleasure travel with a business trip
* Small world – what are the odds of meeting, in South America, Samoans with mutual friends?
* Wildlife experiences – swimming with fur seals
* Conservation efforts are effective/ineffective in the Galapagos
* The benefits of a good guide
* Surprise at how developed some of the islands are
* How to pick the best Galapagos cruise ship

... and so on. The point is that the writer may not know what the story is about until he writes it, and then the theme will emerge.

Kids, Try This at Home

········· MAKE A MIND MAP ········

Made popular by Tony Buzan, a mind map is a way of exploring directions your article might take. There are lots of ways to do this; probably best done with someone else asking probing questions and helping you see possible directions and links.

For example, on a big sheet of paper, start with a central theme or idea or situation. Then start surrounding the central theme with balloons that contain possible related ideas. The hope is that by getting all the possibilities on paper, one of them will jump out and say, "I'm your Big Idea, write me."

MIND MAPS IN ACTION

I visited the so-called Jumping Cat Monastery on Inle Lake in Burma. I found a bunch of cats, all named after celebrities, jumping through hoops. A trickle of tourists. Some bored monks. An architecturally important temple. Lots of oversized Buddha images. I then went to the Mount Popa area, some two hundred kilometers to the west, and was struck by the mystical vibes and sanctity of the place. Too many people living an abstract life compared to my regulated left-brain upbringing. But it wasn't all fluffy, mystical stuff for the monks, nor was it all logic and analysis for me. Shades of gray. Surprising life outlooks. Too much going on. How to put it all into a personal travel story? How could I relate all this to my reality (and that of the reader)?

I made a mind map that roughly looked like the one on the following page. Putting key points down in this way helped me structure the story and see what it's really about.

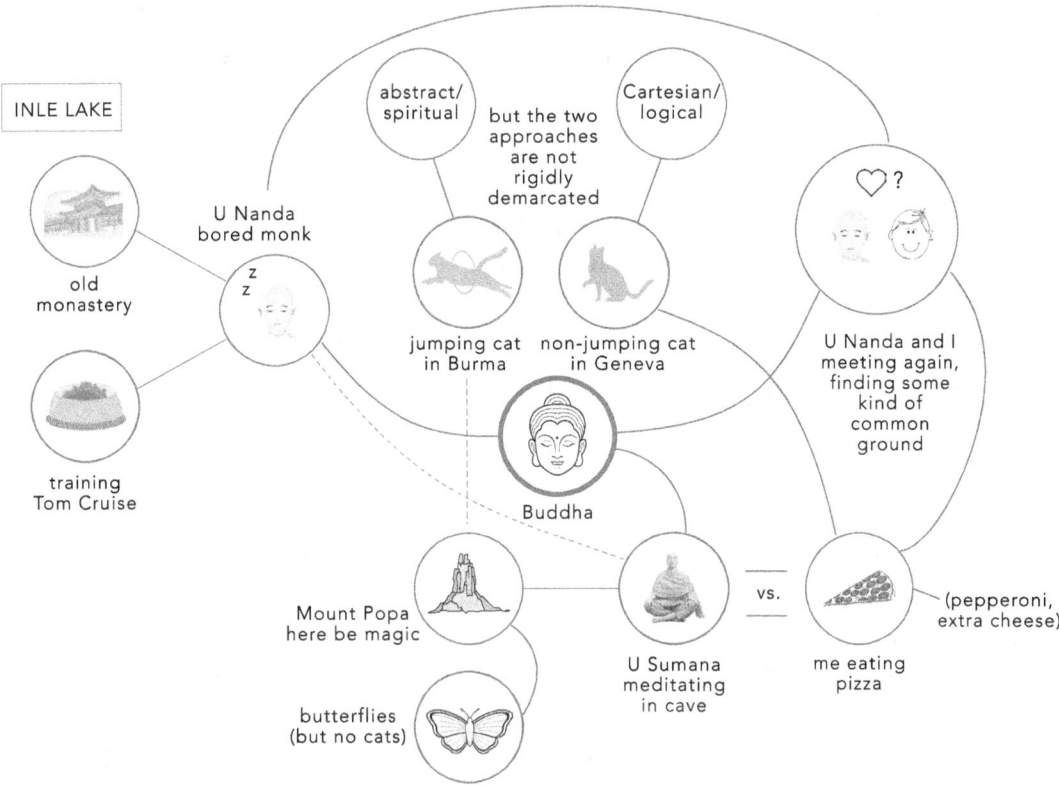

And here's the article. You'll see I used six questions, lots of scenes, a bunch of conflicts, and a few names and foreign phrases. I don't expect people to necessarily remember the Burmese word for "walking meditation" or the instructional phrase telling a cat to "jump," but these details help convince the reader that I was there and did my homework.

"Come on, Brochette, jump through this hoop. Arnold Schwarzenegger can do it – it can't be *that* hard."

Our ginger cat in Geneva was doing what cats everywhere do – exactly what she felt like. Which at this moment was not jumping through a hoop.

I was trying to accomplish a similar *coup de persévérance* to that which some monks in Myanmar have achieved. Teaching cats parlor tricks. But Brochette wasn't buying it. What did the monks have that I didn't?

Lots of patience and an abundant supply of Friskies, as it turned out.

I was introduced to the famous jumping cats at the Nga Phe Kyaung monastery, on Inle Lake.

The "jumping cat monastery" is a key stop for the trickle of tourists who visit Myanmar. There I met Venerable U Nanda, 25, one of a dozen resident monks.

"It's easy to train cats," he said, somewhat reluctantly putting down his Burmese comic book.

With a large dose of ennui, he explained that you simply start when they're kittens, scratch them under the chin, say *kon*, and reward them with kitty treats.

Obviously, it works. Every 30 minutes or so, when a group of visitors would accumulate, San Win, an assistant in the monastery, would put the cats through their paces.

"What's that one called?" I asked, pointing to a black and white tabby.

World-weary U Nanda explained, "That's Leonardo di Caprio."

"And this one?"

"Demi Moore."

"Can I try?"

I held the wire hoop in front of Arnold Schwarzenegger, paradoxically one of the skinnier cats in the temple. I gave him a little nudge, ordered him to *kon*, and after he jumped I rewarded him with a biscuit.

Meanwhile Tina Turner was curled up on my backpack, asleep. "Don't leave your things on the floor," U Nanda instructed. "She pisses everywhere."

After a while U Nanda started to open up. Perhaps he saw that since I wasn't going to go away, he might as well have a discussion. I was interested in Buddhist history; he was interested in conjugating English verbs.

Throughout our conversation, the abbot, Sayadaw Kite Ti, 68, kept his distance and read a book. I don't read Burmese, but from the pictures of cowboys and horses I could be pretty sure that it wasn't a religious text. He didn't glance up as visitors stuffed relatively generous contributions into the offerings boxes.

A few days later, in another part of Myanmar, I trekked an hour up a butterfly-enhanced forest path on Mount Popa, arguably the most mystical hill in this most mystical of countries, to visit a hermit monk named U Sumana.

Hesitantly, I approached the cave and saw a young monk preparing a fire. I asked if I was disturbing him. Popping in unannounced suddenly seemed like a stupid idea – the last thing I wanted to do was get in the way of his accumulation of karma points. Nevertheless, for a recluse, Venerable U Sumana was remarkably outgoing. He had finished his morning prayers, he explained, and invited me to sit on the ledge and chat.

Several years earlier, U Sumana took over the cave that had been the home of U Jermani, a legendary monk who meditated in this damp, isolated ledge for 50 years. U Sumana had few possessions, few clothes, and his diet consisted of a handful of rice and some vegetables. To me such isolation, deprivation, and rigor would be purgatory. I like my diversions too much – Beethoven, a fine wine, golf, pizza, and the company of friends. U Sumana, though, had a different view of his adopted home. "It's shady and cool. It's easy to get water. I'm in the middle of nature and there's no one around to distract me from my prayers." He had bright eyes and an easy smile. He explained he had seen this cave in a dream and journeyed here from distant Mon state.

My rational, Cartesian mind was racing. "But what do you do all day?" I asked.

U Sumana, 30, explained simply: "I meditate." Sometimes sitting. Sometimes moving. He showed me his walking meditation. Very, very slowly, I tried to replicate his movement – I roll from my heel to the toe and hold the opposite foot in the air before placing it down. I concentrate on the action. He explains that this type of practice, called *zingyan shouk chin*, will clear my mind. Help me to develop patience. Just like training a cat, perhaps.

Back at Inle Lake I sought out U Nanda. I felt I had unfinished business with the young monk, a feeling that there was more to him than a saffron-robed feline-inclined impresario.

"You again," he said when I walked in. He wasn't hostile, but he wasn't overly welcoming.

I deliberately avoided the handful of curious visitors watching Brad Pitt and Michael Jackson leaping about on the linoleum. "Tell me about the temple," I asked. And he did. He showed me around the 160-year-old monastery, the oldest on Inle Lake. Proudly, he turned on lights so that I could better see the six two-meter tall Buddha images made out of lacquerware, and the gilt-encrusted wooden statues and carved pillars. He took me into the abbot's room to show me old, sacred Buddha images. In half an hour of looking through different eyes, the monastery for me had evolved from a tourist site into a combination art museum and place of worship.

"What do you do?" he eventually asked me.

"I'm a journalist."

"Then tell people the monastery is more than cats. It's Buddha."

—Paul Spencer Sochaczewski. "Jumping Through Buddhist Hoops in Myanmar." *Curious Encounters of the Human Kind – Myanmar.* Geneva: Explorer's Eye Press, 2015.

THE READER WANTS IT ALL

This is a bipolar book. On the one hand I'll encourage you to find your voice, to heat up your story, to explore emotion and elegance.

On the other hand, good writing requires respect for structure, grammar, logic.

Put another way, the reader wants it all – emotions *and* structure, creativity *and* accuracy, insight *and* facts.

TWO BASIC REFERENCES

There are a zillion books out there about how to write better. I've got a couple of shelves of writing books. They're all helpful, and truthfully, some of them might resonate with you more than my book does. So be it.

But the two basic references you must have are:

* *The Elements of Style*. Strunk, William Jr. and E. B. White. New York: Harcourt Brace, 1919. New York: Macmillan, 1959.

* *100 Ways to Improve Your Writing*. Provost, Gary. New York: New American Library, 1985.

 Kids, Try This at Home

· · · · · · · · · ZEN-MUSIC-SPEEDWRITING · · · · · · · ·

Remember during art class when the teacher said: "Draw anything you like; be creative!"
I used to sit there in a panic. Be creative! I was stuck and so were my friends.

But if the teacher had said: "Draw a farm house on another planet, with domestic animals that look like George W. Bush, two children with long red hair and wearing funny hats, ice cream-eating flowers, a triple sun, giant flying alien radioactive squirrels and spaceships in the form of hamburgers," I would have produced something pretty interesting and personal, as would all my pals.

Sometimes you need structure in order to be creative, and Zen-Music-Speedwriting takes away some of the angst of forced creativity.

Like a high school chemistry experiment, this works best under adult supervision.

It's a writing sprint, preferably done with at least one friend. It's a way of telling the Boring Editor to get off your shoulder and bother someone else for a while. (Boring Editor is the nagging feeling that "you're not clever enough to write," or "who cares about your story?")

1. Have a friend choose a few musical cues – pieces of music (without words) that might be energizing, melancholy, whimsical, exotic. I've indicated (in parentheses) some of the music I use in my workshop.

2. Your friend gives you the first few words you will write, such as:

    "Deep in the forest I met ..."
    (Mendelssohn. Symphony no. 4. First movement)

    "The old lady looked in my eyes and told me ..."
    (Shiv Kumar Sharma. Music of the Mountains. Track 7)

    "Would you like to dance, the good-looking man/woman said ..."
    (Various artists. 16 Grandes Tangos for Export. Track 1)

    "I was afraid, but I opened the ancient wooden gate ..."
    (Conan the Barbarian. Riddle of Steel/Riders of Doom. Track 2)

    "Was it good for you too? I asked ..."
    (Mozart. Concerto for piano and orchestra no. 21, second movement)

"I think it's time to get out of here ..."
(Glinka. Overture to Russlan and Ludmilla)

3. Your friend turns on the music, gives you the first few words, and tells you to start. Then you write for one minute at full blast. Don't take your pen off the page, don't stop to think, don't worry about punctuation or legibility or lawsuits.

4. Do not show what you wrote to anyone. It's private. It's an exercise. Repeat three times per day.

Maybe playing loud music would help.

LOOK FOR GENERATIONAL PATTERNS IN FAMILY STORIES

A student in one of my writing classes wrote about her trepidation in letting her nine-year-old daughter go off, unchaperoned, with some local children while the family was staying at a rural eco-hotel in Bali. Her story was fine, but a new dimension evolved when she considered generational patterns. How did the writer's mother treat her when she was that age – did her mother give her freedom or was she smothering? And how would she advise her own daughter, in fifteen years' time, to raise her own children?

∽

In this personal essay, actor Kirk Douglas introduces a generational dynamic through two voices – his own and that of his father, who becomes an equally important main character.

My father, a Russian peasant, came to this country in 1910. Like all of his pals, he smoked. It's hard for me to picture my father without a cigarette in his mouth.

After many years of smoking, my father was told by his doctor that he would die of cancer if he did not stop smoking. So he quit cold turkey. Here's how he did it: he always carried one cigarette in the breast pocket of his shirt. When he felt the urge to smoke, he'd take the cigarette out and look at it fiercely. With a growl, he would say, in his Russian accent, "Who's stronger? You – me?"

He would glare at the cigarette: "I stronger." And he'd put the cigarette back in his pocket. He did that for a few years, but it was too late. He died of cancer at age seventy-two.

During my college years, my Navy service during World War II, and my years as an actor on Broadway, I never smoked. Then Hollywood beckoned, and I answered. My first picture was "The Strange Loves of Martha Ivers," with Barbara Stanwyck and Van Heflin, in 1946. I was intimidated, but proud to be playing the role of Miss Stanwyck's husband. I arrived at the set, very excited, to do my first scene with her. But I had spoken only a few lines when the director, Lewis Milestone, stopped the action and said, "Kirk, you should be smoking a cigarette in this scene."

"I don't smoke," I replied timidly.

"It's easy to learn," he said, and had the prop man hand me a cigarette.

I continued with the scene, lighting and smoking my first cigarette. Suddenly, I began to feel sick to my stomach and dizzy.

"Cut," yelled the director. "What's the matter with you, Kirk? You're swaying."

I rushed to my trailer to throw up.

But Mr. Milestone was right. It's easy to learn to smoke. Soon I was smoking two to three packs a day.

At that time everyone smoked, and the cigarette was the favorite movie prop. Many actors have trouble with their hands. Should they put them in their pockets? Should they put them behind their back? Do they have them at their sides? The cigarette answered the question. You take one out of the pack, you tap it, light it and inhale deeply. Then you exhale. If you are clever, you can learn to blow smoke rings. You can point with a cigarette. You can tap the ashes into an ashtray, and put it out gently in the ashtray or fiercely – whatever the scene requires. Paul Henreid had a worldwide hit in 1942 lighting two cigarettes at once in "Now, Voyager."

When I became famous, tobacco companies supplied me with cartons of cigarettes every month. One day in 1950 I was in my den, smoking as usual. I exhaled and through the smoke I saw a picture of my father on my desk. I thought of him on his deathbed. I stubbed out the cigarette in the ashtray. I took one cigarette from the pack and threw the rest in the wastebasket.

I held up the cigarette and studied it. My father's words came to me: "Who's stronger? You – me?"

"I stronger." I put the cigarette in my shirt pocket and never smoked again ...

—Kirk Douglas. "My First Cigarette, and My Last."
The New York Times, May 16, 2003.

DON'T TRUST YOUR MEMORY

Something that is vivid today (the name of your guide, the price of the hamburger in Oslo, the numbing pain of the wooden bus bench) will become fuzzy. Take notes.

Kids, Try This at Home

FIND THE VIBRATION

Do this with a friend. Tell her all about your recent trip. Let her ask questions about the trip itself: How did you feel? Were you surprised? What was he like? The objective is to force you to tell the story in all its glory. Surprising what comes out when you have a real-life interrogator.

What you'll find is that during the retelling, one incident/encounter/character will have more energy and vibrancy than the others. This could be a good insight into what the story is really about, or at least provide a place to start.

THE QUEST

Recognizing Your Hero's Journey

You're on a hero's journey

**Buddha. Aung San Suu Kyi. Mother Teresa. Luke Skywalker.
Eleanor Roosevelt. Genghis Khan. Mahatma Gandhi.**

What do they have in common?

They all had their own hero's journeys, specific to them, but with common archetypes.
Add yourself to that list.

REMEMBER JOSEPH CAMPBELL

Joseph Campbell was a philosopher who wrote *The Hero with a Thousand Faces*, which summarized the archetypes found in the mythologies of hero's journeys throughout the world.

Make your writing bigger by realizing that you, too, are on a hero's journey.

Useful Advice from Someone Who Wrote Pretty Well

"It was a long journey, but if it was any shorter I wouldn't have arrived."

—Anonymous Irish sage

THE QUEST POWERS YOUR STORY

A hero is on a quest.

It could be big: To act proudly when disaster strikes. To dispel ancient demons. To get over the loss of a loved one who died too young.

It could be prosaic and measurable: To overthrow a dictator. To win a race. To smuggle drugs, make some money, and not spend the rest of your life in a Turkish prison.

It could even be mundane: To get a date for the prom. To get into Harvard. To find the source of the original Pizza Margarita in Naples.

Simply put, a hero's quest can be stated as, "I set out in search of ... and discovered ..." What's *your* quest about?

 Kids, Try This at Home

THE MAGIC SENTENCE TO STRUCTURE YOUR HERO'S JOURNEY STORY

Fill in the four blanks and you will have a big head start on understanding your quest:

I went to _____ looking for _____ and was surprised to find _____ which taught me _____ .

A QUEST DOESN'T HAVE TO BE EARTH-SHATTERING

Maurice Herzog was the first man to climb an 8,000-meter mountain – Annapurna. At the end of his book *Annapurna: The First Conquest*, he pointed out that life's challenges take many forms by saying, "There are other Annapurnas in the lives of men."

FOCUS YOUR QUEST

Have a single goal.

Let's say you are writing a story for a travel magazine about food in Singapore.

A typical article would be something along the lines of:

Singapore has many different kinds of food.

It's all delicious.

I ate satay and it was good.

I ate Hokkien fried *mee* and it was good.

I ate Indian fish head curry and it was good but too spicy for me.

I didn't get sick; hygiene is very good in Singapore.

I gained five kilos.

But what you *could* do would be to focus on one type of food, let's say the grilled skewers of marinated meat called satay.

That's better; you've narrowed it down and created a focus.

But it's still static.

So how can you increase the dynamics of the story?

Well, you could add an active verb that indicates you're on a quest: "I'm looking for the best satay in Singapore." This will force you to speak with people you might not otherwise have met. It will force you to gaze into the history of satay, and the cultural role of food in Singapore society. It will force you to write in scenes with details and emotions. It will force you to ask questions, which are the locomotives of a quest story. Can you make us smell the embers of the charcoal? Can you make us taste the spicy peanut sauce? Satay is eaten by all Singaporeans, but it is essentially a Malay/Indonesian dish – what is the role of the minority Malays in Singapore? How does Singapore function as an ethnic and religious melting pot? How has an eclectic Singaporean cuisine enhanced nation building?

❦

I've based many of my most successful personal tales on (often obscure) quests. Quests can *always be expressed by questions*. Why does the Sultan of Yogyakarta worship a mermaid queen? Why is the white elephant revered in Thailand? Do real Hobbits live in Indonesia? How close are we to orangutans? Why do we have a need/fear relationship with nature? Are there really tiger magicians in the forests of Sumatra?

Here's how I started my article on my quest to find Waltzing Banana Island.

Some people with stardust in their eyes and too much red wine in their veins spend their lives searching for Atlantis or Eldorado. Other adventurers windsurf across the Pacific or attempt to ride every attraction at every Disneyland.

I have a simpler quest. I'm looking for "Waltzing Banana Island."

Since I was a kid growing up in a New York suburb, I've been intrigued by distant pastures. It was armchair imagining, mostly, writing school reports about Tibet and reading *The Wonderful Flight to the Mushroom Planet*, the first book I ever read that had no pictures.

"Waltzing Banana Island," or to put it in its correct Indonesian-French nomenclature, "Pulau Valse Pisang," is a tiny speck of land in far eastern Indonesia. My search for the island is devoid of socially redeeming value; I'm simply intrigued by how it got its name. A misspelling of the Dutch *valsche*, which would make it the "False Banana Island"? A secret hideaway for Carmen Miranda? An abundance of fruit trees, or a crescent shape? Or, more romantically, perhaps it was named by French explorers aboard the Astrolabe who charted eastern Indonesian waters in the mid-19th century. Since the banana is a euphemism throughout Indonesia for the male sexual organ, perhaps the lonely French sailors found the local lovelies *très charmantes*, musically inclined and welcoming.

—Paul Spencer Sochaczewski. "Journeys Without a Map."
Travel and Leisure, December 2005.

❦

Quests don't have to be earth shattering. Sarah Warwick used a quest theme, and an anecdote lead, to write about the surprisingly big food (four Michelin-starred restaurants) of tiny Le Bourget-du-Lac in eastern France. (Pity that either she or the editors misspelled and misgendered the name of the restaurant Le Bateau Ivre, incorrectly writing *La* Bateau Ivre. It may not matter to non-Francophones, but a French-speaking reader will just shake her head at the schoolgirl mistake.)

Olivier Parpillon twists his fingers around the *lavaret*, untangling strands of nylon net from its gills. The silvery fish gulps desperately at the air in a succession of small wet pops. With a casual movement born of years of practice, Parpillon then flings it across the boat in a twirling arc that lands it in a plastic crate among the moist, shiny corpses of its brethren.

The whitewashed bottom of his small fishing boat is spattered with tiny, oily circles that gleam like yellowed sequins. Around us a gentle drizzle starts to fall. Unperturbed, Parpillon carries on untwisting and untangling while I, cozy in an oilskin jacket and still bleary from interrupted sleep, look on with something akin to wonder.

It's not every day one gets the chance to join a French fisherman on the calm, dawn-lit waters of an alpine lake. But my journey out with Parpillon this morning – an exercise that involved a 4 a.m. wake-up call – isn't born out of idle curiosity. I'm here to gain a better appreciation for the produce that ends up in the restaurants of a very special French village, and to follow these fish on their journey from lake to kitchen to plate.

—Sarah Warwick. "The Bounty of Bourget." *Destinasian*, December 2012/January 2013.

A Quest Is a Journey with a Goal

A.J. Jacobs is a master of the quest-book, which he sometimes introduces using an elegant "list" lead. (But I wish he wouldn't use an apostrophe for the plural of A.)

I know the name of Turkey's leading avant-garde publication. I know that Bud Abbott was a double-crosser and John Quincy Adams married for money. I know that there's a heated controversy over who invented the accordion. I know that dwarves have prominent buttocks.

I know that Hank Aaron played for a team called the Indianapolis Clowns and that the British tried to tax clocks in 1797 (big mistake). I know that Adam of Bible fame lived longer than the combined ages of the correspondents of *60 Minutes* and *60 Minutes II* (930 years, to be exact). I know that absentee voting is huge in Ireland. I know that South America's Achagua tribe worshipped lakes, that the man who introduced baseball to Japan was a communist, and that Ulysses S. Grant thought Venice would be a nice city "if it were drained."

I know all this because I have just read the first 100 pages of the Encyclopaedia Britannica. I feel as giddy as famed balloonist Ben Abruzzo on a high altitude flight – but also alarmed at the absurd amount of information in the world. I feel like I've just stuffed my brain till there are facts dribbling out of my ears. But mostly, I am determined. I'm going to read this book from A to Z – or more precisely a-ak to zywiec. I'm not even out of the early A's, but I'm going to keep turning those pages till I'm done. I'm on my way. Just 32,900 pages to go!

—A.J. Jacobs. *The Know-It-All.* New York: Simon & Schuster, 2004.

∽

And Jacobs again. Note how he uses his beard as a Story of One to introduce the Story of Many (see Writing Tip #8 and Glossary).

As I write this, I have a beard that makes me resemble Moses. Or Abe Lincoln. Or Ted Kaczynski. I've been called all three.

It's not a well-manicured, socially acceptable beard. It's an untamed mass that creeps up toward my eyeballs and drapes below my neckline.

I've never allowed my facial hair to grow before, and it's been an odd and enlightening experience. I've been inducted into a secret fraternity of bearded guys – we nod at each other as we pass on the street, giving a knowing quarter-smile. Strangers have come up to me and petted my beard, like it's a Labrador retriever puppy or a pregnant woman's stomach.

I've suffered for my beard. It's been caught in jacket zippers and been tugged on by my surprisingly strong two-year-old son. I've spent a lot of time answering questions at airport security.

I've been asked if I'm named Smith and sell cough drops with my brother. ZZ Top is mentioned at least three times a week. Passersby have shouted, "Yo, Gandalf." Someone called me Steven Seagal, which I found curious, since he doesn't have a beard.

I've battled itch and heat. I've spent a week's salary on balms, powders, ointments and conditioners. My beard has been a temporary home to cappuccino foam and lentil soup. And it's upset people. Thus far, two little girls have burst into tears and one boy has hidden behind his mother.

But I mean no harm. The facial hair is simply the most noticeable physical manifestation of a spiritual journey I began a year ago.

My quest has been this: To live the ultimate Biblical life. Or more precisely, to follow the Bible as literally as possible. To obey the Ten Commandments. To be fruitful and multiply. To love my neighbor. To tithe my income. But also to abide by the oft-neglected rules: To avoid wearing clothes made of mixed fibers. To stone adulterers. And, naturally, to leave the edges of my beard unshaven (Leviticus 19:27). I am trying to obey the entire Bible, without picking and choosing.

—A.J. Jacobs. *The Year of Living Biblically*. New York: Simon & Schuster, 2007.

∽

A quest doesn't have to be of earth-shattering importance; it's ok to have fun on the journey (especially if there's a magazine article at the end of the tunnel).

Everything these last couple of months has had something to do with the Olympics ... Last month on Fire Island I saw a sassy troop of drag queens re-enact the entire 1996 U.S. women's gymnastics team floor exercise. (You haven't seen true drag until you've seen a fortysomething man do vintage Kerri Strug.) Naturally, after my trip to the Super Bowl earlier this year, I just assumed I'd soon be winging my way to London to see the games of the XXX Olympiad. But, to my shock and disappointment, *Vanity Fair* told me they'd rather spend the money on making a magazine. So I decided to take things into my own hands. I had the Olympic bug and ... I wasn't about to miss out on all the fun and frenzy. I decided I'd do my own Olympics, here in New York. Since I'm workout-obsessed, I'd take every exercise class I could find that was Olympic-themed. A chance to humiliate myself in front of my friends and peers? Check. An opportunity to throw on a bathing cap and synchronize swim with a bunch of sassy gals? Hell yeah, game on! Oh, and you would like me to wear the actual uniforms for the purpose of the pictures? O.K., what could possibly go wrong?

So I tackled the sports head on and had some great workouts, some good laughs, and a little agony along the way. What did I take away from this experience? That at 37 I am a little long in the tooth for every sport and that I was not so comfortable being photographed in a Speedo (but I like it now).

—Michael Carl. "Work Out Like an Olympian." *Vanity Fair*, July 28, 2012.

∽

A quest gives you an opportunity for purposeful travel.

I had come to follow in the footsteps of the 18th-century painter Nainsukh. Many of his works are now in the world's leading museums, but murals influenced by his innovations can still be found on temple walls all over the Himalayan foothills. I planned to see the landscapes, villages and palaces that he lived in, as well as the best of the frescoes that were painted in the tradition that he helped to change forever: it was to be a sort of Himalayan equivalent of the Piero della Francesco trail through Tuscany, Umbria and Le Marche.

—William Dalrymple. "Treasure Among the Tree Trunks."
Financial Times, December 1–2, 2013.

———————

A GOOD QUEST GATHERS CURIOUS LITERARY ASTEROIDS

Having a quest provides the opportunity to bring in wandering asteroids – intellectual tangents related to the main quest.

In *Shopping for Buddhas*, Jeff Greenwald's quest is to find and buy the "perfect" Buddha statue in Kathmandu. The reader continues to turn the page because the basic quest-question is so intriguing – "Will Greenwald find the perfect Buddha?" Along the way, Greenwald gives us insights and scenes about life in Kathmandu, the antique business, how to identify real antiques and how to identify fakes, what it means to be a Buddhist in a city where a majority of people are Hindu, how good (and bad) luck sometimes descends when you least expect it, and perhaps most interesting, speculation on what Buddha himself might have made of this quest.

Here's how he adds a layer of personal philosophy to his quest:

A half-naked priest raked through the embers of a smoking cremation ghat. We watched from a distance as he poked at something black and egg-shaped. When we came closer to investigate, I saw that it was a human head – and the black, roasted remains of a torso, tiny and twisted. The head seemed to be thrown back in a gesture that was both agonized and inspired. There was something triumphant and ultimate about it, like a face contorted during childbirth.

"Where is that soul now?" Karen wondered. I knew the local answer. The spirit, blind and helpless, would have begun its passage through the Rivers of Fire, clinging to the tail of a sacred cow. Ah, the imagination that goes into creating what comes next! And the aching sigh of mortality; our smooth, warm bodies crackling into ash, skulls bursting with a pop, limbs falling away. We stood still and silent and watched the head in the flames, teeth grimacing at the sky.

"An inevitable turn of events, I'm afraid," I muttered.

And then I realized that, if you take away the words "I'm afraid," what I'd said was essentially Buddha's primary teaching: death is inevitable. The whole trick lies in somehow coming to terms with that fear.

What, I asked myself, is $650 [the cost of the "perfect" Buddha he was considering buying] if it can help me sizzle those two words – "I'm afraid" – out of my life? What price enlightenment? Is it a bargain basement commodity, or do you get it when and where you can, damn the expense?

—Jeff Greenwald. *Shopping for Buddhas.* San Francisco: Harper & Row, 1990.

Another example: a friend wants to ride a bike across America. Now this is a big challenge with plenty of conflicts and challenges – what bike to choose, what equipment to take, how to convince his wife that he won't be around to mow the lawn for six months. No doubt he can write an interesting personal memoir out of the experience. But my friend is adding layers to the quest – he is an expert on climate change and plans to give lectures on global warming (or is it cooling?) at schools along his route. This extra dimension opens interesting literary asteroids – will he arrive at his destination on time, how will the students react to his message, how will their parents behave, will he see evidence along the way that supports his beliefs or will he uncover evidence that forces him to challenge his understanding of the science?

QUEST AS SEARCH FOR AN INDIVIDUAL

A quest can be a search for a particular individual, and that person can be the poster boy for a more far-ranging exploration of ideas.

I started a chapter in a book with the quest for the last *perkenier* and then wrote about the Dutch colonial period, the search for spices, how tiny Banda was the only place in the world where nutmeg grew, how this isolated tropical island changed global history.

I sought out the last *perkenier* of Banda.

In 1992, when I took a tiny boat from the main island of Banda Neira to the adjacent island of Banda Besar, I found Wilhelm "Benny" van den Broecke sitting on his porch, as if he had been expecting me.

—Paul Spencer Sochaczewski. "The Last Perkenier."
An Inordinate Fondness for Beetles, Singapore: Editions Didier Millet. 2012.

∞

Here's one of my quest-type personal travel stories, total length just 800 words. Note the Nancy Reagan dilemma (see Writing Tip #3 and Glossary) – I didn't remember where I had first seen the girl who is the subject of my quest – that's the problem that might prevent me from achieving my goal.

In 1979 I took a black and white photo of a young girl in Ladakh. She was perhaps ten. She wore a rough robe of homespun wool, she carried a slate on which she used a stick dipped in muddy water to write her alphabets, she carried a simple brown canvas army-style book bag slung over her shoulder.

I have no idea what she was thinking, but to me her gaze says, quietly, "Watch me. I'm going to surprise you."

I sought her out in April 2005.

There was a slight problem though. I didn't remember where I had taken the photo.

One of the benefits of being a somewhat organized pack rat is that I keep my old journals. I found my notes from the trip, twenty-six years earlier. At a village I had identified as Bongzo, I had written about a little girl, whose "hands were rough with ingrained dirt, the texture of sandpaper." We had arithmetic as a common language, and I wrote "2 + 2" and watched her stroke the numeral "4." I gave her a ball point pen. "The girl's eyes lit for a moment with immediate recognition," I had written. "After realizing the pen was for her she grabbed it and in one motion hid it inside her maroon robe."

In 2005 I was in the remote Himalayan region of Ladakh for a weekend, to write an article about the golf course in Leh, which, at 3,445 meters, is the world's highest. I had a free day, and understanding my esoteric interests, my guide, Tashi Chotak Lonchey, had taken me to the monastery that I had visited twenty-six years earlier (yes, one of the monks was still alive and he recognized himself in a photo). After a cup of butter tea we decided to drive several hours to visit a sacred forest, an ancient juniper tree grove in Hemis Shukpachan. After driving for about an hour we passed a small village and I saw a sign that said "Basgo." "Maybe this is the place where you took the picture," Tashi suggested. Bongzo? Basgo? Close enough to be worth a stop.

None of it looked familiar. My only thought was that in 1979 my friend David and I must have stopped here for a tea break during a bus ride to Ridzong Monastery further along the same road.

Tashi and I stopped at a large house near the road and showed a blowup of the young girl's photo to an old woman. "It could be Tsewang," she said after some thought. "Her husband Tashi Angchok is just up the street."

We found Tashi Angchok working at the family restaurant. He offered us tea as he studied the photo. "The smile looks similar to my wife's," he said. But the problem was that his wife, Tsewang Dolma, the reputed girl in the photo, wasn't around since she was teaching at Tridho, a one-class school some three hours away, near the Chinese border.

He took the picture to his mother-in-law, and came back with a handful of old photos showing his wife as a young girl. The mother said that my photo seemed to be that of her daughter, but she wasn't too sure.

We still had a long program ahead of us that day, so we left the photo with Tashi Angchok, told him we would be back at the end of the afternoon, and went to explore the sacred forest in Hemis.

It was almost sundown when we got back to Basgo.

"It's her," Tashi said confidently.

We asked how he knew.

"I showed the picture to Tsewang's sister but didn't say 'is this Tsewang?' I simply asked 'do you know this girl?'" he said, quite proud of his detective skills.

"She said, 'yes, that's my little sister.'"

So, just like that I had found a family who invited me to dinner next time I'm in Ladakh. Then I'll get a chance to actually have a conversation with this girl, now a grown woman, whose photo and spirit has graced my home for a quarter of a century.

—Paul Spencer Sochaczewski. "The Girl by the Side of the Road."
Curious Encounters of the Human Kind – Himalaya. Geneva: Explorer's Eye Press, 2015.

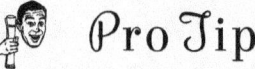
Pro Tip

Morph Your Metaphors

A quest can have multiple layers. In The Snow Leopard, Peter Matthiessen embarks on a big existential quest – to deal with the recent death of his wife, as well as a more precise (and quantifiable) quest – to see a snow leopard in the mountains of Nepal.

Of course it's not so clear-cut – the snow leopard morphs into a metaphor for the elusive search for the meaning of life. Good quests are like Joseph Campbell's Scene-Shifters – they fiddle with reality and logic, like a child's kaleidoscope shifts those colored bits of glass.

QUESTS AS BOOK THEMES

Many nonfiction books are based on quests, and the following two examples couple the quest of the literary/mythical heroes (Rama and Kim respectively) with the quests of the authors to symbolically follow in their footsteps.

Jonah Blank embarks on a quest to find Rama – specifically to understand modern India through the device of visiting people and places related to Rama, an avatar of Vishnu whose story is inseparably woven into the fabric of India. Note too the elegance of his writing and the use of Triple Whammy – The Rule of Three (see Glossary and Writing Tip #7), which I've indicated in [brackets].

Imagine a story that is the *Odyssey*, Aesop's *Fables*, *Romeo and Juliet*, the Bible, and *Star Wars* all at the same time. Imagine a story that combines adventure and aphorism [1], romance and religion [2], fantasy and philosophy [3]. Imagine a story that makes young children marvel [1], burly men weep [2], and old women dream [3]. Such a story exists in India, and it is called the Ramayana.

> —Jonah Blank. *Arrow of the Blue-Skinned God.* New York: Touchstone, 1992.

An appreciation of Rudyard Kipling's novel *Kim* provided the trigger for Peter Hopkirk's quest for an understanding of the Great Game being played in the Subcontinent:

For it was *Kim*, more years ago than I care to remember, which first introduced me to the intoxicating world of the Great Game … So spellbound was I by this glimpse into the workings of the Indian secret service that I carried a copy of *Kim* everywhere, even if much of it was lost on me … The quest was to last a lifetime, and has still to run its course.

> —Peter Hopkirk. *Quest for Kim.* London: John Murray, 1996.

———————

TRIGGER INCIDENT

If you're writing a personal quest story, consider whether there was a trigger incident – did something dramatic happen that caused you to embark on your journey?

For example, in *Shopping for Buddhas* Jeff Greenwald started his quest to find the "perfect" Buddha statue after a near-death experience while on a trek in Nepal. "Lucky, so very lucky to be alive," he wrote.

———————

TWO TYPES OF QUESTS:
REJECTION OF STATUS QUO & SEARCH FOR SPECIFIC GOAL

A quest generally takes on one of two structures (which are often intertwined): The Rejection Quest and the Directed Quest.

In the Rejection Quest the writer is running away; she wants no part of growing up in a middle-class suburban Chicago family, or is fed up with an unhappy marriage (as was done in the film *Thelma and Louise* and in the book *Eat, Pray, Love*) and sets off to find, well, she's not sure what she's going to find, but she just has to get the hell out of town. In the Rejection Quest the goal might be vague but becomes clearer as the journey evolves.

In the Directed Quest the writer sets off with a specific goal in mind – to learn to cook Italian food and find an Italian husband, perhaps not necessarily in that order. To become an Olympic athlete. To discover a practical way to harness nuclear fusion. To bicycle around the world. To study Asian art at an age when most people are happy just puttering in the garden.

THE ADOLESCENT ITCH

Quests often link to a coming of age, a rite of passage.

Many participants of my writing workshops tell about formative, often life-changing experiences. Dealing with an addiction. Family tragedies. Joining the Peace Corps or the armed forces or Médecins Sans Frontières to work in strange lands.

Some of these experiences are rites of passage, and they are wonderful devices on which to build a story.

The key to a rite of passage is often an "adolescent itch for self-imposed exile," as American neuroscientist Robert Sapolsky writes:

We know that following this urge is one of the most resonantly primate of acts. A young male baboon stands riveted at the river's edge; an adolescent female chimp cranes to catch a glimpse of the chimps from the next valley. New animals, a whole bunch of 'em! To hell with logic and sensible behavior, to hell with tradition and respecting your elders, to hell with this drab little town, and to hell with that knot of fear in your stomach. Curiosity, excitement, adventure – the hunger for novelty is something fundamentally daft, rash, and enriching that we share with our whole taxonomic order.

You could do worse than recognizing the power and dynamics of the rite of passage and making it the central theme of your personal story.

Useful Advice from Someone Who Wrote Pretty Well

Notice how many of the Olympic athletes effusively thanked their mothers for their success? "She drove me to my practice at four in the morning," etc. Writing is not figure skating or skiing. Your mother will not make you a writer. My advice to any young person who wants to write is: leave home.

—Paul Theroux

 ## Kids, Try This at Home

· · · · · THE HERO'S JOURNEY WORKS FOR NGO CAMPAIGNS · · · · ·

This is a bit tangential, but if you're working in a non-governmental organization preparing a strategic campaign (let's say you're with a disease-related NGO and your goal is to convince a health ministry to reimburse people for a specific diagnostic test) then you might structure your lobbying campaign as if it was a mythic tale out of Joseph Campbell's playbook. No doubt you'll see these archetypes:

Grail – what's the ultimate goal?

Damsel in distress – who are you fighting to save?

Dragon – who/what doesn't want you to achieve the goal?

Allies – who's on your side?

Armory – what weapons are at your disposal?

Gatekeeper – is there one person who can open a door?

Mentor – who can give you helpful advice?

Opposing armies – who actively doesn't want you to win? Is there a way to convert or work with them?

Infidels – who is shaking things up just to make your life difficult?

Pesky foreigners – who is stealing your resources?

Knights – who will fight on your behalf? What reward can you give them?

King/God – is there a higher authority you can invoke?

Make your quest bigger by recognizing your inner dream.

Pro Tip

Learn from Film Heroes

Christopher Vogler's book The Writer's Journey reveals how the world's iconic films – Gone with the Wind, The Wizard of Oz, Star Wars, Casablanca, Die Hard – follow the classic structure of the hero's journey.

Illustration: Tom Gauld.

A Good Quest Has Legs

A good quest can be odd, difficult, and doesn't have to have redeeming social value. A good quest has levels and opens up new narrative pathways in the story.

❧

Here's my lead for a story about my search for Hanuman's Mountain.

> It takes a chunk of Hindu chutzpah for a remote Indian villager to stay angry at one of the most popular gods in the pantheon, but Padhan Patti feels she has a good reason.
>
> "When Lord Hanuman came here to retrieve the medicinal plant mountain, he promised to bring it back," the 50-something woman says, referring to a pivotal scene in the classic *Ramayana* epic. "But he didn't." Padhan Patti promises that when I hike another few hours to a vantage point, I will see a huge "bleeding" scar on the side of Dunagiri mountain where the flying monkey god Hanuman is said to have sliced off a big chunk of mythological real estate.
>
> Padhan Patti says she still respects Hanuman, the flying monkey god, because after all he is the Hindu epitome of loyalty, devotion and good works. Nevertheless, to register her disappointment in his lapse to keep his word she, along with several of her neighbors, refuses to take the *prasad*, or communion, at the village's annual Hanuman festival.

I then explain why my quest brings me to northern India.

> Some people search for Mount Ararat, where Noah landed. Others seek Atlantis, or Solomon's temple, or the rumored companion city to Machu Picchu. I am searching for a mythical medicinal-plant mountain from a fable that provides entertainment and moral guidance for hundreds of millions of people.

And set the Ramayana in context.

> Clearly, Hanuman's role in the *Ramayana* is a story for the ages.

Having huge religious and cultural influence, with some of the story lines and moral impact of the western Bible, the *Odyssey*, and the Ring Cycle, the Ramayana tells of how the wife of Indian Prince Rama (an avatar of Vishnu, one of the most powerful Hindu deities) is kidnapped by the ten-headed demon Ravana, who spirits the woman to his well-protected redoubt in his kingdom called Langka, in what is now Sri Lanka. During the numerous battles that ensue, Lakshmana, Rama's devoted brother, is mortally wounded. The only thing that can save him is *sanjivani*, a combination of medicinal plants that only grow in the high Himalaya. The royal physician bemoans: "But we're stuck here in Sri Lanka and the plants grow in the mountains near Tibet. Who we gonna call?"

This is when Hanuman comes to the rescue. The monkey god flies some 2,600 kilometers to the medicinal plant mountain (soaring at a speed of roughly 660 km an hour, according to R.P. Goldman, from the University of California at Berkeley, who made his calculation based on the writings of ancient scholars). And then, depending on which of the many versions of the story you read, Hanuman either forgets which plants were on the shopping list or the plants hide in fear when they see this big flying monkey coming in for a landing. Either way, he rips up the mountain and carries it back to Sri Lanka. After one whiff of the healing herbs, Lakshmana is back in business, enabling Rama and his brother to win the final battle, rescue Rama's wife Sita, and return home for a bittersweet finale. In most versions of the story, after the medicines have worked their magic, Hanuman puts the mountain back on his shoulder and flies again over the subcontinent to replace the mountain in its rightful place.

For the quest to be worthwhile it helps if there is physical or psychological pain. But what is the philosophical drive that underpins this particular quest? What do I hope to find?

I was exhausted but thrilled as my friend Gopal Sharma and I walked up the steep, narrow path to Dunagiri village. I've wanted to find Hanuman's mountain for some 30 years. Partly it was the quest for something that is inherently "unfindable," but I was also intrigued by an unintended side benefit. It is difficult to fly over a subcontinent carrying a mountain like a pizza delivery guy without bits of earth falling to the ground. Where these clumps of medicinal-plant dirt fell, sacred forests sprouted. These holy groves, places rich in healing herbs and generally protected by the local communities, can be found throughout Asia, and during my work in nature conservation I took a particular interest in their existence and the practical, cultural, and spiritual benefits such natural gardens provide to local people. How interesting it would be, I thought, to find the mother lode of these sacred forests.

My own wounds are acting up – my knees, never too strong while walking in a shopping mall, are lurching under the stress of climbing a goat track above the timber line. I'm constantly out of breath. And, although it's only mid-September, it's starting to snow.

Then I described how difficult it was to look for this mountain – this is a classic Nancy Reagan problem (see Writing Tip #3 and Glossary) – if it had been easy to find the mountain, then the value of the quest would have been diminished.

A strong story has strong characters, in this case Hanuman, Gopal Sharma, and Padhan Patti – all related to Dunagiri mountain (note the "scar").

But where was this elusive rock? I read dozens of books, spoke to a gaggle of scholars. Some Ramayana versions give poetically vague directions – "Go over the sea and north into the far high Himalaya. At night from the air you will easily see the glowing Medicine Hill of Life, crowned with herbs long ago transplanted from the Moon." Another version of the Ramayana places the medicinal-plant mountain between the (mythical) Rishabha mountain, full of fierce animals, and the (very real) Mount Kailash, in Tibet. Yet another instructs Hanuman "to fly 9,000 yojanas to the red mountain, then another 9,000 yojanas to the blue mountain," and on and on (Indian scholars who calculate such things estimate that one ancient yojana is equal to approximately 13 to 16 kilometers). N.C. Shah, of the Central Council for Research in Indian Medicine in Lucknow, pointed me toward Dunagiri by noting that Hanuman's mountain was located "where *kshir*, or ocean, was churned for *amrita*, ambrosia, and where existed two hills, namely Chandra and Drona." An Indian conservation official said no, the mountain is in his home state of Tamil Nadu, in the south of the country. More prosaically, a friend in Mumbai asked, "Why are you interested in this crazy goose chase in the first place? No Starbucks in the mountains."

Eventually, Ajay Rastogi, a friend in Delhi with whom I had worked during my tenure at the WWF-World Wide Fund for Nature, said that he had heard about a village where some folks refused to share in Hanuman's communion. Ajay couldn't make the trip but he introduced me to Gopal Sharma, a tough Indian mountaineer and adventurer. Gopal Sharma had twice summited 7,817 meter Nanda Devi (in one climb he survived a night bivouac without a sleeping bag at 7,600 meters, and on another attempt survived a 400-meter fall).

After a comfortable overnight train from Delhi to Haridwar, a holy city where the Ganges leaves the mountains and enters the plains, Gopal and I drove for twelve hours to Joshimath, an Indian hill station in the state of Uttaranchal that suffers from the ugly unregulated construction and traffic of most such resorts. The next morning, driving towards the border with Tibet, we drove another two hours to the trailhead, altitude 2,578 meters, in the general vicinity of the Nanda Devi Sanctuary.

And during the article I continue to struggle against the physical elements and investigate the role of sacred groves, and their medicinal plants, throughout the subcontinent.

I hike in the Alps on weekends, and am no stranger to the mountains, but I soon tired and huffed and puffed my way to our campsite at Dunagiri village at 3,651 meters, about one and a half times the altitude of Aspen, Colorado.

This was Ground Zero for my search. The hundred or so villagers in Dunagiri (the village, and the mountain of the same name, are sometimes referred to as

Dronagiri) were curious, polite, and after a while quite willing to answer the strange questions of an out-of-breath foreigner. You can't see the 7,066-meter Dunagiri mountain from the village, and Gopal and I hiked up a few hundred meters to get a good view. We were lucky with the weather and the snow-covered mountain shone like a beacon. We clearly saw the gash where part of the mountain was sliced off, and it only took a bit of imagining to visualize Hanuman morphing his hand into a cosmic machete to chop off the huge chunk of rock. Near our lunchtime picnic spot, in the meadows, we found one of the medicinal plants on Hanuman's shopping list, *visalyakarani*, which in Sanskrit means "removing spikes and arrows." G.S. Rawat of the Wildlife Institute of India subsequently identified the plant as *Morina longifolia* (Dipsacaceae), used locally to heal wounds.

The search for healing plants in the Himalaya has a basis in fact. Scientists and local people alike know well that the Himalayan region is a treasure chest of important medicinal plants that form the heart of the Ayurvedic system of medicine used to treat Lakshmana, and that remains the medical system of choice for tens of millions of Indians, Nepalese, and Sri Lankans.

And I finish in a circular structure, not far from where I started, but with movement in the story.

We returned to the village to say goodbye. I just wanted to be clear that I had the story right, and asked Padhan Patti to confirm that she really was upset with Hanuman because he didn't return the mountain. She nodded, but added a new fillip, another reason for being perturbed. She told the story with a familiarity and acceptance that was as if she was recounting a family tale that happened, say, a generation ago, like my father's war stories. Hanuman flew in during a whiteout, she said, and couldn't find the mountain. Unlike most modern men he stopped to ask directions. The only person in the village was an old woman, an ancestor of Padhan Patti's. The old woman pointed in the direction Hanuman was to fly. "I can't see it and I'm in a hurry," Hanuman replied. So he put her on his shoulder and she navigated while he soared. They arrived, Hanuman said "thanks, have a good life," grabbed the mountain and flew away, leaving the little old lady alone in the middle of a blizzard.

—Paul Spencer Sochaczewski. "The God Who Flew Off with a Mountain." *Curious Encounters of the Human Kind – Himalaya*. Geneva: Explorer's Eye Press, 2015.

WRITING TIP #1

You Have a Choice

RECOGNIZE THAT YOU HAVE OPTIONS

In writing, as in other aspects of life, you have choices. One of the most important writing choices you make concerns how cold, or how hot, you want your story to be.

Cold writing is impersonal, academic, aloof. Hot writing is effervescent, endearing, intimate.

Cold writing provides information. Hot writing tells a story.

Cold writing deals in facts. Hot writing offers interpretation.

COLD OR HOT?

Here's the dilemma. Many people who want to write personal stories have been so conditioned by years of writing academic studies and business reports that they don't know how to write informally, about themselves. It's as if they have been caged for so long that when a good Samaritan opens the door, they are afraid to step outside. They find security in the self-imposed prison of "boringnicity."

But the paradox is that every day these otherwise normal people tell their friends and families stories full of conflict, characters, dialogue, setting, and passion. Their conversations are hot, so why is their writing cold?

CONTRADICTORY WRITING

Creative nonfiction is based on a conundrum.

On the one hand good writing requires the research, structure, and accuracy of a journalist. But you also need to be a mesmerizing storyteller invoking human emotions. Good writing requires cohabitation between cold writing and hot writing.

When you write cold you risk getting zapped.

YOU HAVE A CHOICE

You choose how cold, or how hot, to make your story.

It's not one or the other. It's a continuum, a range of options. Most beginning writers write in a default cold mode. Cold writing is safe, but boring. This book will help you learn techniques to heat up your story.

Your choices will depend on what your own comfort zone is and what the expectations of the audience are.

If it makes you feel better, perhaps seventy percent of the participants in my workshops are comfortable writing boring academic or business reports but are uncomfortable when they put themselves into the story, even though they use "I" constantly in conversation. Boring writing has become their default positions.

Obviously you have to understand and respect the expectations of your target audience – a scientific paper in a peer-reviewed academic journal is *expected* to be cold. But there are times when you will get your message across more forcefully when you heat up your writing or presentation.

Your reader is a normal person with emotions, beliefs, and a sense of humor. Treat him with humanity.

FIVE TIPS TO BREAK OUT OF ACADEMIC/BUSINESS/COLD WRITING

Every time I run my workshop, I'll have a few people who write comfortably for work, but who freeze when writing their personal stories.

Here are five suggestions, each of which will be explained later in the book.

1. **Explore your voice.**
    You don't have the same voice at work as you do in the pub. Explore the pub voice.

2. **Write like you're speaking to a friend.**
    You're not writing for Wikipedia, you're writing to your best pal.

3. **Start with "I" and an active verb.**
    This can be liberating. See where it goes and how it feels.

4. **Write in scenes.**
    If you can write one scene, just a couple of paragraphs, you've broken the back of the problem.

5. **Become friends with the Nancy Reagan Principle.** (See Writing Tip #3 and Glossary)
    Recognize the importance of conflict and problems that force the hero to make a choice.

INTIMACY IS HOT

When I said your job is to get the reader to turn the page, it's another way of saying "create intimacy" with the reader by writing hotter.

"Your book nauseated me. Did you do that on purpose?"

Hotter stories evoke visceral responses.

HEAD AND HEART

You need both. We think (sometimes overthink) with our brains. We believe rational, well-explained arguments.

But we are emotional animals. Even when confronted with facts, many people will ignore the science and vote with their heart – I'm thinking here of themes like evolution and climate change, love and politics.

If your story can involve the head (cold) *and* heart (hot), you're more likely to make contact with the reader.

THE CONTINUUM

Here are some of the options. Remember, this is not either/or, it's a continuum.

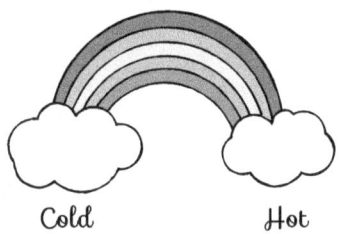

Cold   Hot

COLD	HOT
brain	heart
third person	first person
school report	campfire tale
Creative Work	Creative Inspiration
statistics	interpretation
facts	opinions
science	philosophy
professor	best friend
lecture	joke
intellectual	emotional
aloof	endearing
chronology	themes
isolated	accessible
hard slog	eureka
binary – black or white	shades of gray

"I worked really hard on this damn report; thank God it's finished."

"I had a great time writing this article and think you'll love it."

HOW TO WARM UP A STATISTIC

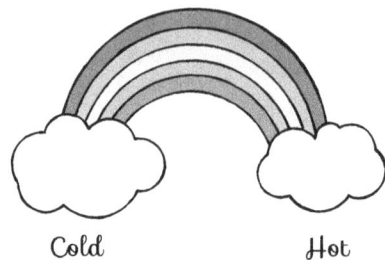

Cold   Hot

COLD

Burma, north to south –
1,286 miles (2,070 km).

Burma land area 261,228 square miles
(676,578 square kilometers).

Area of US state of Ohio: 44,824 square miles
(116,096 square kilometers) compared to
area of Switzerland 15,940 square miles
(41,285 square kilometers)

The off-Broadway show *The Fantasticks* ran
for 42 years and 17,162 performances.

The show opened in 1960 and closed in
2002.

HOT

Longer than Chiang Mai to Singapore, about
the distance from Boston to Miami, or
St. Petersburg to Crete.

Three times the size of the UK.

Three Switzerlands can fit into Ohio.

It was the world's longest running musical.
It ran longer than *Cats* and *Les Misérables*
combined.

The Fantasticks opened almost a decade
before Neil Armstrong walked on the moon,
before Woodstock, before Elizabeth Taylor
received an Academy Award for *Butterfield 8*,
before Wilt Chamberlain completed the first
of his seven consecutive years as basketball's
top scorer. It opened when Dwight
Eisenhower was president and closed when
George W. Bush was president.

COLD-HOT - EXAMPLE OF HOW IT WORKS IN PRACTICE

Here's the evolution of cold to hot in an article I wrote about seeing Komodo dragons in Indonesia. Look at the evolution from third person to first person, the increasing use of dialogue, the introduction of characters and conflict (danger), creating scenes instead of narrative, and the use of details.

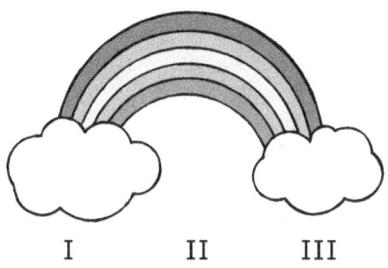

I   II   III

Version I - Cold (first draft)

The Komodo dragon, Latin name *Varanus komodoensis*, was not discovered until 1912. It is the world's largest monitor lizard and grows to three meters in length. It is an ancient creature.

They are voracious and feed on young deer, wild pigs, and sometimes even attack wild horses.

They are also cannibalistic.

They have several snake-like characteristics: a forked tongue and the ability to disjoint their lower and upper jaws in order to swallow large chunks of prey.

Dragons lay their three dozen eggs in nests made of dirt and leaves that have been abandoned by ground-dwelling megapode birds. The decomposing detritus provides the heat to incubate the dragon eggs, but the female has to keep guard to ward off other predatory dragons. They can move quickly, and tourists are warned to be careful when around the dragons.

Version II - Warm (second draft)

We saw several adult Komodo dragons, the world's largest monitor lizards, weighing as much as seventy kilograms, hanging around the staff quarters of the national park station, attracted to the smells of lunch being cooked. The park ranger warned us that while they look slow, they can move quickly.

Along the trail we saw a female dragon guarding her eggs. She flicked her forked tongue; the guard explained that this is one of the Komodo dragon's several snake-like characteristics. Another snake-like attribute is the dragon's ability to disjoint its lower and upper jaws in order to swallow large chunks of prey.

Dragons lay their three dozen eggs in dirt and leaf nests abandoned by ground-dwelling megapode birds. The decomposing detritus provides the heat to incubate the dragon eggs, but the female has to keep guard to ward off other predatory dragons. We shuffled within a meter of one such female. While she seemed more intent on her nap than breakfast, I was reminded that these reptiles are voracious and unpredictable. The park ranger told us to be careful; dragons have been known to attack tourists.

Version III - Hot (final)

I wasn't prepared for my first encounter with Komodo dragons. Just big lizards, I had thought.

But up close they looked like renegades from a bad horror film – lazy, nasty-looking brutes.

Although wild, the paradox is that the six animals we saw as we disembarked from our Zodiac had zero fear of people and were lounging around the staff quarters of the national park station, attracted to the smells of rice and curry being cooked. "Don't get too close," Abdurahman, the park ranger guiding us said. "They look slow but they can move quickly."

After half an hour of hiking along a hilly trail, our footsteps crackling the desiccated undergrowth, Abdurahman motioned for us to shut up and slow down. Cautiously, we crept up on a female dragon, almost as long as a car and weighing as much as a man, guarding her eggs.

"Don't startle her," Abdurahman, a slight young man who grew up with Komodo dragons roaming through his village, cautioned. She was lying just a meter away, too close for my comfort zone.

She blocked the path and Abdurahman, armed only with a flimsy stick, edged us past the animal.

She flicked her forked tongue. I recalled my pre-trip reading: the quick-moving dragon doesn't kill its prey immediately; it snaps at the deer or wild pig and the dragon's toxic saliva slowly incapacitates the victim. The dragon follows the wounded animal for hours, even days. Then, like a snake, it disjoints its upper and lower jaws in order to swallow large chunks of meat.

But instead of quickly moving out of snapping-range, Abdurahman paused to give us a biology lesson. "See those mounds?" Abdurahman asked. We bent down to examine four piles of dirt and leaves.

"They look like megapode nests," Clara, a woman in our group noted.

I wanted to suggest that maybe we could continue this discussion a bit farther from the dragon momma-to-be, but Abdurahman took up Clara's observation, explaining that dragons often lay their three dozen eggs in nests abandoned by ground-dwelling birds. The decomposing compost provides the heat to incubate the dragon eggs, but the female has to nevertheless keep guard to ward off other predatory cannibalistic dragons.

Finally, gingerly, we shuffled past the female dragon. While she seemed more intent on her nap than lunch, I was reminded of the Swiss man, Baron Rudolf von Reding Biberegg, who during a visit to Komodo in 1974 fell and injured his knee. His guide returned to a village to seek help. All the search party found hours later was the man's hat, camera, and a bloodstained shoe. Von Reding, 79, a seasoned hunter, made the ultimate contribution to nature conservation – he fed himself to an endangered species.

INCORPORATING COLD AND HOT IN A "COLD" NEWS FEATURE

By putting herself in the story from the beginning, Jane Brody makes an already hot subject (breast cancer, possible new treatment) even hotter. Brody has breast cancer and she is taking tamoxifen; her words take on added power.

Having completed the first two phases of treatment for an early breast cancer – a lumpectomy and six weeks of radiation therapy – I have now begun the third and, in a way, the most exciting phase: five years of daily treatment with the drug tamoxifen.

—Jane E. Brody. "Round 3 in a Cancer Battle." *The New York Times*, May 17, 1999.

INCORPORATING COLD AND HOT IN A PERSONAL ESSAY

Boxing and brains.
Photo: Eric Nelson

Here's one way to mix cold and hot. The author's inclination is to write cold – she has a Ph.D. in neuroscience and most everything Melissa Ray's written previously has been for publication in scholarly journals. But she catches our attention by the hot elements in her story. She asks a big, hot question – does boxing scramble a fighter's brain? And she makes it even hotter by asking, "does boxing scramble *my* brain?"

She wrote this as a blog, and I like the way she avoids the usual blog blandness and creates a fully formed story with conflict, scenes, not taking herself too seriously, and a circular structure. I also like the way she invites readers' comments in a separate addendum. She quotes experts, which makes her look smarter. I also think she's creating an interesting niche for herself, the articulate female neuroscientist who is a world-class Muay Thai fighter. Or vice-versa.

Ray starts with an anecdote lead, with plenty of conflict. She also sets up a Scheherezade Scenario by forcing the reader to ask: "Will this woman ever win a fight?"

I remember the bell dinging and a sober male voice announcing "Round one ..."

I breathed deeply and stepped towards the centre of the ring. It was my third fight. The venue was a grimy working men's club in Leeds, England, and my opponent a popular local girl with vociferous support. I was 26 and had trained with a Muay Thai master for about three years and was, I thought, in top physical condition. *I can take her*, I remember thinking. *I'm bigger, maybe quicker. And I've been studying the moves of the great Muay Thai boxers of Thailand.*

However, I lacked experience and had watched relatively few Muay Thai fights in person, relying instead on fight videos for inspiration.

My opponent, dressed in her gym's apparel of green shorts and a mustard yellow top, immediately started punching wildly – throwing big looping hooks.

Hold on – this isn't what happens in the videos!

One problem with studying videos of professional fighters is it left me with unrealistic expectations of how my own fight would progress. In the bouts I had watched, especially those in Thailand, the boxers would start slowly – tentatively feeling each other out in the first round. I was foolishly unprepared for my opponent's immediate onslaught. I tried to emulate my Thai heroes – mainly using my legs to throw controlled kicks to the body or lower leg. In contrast, my opponent rushed forward with fists flying and not a single kick thrown. One of those big hooks connected with my left temple. And then, nothing. The fight was over. It was less than a minute into the bout – probably even less than thirty seconds. I had, in boxing jargon, been "caught cold." My memories of the event are patchy. I don't recall experiencing any pain. I do remember my visual field gradually narrowing to darkness and the roar of the crowd petering out to silence. My next recollection is being in the changing rooms asking my trainer what happened. To this day I have no memory of the fight ending, congratulating my opponent, bowing and leaving the ring, and making my way backstage.

So, I took a severe blow to the head and lost the bout.

In time I would learn to deal with defeat, and how to win more than my share of fights.

Here are the first two of eleven questions in the article (and three more in Ray's end note) that keep the reader engaged.

But what about that punch to my left temple, and hundreds more I experienced during my eight-year fight career? Did they scramble my brain?

Here she shifts gears by giving us some backstory and explaining that her interest in brain physiology is both scientific and personal. Note the Nancy Reagan word "but" in the second paragraph below.

During the time I was training for that fight, my "day job" was studying for a Ph.D. in neuroscience (the study of the brain) at Newcastle University. Given my academic background, I take a particular interest in the risk of damage to the brain caused by blows to the head.

Muay Thai can be brutal. But there a good side to this Thai martial art – the respect and camaraderie between opponents. I know no other sport in which contestants can go from pounding each other to bowing at each other's feet within a matter of seconds.

Often likened to a game of chess (with violence), Muay Thai involves complex strategies for attack, defense and counter-attack, and requires the boxer to master a range of techniques. To train in Muay Thai is mentally as well as physically stimulating.

Elaine Perry, my mentor and professor of neurochemical pathology at Newcastle University, explains that when a person learns a new skill, this encourages the generation of new nerve connections in the brain.

I try to remember this as my trainer works me on the pads to near exhaustion – repeating the drills again and again. "Faster ... harder ... more turn in the hips ...," he bawls at me. As I kick, the ache in my hamstrings reminds me the technique is being committed to memory. The stiffness in my shoulders from punch combinations reminds me that nerve connections are being formed. This must be good for me.

The brain also has a regulatory process in which unused nerve cells are eliminated; so any activity that stimulates and encourages learning is beneficial to brain cell maintenance and function. The phrase "use it or lose it" applies to the brain as much as to the muscles. According to scientists from a Princeton University research team, vigorous exercise promotes the growth and survival of cells in an area of the brain involved in learning and memory. Increased blood flow during exercise has further beneficial effects of promoting the transport of oxygen and nutrients to brain cells. So perhaps Muay Thai helped me with my academic challenges?

Here Ray introduces a second "no" word – "but" – with a question, which forces her, and the reader, to look at things from a different point of view.

But what happens to these brain cells after a punch to the head, like the one I experienced that gloomy March afternoon in 2004?

As I learned all too quickly, there are different grades of blows. A knockout (KO) blow to the head is a fight-finishing strike – often associated with loss of consciousness caused by trauma to the brain stem following the sharp rotation of the skull. Memory loss and concussion are other adverse effects. Strikes to the head can be concussive without causing a KO and these are more difficult to recognize – symptoms of headache, confusion, memory loss, or dizziness might not appear until several hours after a bout. Repeated subconcussive blows – which can be sustained within a fight or during sparring – can also cause changes within the brain and loss of its cells.

According to the regulations, after a KO loss a boxer should not be allowed to compete again for at least thirty days. From what I have observed in Thailand, where I lived and practiced Muay Thai for six years, this rule is seldom enforced, especially in the provinces. Financial considerations tend to take precedence over safety considerations – fighters may have families to feed or gyms have overheads to be paid. About five years ago, while training in Chiang Mai in northern Thailand, I met one teenage boy named Deng who fought four times within a ten-day period, losing by KO on two occasions. After one of those KOs he was back in the ring only two days later, going on to win the ensuing bout. While I admired his tenacity, I did wonder what level of damage might have been inflicted on his adolescent brain.

Opponents of combat sports cite the cases of boxing legends Muhammad Ali and Freddie Roach to argue that boxing is dangerous and should be more strictly regulated.

Both former fighters developed symptoms of Parkinson's disease in their thirties and forties, including shaking, stiffness, and slowed speech and movement.

See how Ray keeps asking questions?

Was boxing responsible for the neurological problems they faced later in life?

The long-term effects of Muay Thai on the brain are unclear. Research is lacking – certainly in the English language – on former Muay Thai fighters and permanent damage that might have resulted from head trauma sustained during fights.

She then uses a Triple Whammy – the Rule of Three:

Probably most commonly considered as a nasty after-effect of a boxing career, dementia pugilistica, or "punch drunk syndrome," is a form of dementia that causes loss of memory, impairs the ability to concentrate, and leads to problems with coordination.

And here she introduces a celebrity to make her point stronger; in doing so she invokes the Story of One to represent the Story of Many (see Writing Tip #8 and Glossary).

Parkinson's disease shares some symptoms with dementia pugilistica but includes marked movement impairment and tremor. Its most high-profile sufferer is 70-year-old Muhammad Ali; I was one of billions of people around the world who watched his brave appearance at the 2012 London Olympics opening ceremony. His frail, trembling figure was a stark contrast to the lightning quick younger Ali who would "float like a butterfly, sting like a bee" in the boxing ring.

Can his symptoms be attributed to his having taken too many blows to the head?

Ali's own physician, Ferdie Pacheco, thinks so. Pacheco said that 70-year-old Ali is in fact suffering from Parkinson's syndrome, which is induced by physical trauma from boxing, and not Parkinson's disease. However, he also said that such a precise diagnosis could only be confirmed at autopsy.

To further complicate matters, aging fighters can be prone to alcoholism or substance abuse.

I remember countless conversations in the gyms in Thailand about former fighters who were lost on whiskey or "yaa baa" (methamphetamine) habits. Did brain trauma lead to these abusive habits? Were there other social factors at work?

Does wearing a head guard help prevent head trauma and resulting neurological disorder?

And she quotes other experts, which gives her credibility – it says she's serious and has done her homework.

In amateur Muay Thai, boxers are required to wear protective gear, including head guards. In Thailand, where most boxers fight professionally and even six-year-old kids fight without such protection, the Thais are bemused by the safety requirement.

Medical experts have different views on whether the wearing of a head guard actually offers any protection against head trauma. Professor Tim Noakes, head of the South African Sports Science Institute, has suggested that amateur boxing is safer than professional boxing because of the wearing of protective headgear and lower rate of KOs. Margaret Goodman, Ringside Physician and chairman of the Medical Advisory Board of the Nevada State Commission, argues that head guards only protect against cuts and facial swellings and do not prevent brain trauma. Sports neurologists have also suggested that it is the repeated subconcussive blows – not the KO blows – that cause most damage to brain health. A group of researchers from the New York Hospital for Special Surgery evaluated 42 professional boxers using tests measuring attention, concentration, and memory. Poor performance in these tests was related to the number of rounds of sparring a boxer had completed (when they were wearing head guards), and not with age, fight record, or history of KO.

After more than eleven years in the sport and more than forty fights, it is clear that I have not been deterred from training in Muay Thai, despite its risks. Even after the KO loss, my feelings were of embarrassment and disappointment in myself rather than any particular concern for my health. Risk of head injury is associated with many other sports (including cycling, football and rugby) and several daily-life activities. In Thailand, for instance, riding a motorbike without a helmet carries a far greater potential risk to health than fighting Muay Thai. People who are concerned about head trauma should not be put off from the sport. It is quite possible to train without head contact and receive the same health benefits. Fighting is another matter but perhaps the risk is part of what makes it so exciting? When I'm in the ring the heady rush of adrenaline triggered by the body's fight-or-flight response gives me a thrill and a feeling of fulfillment that overrides any fear of injury.

And she concludes with a satisfying circular structure, closing the Scheherazade Scenario (see pg. 112) loop.

> My subsequent bout was in an amateur tournament in Prague, Czech Republic against a tricky Turkish girl, well known on the international scene. I listened to my trainer's last-minute instructions and tuned out as the referee explained the rules in a language unknown to me. I bowed to my opponent with respect. And then the fight commenced. *Guard up, guard up!* I was not going to make the mistake of the previous bout – this time my left hand shielded my temple throughout the fight. We traded kicks, punches, and knees for the full three rounds, after which I felt tired but confident of victory. The result was announced and the referee held my right arm aloft to present me as the winner. I remember every moment.
>
> Request to readers: I am interested in hearing your views on this subject.
>
> Have you ever worried about damaging your brain through Muay Thai? How many of you have been knocked out during a fight and what are your memories of the experience? What are your views on wearing protective headgear – should it be made compulsory or do you feel it would "water down" a fight and make it less interesting?
>
> —Melissa Ray. "Muay Thai on the Brain." Participant in my writing workshop. Published in author's blog.

USE SPECIFIC COMPARISONS TO MAKE THE STORY HOTTER

Here's a fact. In 2010, gamblers in Macau bet about six hundred billion dollars.

Sounds like a lot? But compared to what?

Look at how Evan Osnos put the six hundred billion statistic into perspective:

> In 2010, high rollers in Macau wagered about six hundred billion dollars, *roughly the amount of cash withdrawn from all the A.T.M.s in America in a year.* [italics added]
>
> —Evan Osnos. "The God of Gamblers: Why Las Vegas is Moving to Macau."
> *New Yorker*, April 9, 2012.

And again:

> The infusion of China's new riches triggered an unprecedented surge of construction, and by 2006 Macau's casino revenues had surpassed those of Las Vegas, until then the world's largest gambling town. *Today, the quantity of money passing through Macau exceeds that of Las Vegas five times over.* [italics added]
>
> —Evan Osnos. "The God of Gamblers: Why Las Vegas is Moving to Macau."
> *New Yorker*, April 9, 2012

HOW TO USE FACTOIDS TO MAKE A MESSAGE HOTTER

I was communications director with the International Osteoporosis Foundation for ten years, and we developed ways to make cold statistics hotter. Some examples of a rainbow progression from cold to hot using osteoporosis factoids:

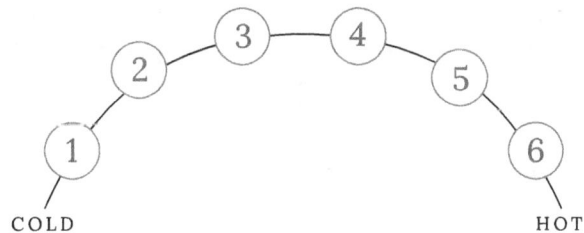

COLD   HOT

1. Osteoporosis affects about thirty-three percent of women over fifty.

2. Osteoporosis affects one out of three women over fifty.

3. Let me tell you the story of Maria Bianchi, a high school chemistry teacher in Milan. She's fifty-five years old and has osteoporosis. She has never hugged her granddaughter, Lucia. Lucia has been told, "Don't hug Nonna, Nonna can break."

4. Maria Bianchi is my neighbor.

5. Maria Bianchi is my grandmother – I've never hugged her.

6. I am Maria Bianchi.

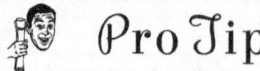

Pro Tip

Moving from Cold to Hot in a Presentation

To make a story hotter, personalize using the Story of One and use of "I", introduce conflict, and give details. Here's how one of my presentations progressed from cold to hot.

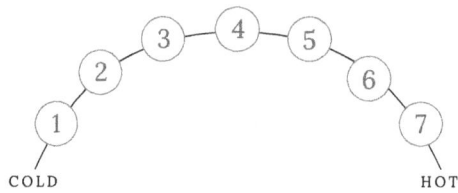

COLD   HOT

1. I stand on stage and say: "Osteoporosis is a skeletal condition characterized by decreased density (mass/volume) of normally mineralized bone. The reduced bone density leads to decreased mechanical strength, thus making the skeleton more likely to fracture."

2. I say: "When you have osteoporosis, your bones become brittle and break easily."

3. I take a rubber Halloween skeleton and bend the bones. I say: "Normal bones can resist moderate stress like this rubber skeleton."

4. I take a pencil and snap it in two. I say: "Osteoporotic bones snap under pressure."

5. I deliberately stumble and fall. The audience is surprised. Sometimes they even come forward to see if I'm ok. I say: "If I had osteoporosis, I certainly would have broken some bones just then – maybe my wrist, maybe my hip."

6. I say: "If I had broken my hip, I have the same risk of dying as if I had breast cancer."

7. I say: "I really did break my hip; could someone please call an ambulance?"

WRITING TIP #2

Tell the Story -
The Little Red Riding Hood Strategy

THE SCENE IS THE KEY

A story is made up of a bunch of scenes.

Master the scene and you give the story its power.

Writing one scene will jump-start a complex project.

Useful Advice from Someone
Who Wrote Pretty Well

In traditional journalism, the basic building block was the fact ... The more facts the better ... All this took place in the name of accuracy and objectivity – certainly not in the name of readability or memorability. The scene has now become the fundamental block around which the writer forms the story.

—Theodore A. Rees Cheney. *Writing Creative Nonfiction.*
Berkeley: Ten Speed Press. 2000.

Kids, Try This at Home

· · · · · · · · · THE PERFECT SCENE · · · · · · · · ·

Grab hold of a kid, and in your best theatrical guise tell him the crucial scene in Little Red Riding Hood (you know the one I mean – Little goes to her grandma's house and finds her grandma looking a bit strange. "Oh grandma, what big eyes you have!" That scene.

It's a classic scene. Not too long, not too short. With clearly defined characters. With plenty of conflict, setting, and details. With a cliffhanger ending that makes the reader wonder what's going to happen next.

The Grimm Brothers did not paraphrase the scene. They did not say:

> Little went to her grandmother's house and saw that her grandmother was looking odd. She asked what was wrong and the grandmother gave her obscure, confusing answers. After a brief exchange the grandmother revealed that she was a wolf and ate the little girl.

Here's what they did write, in a memorable scene:

> When Little Red Riding Hood arrived at her grandmother's cottage, she was surprised to find the door standing wide open.
>
> "Good morning, Grandmother!" she called out as she went inside, but she got no reply.
>
> Then Little Red Riding Hood began to feel rather uneasy. She went up to the bed and drew back the curtains.

There lay her grandmother, with her cap pulled down to her eyes and the bedclothes pulled up to her chin, looking very strange.

"Oh, Grandmother!" she cried. "What big ears you have!"

"All the better to hear you with, my dear," came the reply.

"Oh, Grandmother! What big eyes you have!"

"All the better to see you with, my dear!"

"Oh, Grandmother! What big hands you have!"

"All the better to hug you with, my dear!"

"Oh, Grandmother! What a big mouth you have!"

"All the better to eat you with!"

With these words, the wolf jumped out of bed and gobbled up Little Red Riding Hood in one mouthful.

Then he climbed into bed, lay down and fell fast asleep. Soon he began to snore. He snored so loudly that the cottage shook.

—Jacob and Wilhelm Grimm. *Little Red Riding Hood*. Retold by Vera Southgate. London: Laybird Books, 1988.

Put another way, don't paraphrase, don't summarize. Write the story in scenes. Show, don't tell. Put in the action, so we can see, hear, and feel what's going on. Use dialogue, conflict, and a Scheherazade ending.

THE FIVE SCENIC ELEMENTS

A scene has five ingredients:

* **Characters**
* **Dialogue**
* **Problem/conflict**
* **Setting**
* **Movement in the story**

WHAT DOES A SCENE IN A PERSONAL ESSAY LOOK LIKE?

Scenes don't have to be long. They do have to incorporate the five scenic elements. What follows are some successful scenes that use characters, dialogue, problems and conflict, setting and movement.

∾

Here's a two-paragraph scene from an article about Steve Prefontaine, a charismatic track star who died too young:

> His fans knew instinctively what had been taken from them in 1975. A memorial service was held for Prefontaine at [University of Oregon's] Hayward Field, where lies the soul of American track and field. The service lasted 12 minutes 36 seconds, which had been Prefontaine's unaccomplished goal for the three-mile run.
>
> A large crowd of mourners sat staring at the empty track. Over the last minute of the service, they began to rise and applaud as if Prefontaine was running before them. At 12:36 the clock froze like a beacon. For a few seconds thereafter, deep silence, and then somebody yelled, "Way to go, Pre!" And the crowd sent him off on a raucous victory lap.
>
> —Ian Thomsen. "It Takes a Nimble Touch to Capture Prefontaine's Elusive Spirit." *International Herald Tribune*, March 21-22, 1998.

∾

Here's another effective scene, a firsthand account of getting tear-gassed at the 2012 *Bersih* ("clean") demonstrations in Kuala Lumpur, Malaysia:

> The entire time, our skin was burning, our eyes were tearing, our noses were running, and we were gagging and vomiting. It was agony. But we couldn't stop. There was no place to stop ... So we shuffled on, trying our best not to fall. I remember an old *pakcik* near me tripping and I grabbed him. A little later on, I myself lost my balance and started to fall. I remember having the panicked thought, 'I can't fall! I'll be trampled!' I didn't fall. A Chinese guy next to me hauled me up and held me

upright. I turned to thank him and saw a really tall Malay guy behind us who kept throwing water from his humongous bottle all over us. A guy to my right shoved some salt into my hands. Another guy poured water over my face. I remember thinking, "Shit! I brought some salt, and now I have salt in my hands, but what the hell do I do with it? Do I smear it on my face? Do I eat it?" Someone told me to put some salt in my mouth. I did it. There was no instantaneous reprieve – the pain was still there, but somehow slowly I realized I was feeling a wee bit better.

Finally the crowd cleared a bit at Jalan Melaka and my vision cleared up enough to see where I was. I saw blood all over the street. I saw old *makciks* and *pakciks* struggling to get to safety. One old *pakcik* was simply sitting there exhausted, in the middle of the divider, minus his footwear. I walked up to him and gave him whatever salt I had left in my hand. Several of us offered to help him up to get him to safety, but he refused. He was simply too tired, too disappointed, and too disillusioned to move.

—Kaur Surin. Facebook public posting.

∽

And a scene from a book about an Indonesian woman from the city living with the Orang Rimba (People of the Jungle) in the Sumatran rainforest:

Indok holds the rat right in front of my face.

"Look friend, this rat is fat, it's delicious." I shudder with dread. The rat is about 30 centimeters away from my nose. Why is it so cute? Is this really a rat? Why is his fur so thick and grey? Could it be a rabbit? Indok proudly tells me all about the rat while plucking its fur. The fur floats through the air like cotton. That rat is still alive! *Astaga!* He is still squeaking! I ask Indok, "Why don't you kill it before you skin it?" She replies, "Ah, it's all the same my friend, the rat's going to die anyway."

"Would you like to try, my friend?" I refuse. I remember the sewer rats in Jakarta. But this one is quite cute; he even resembles Mickey Mouse! Regardless, he is still a rat to me.

I curiously ask how she plans to cook the rat; it seems a bit small for a family meal. "What about Rantai and Ngali? Will they get a share?" She answers that they are not allowed to eat rat because it is taboo for girls. Here's my chance!

I exclaim "Well, I'm already like an Orang Rimba. So I will obey the rules and not eat rat like the girls here." Indok laughs and expresses how delighted she is that I am following the customs of the Orang Rimba. Phew, thank God I got away with that one.

—Butet Manurung. *The Jungle School*. Jakarta: Yayasan Sokola. 2012.

And another scene in which Manurung offers condolences to the widow of the recently deceased tribal chief:

She looks morose, her eyes are lifeless, gazing. She is whimpering, although no tears are apparent.

... I hug her, stroke her back, and without realizing it, I am in tears ...

"It's okay ... Everything will be all right ... be patient my friend," I try to console her.

Still sobbing in my arms, she opens the plastic gift wrap exploring the content and whispers, "Friend, did you bring some instant noodles?"

"... *Aduh*, I did not my friend."

The sobbing starts again, still without tears. I have the urge to laugh, but control myself as best I can.

"What about sardines?"

... This is dreadful. The wailing grows louder, still without tears. I try to comfort her. At the same time, I begin to feel irritated. How can craving food be more important than grieving for her husband? I withdraw, saying I am exhausted from carrying the rice, sugar, and biscuits for her. I plead with her not to ask for things that I do not have. She nods in a fluster.

—Butet Manurung. *The Jungle School*. Jakarta: Yayasan Sokola. 2012.

Here's a scene in which Harry Rolnick and photographer John Everingham try to smuggle odiferous durians onto a flight in southern Thailand:

So that night, after we had procured two dozen big fruit, each about the size of a football, we searched around for a way to hide them from nosy airline personnel.

First, we scraped together tinfoil and plastic bags from a dumpster near the hotel and a tiny hardware shop. Then, under the sky on the beach, we took reams and reams of plastic, covered each durian carefully, and canopied it with tinfoil. To finish the operation, we put each fruit into the bags John usually uses for sealing rolls of film in tropical climates.

To be on the safe side, though, we took this bundle of plastic-wrapped, foiled, bagged fruit and locked it in a big suitcase, which we could store in the baggage compartment. To celebrate these labors of Hercules, we shared a durian, and prayed that the gods would bless our efforts.

The next morning we innocently, insouciantly checked the contraband suitcase into the luggage compartment of Thai Airways and boarded. The plane was due to leave at 10.00 A.M., but as usual it was running late, and at 11.00 A.M. we were still on the ground. Hardly serious, we thought.

That, though, was when the stewardess stood in front of the plane and asked for our attention. Being Thai, she tried to speak loudly, but her voice came out in a whisper announcing a serious problem on board.

In the translation from Thai, she said: "Somebody on this plane is not polite. Even though we have rules, a passenger has brought many durians on board. And the aroma has reached the cockpit. And the pilots are very unhappy. They will not leave the ground."

She was silent, thinking what next to say. Then she must have remembered her school days.

"Would the impolite people," she asked, "please raise their hands?"

We looked around to see if somebody else would take the blame. But John finally owned up to his crime and reluctantly obeyed, raising his hand like a schoolboy caught smoking. Then I raised my own hand, almost prepared to ask the teacher if I could make a wee-wee. Our stewardess looked embarrassed to see such nice foreigners feeling so guilty. She darted back to the cockpit, and then returned.

"Please," she said in halting English. "Please do something with the durian. Please go outside. We will find the durian for you. We will help you." Both John and I prayed silently that she wouldn't cry.

After a moment of silence, a magisterial "harrumph" came from two seats behind us. First, a short elderly man, dressed in wrinkled khakis laden with ribbons and medals, stood up. He was a colonel in the Royal Thai Army, now retired, but still ready to do his duty. He asked us with avuncular kindness how many durians we had. We told him we were carrying them for friends in a country that was bereft of durian [Everingham was planning to take them to durian-challenged Laos]. Like military orderlies from *A Farewell to Arms*, we were carrying blood to the wounded in an Asian Catalonia.

The colonel hesitated for a moment and then declared his plan to the other passengers. In military language, he announced that if it was all right with the farangs (us), everybody would disembark and share the durians together.

"It is," he said in Thai, "fair. It is the Thai way ..."

The stewardess darted back to the cockpit and the pilots agreed to the plan. The controls were dis-controlled, the doors opened, and every passenger disembarked. Our suitcase came out of the hold, bags were opened, storage container unglued, tinfoil removed, plastic unwrapped, and one of the passengers (presumably a terrorist) took out a carving knife to cut open the fruit.

Thus, for the next hour, while the plane lolled on the runway, we sat on the tarmac and ate durian and told stories and laughed and became soppy with the fruits and our new friends: passengers, pilots and, of course, our newest friend, the stewardess ...

When we finally boarded, a mere ninety minutes late at high noon, every breath we took over the next two hours back to Bangkok breathed out the delicate aroma of Limburger cheese, old socks, and that oh-so-sweet taste of Thailand.

We, the fellowship of durian lovers, soaring as near to heaven as our sulfuric odors would allow. As durable, acrid, and luscious as life itself.

—Harry Rolnick. *Spice Chronicles: Exotic Tales of a Hungry Traveler*.
Santa Ana: Seven Locks Press. 2006.

Another Rolnick scene, in which he releases his special brand of punmanship:

When going to a funeral [in Toraja, southern Sulawesi, Indonesia], you are expected to visit the market and offer a sacrificial animal or two. Most buy a pig. Rich Torajans may offer a buffalo ...

Once guests pile into the arena, they become part of an enormous abattoir cum food-processing plant. As each animal is taken by hand (or paw), the shaman – literally the master of ceremonies – screams out his thanks ... to the rest of the crowd that Mr. Shakli and his esteemed family have offered a big pig or a huge buffalo in order to show their respect for the body. Everybody in the stands shouts out deafening approval, and the pig, about to join the din with a great squeal, is silenced when an assistant shaman bashes it over the head with a six-foot-long frying pan ...

I had only a vague idea of the Torajan ceremony, and being invited, thought myself honored ... I asked my guide what kind of gift I should offer.

"Oh," he said, "since you're a foreigner, they'll be thrilled just to have you at all. Nobody expects much, so you can just bring a carton of cigarettes ...

I bought a carton of Marlboro Lights, feeling suitably generous ... I got in the noisy line of animals and merrymakers from the district ...

Just in front of me were six very jolly Germans. So jolly were they that they had gone to the market, and they had brought their own swine to the ceremony. How wunderbar! How native! How schwein-respecting!!!

The Frankfurt sextet ... triumphantly hoisted it on their broad shoulders and jostled their way into the arena ...

This was the portion of the ceremony when the shaman, his head-feathers dancing in the wind, shouts out which family contributed what. So when it came time to describe the foreigners' contributions, he was literally beside himself ...

"Here ... here in our very presence are German people. They are from Germany. Which is near to Holland." (The Indonesians still have grudging admiration for the old colonizers.) "They are heroes for Torajan people. Because they respect Torajan people ...

"And in our honor they have carried a pig. Not an ordinary pig but a pig of immaculate quality. This pig will feed far more people than any normal pig. And the Toraja people should cheer our German friends wildly ..."

Then the Torajans did cheer. Led by the shaman, egged on by the sow-chefs, echoed by the strainer-people and official boilers – and, of course, augmented by the damned pig – the stand screeched louder and louder and louder, until the whole arena was on its feet.

That was when the Germans broke the rules. They rose from their seats in the stands and marched, then trotted, then ran on to those killing fields like first place winners at the 1936 Olympics. They stood beside the writhing pig, taking pictures of themselves, posing with the jubilant shaman and his exhilarated minions, and the crowd went into near hysterics. This, I thought, again discourteously, was what the Nuremberg rallies must have sounded like ...

And now the crowd suddenly hushed. Because now, said the shaman, this ceremony would be blessed. Blessed with yet another foreigner.

The shaman, finishing with the prancing Germans, looked straight through the arena into my eyes and pointed. The crowd followed the pointing fingers to my destination in noisy expectation. What, they wondered, could possibly be more imposing, more moving, than a German pig?

The shaman shouted out his question to my guide, who shouted something back.

I didn't understand the words of my translator. But somewhere in the sentence, I heard the world "Marlboro" talktalktalktalk Marlboro Lights talktalktalktalk ...

The shaman looked at me, looked at the ground, then shrugged his shoulders. Then he shouted out the news to the multitudes.

"The other foreigner," he proclaimed, "has brought a carton of cigarettes."

The arena was silent.

"Foreign Marlboro cigarettes," he shouted, hoping this would put icing on the cake.

For a moment, a hush fell over the crowd. And then, bless their modified Christian charity, they politely clapped. I smiled. I waved with the enthusiastic wave Queen Elizabeth gives from her car. More precisely, I gave a microwave ... The family of the deceased, bless their hearts, did have a genuine nobility. They came through the stands and happily took the carton of cigarettes and thanked me. Shaking my hand, smiling, telling my translator that I was a kind man. They were kind, civil, polite. To the stares of the multitude, they opened a pack, lit up a Marlboro, shook my hand, and marched back to open ground near the boiling cauldron, waving their cigarettes triumphantly.

—Harry Rolnick. *Spice Chronicles: Exotic Tales of a Hungry Traveler.*
Santa Ana: Seven Locks Press. 2006.

∞

And to break the rule, here's a scene with just one character, no dialogue (but plenty of details), and a powerful understated conflict – Wadler has breast cancer and might die.

> I remember I have to make my decision about the scar. I put on a bandeau bra that is the skimpiest I own and a skinny little Nicole Miller dress, deep purple, with spaghetti straps, that I wore when Nick took me dancing at the Rainbow Room. I loved that night. I had a thirties evening bag that I had got for 40 francs at a flea market in Paris and a Deco rhinestone bracelet from an estate sale in New York, and as I get dressed I wonder about the women who had owned the bag and the bracelet, and where they had worn them, and if they had been as happy as I. Then I take off the dress and turn down the top of the bra a little bit and trace the edge with a ballpoint pen. As I do, I start to cry. I don't have a perfect body by model standards, my breasts are different from what they were in my twenties, but they are my breasts, it is my body, and I like it very much. Now I am making a mark that says, "Cut me."
>
> —Joyce Wadler. "My Breast: One Woman's Cancer Story."
> *New York Magazine*, April 13 and April 20, 1992.

∞

Here's a scene that has conflict, dialogue, and movement, as Jeff Greenwald takes his friend to see a Buddha statue in Kathmandu that he is thinking of buying, a statue that on first viewing met all his criteria for "perfection."

We strolled past the pagodas, into the shopping district, through an ever-narrowing maze of alleyways until – right on time – we located Tashi's shop.

It was closed! Bright blue shutters boarded the windows, and a big, black Chinese "Friendship" brand padlock bolted the door. What to do? We planted ourselves on the step.

We waited; and waited. I started to get a little bit irritated. Where the hell was this guy, anyway? After another fifteen minutes I was a lot irritated. Who did this arrogant son of a bitch think I was? Time, I determined, to adopt a somewhat more aggressive strategy. Where, to begin with, did this clown live?

After asking around at the neighboring shops, we were directed to the sculptors' district. The setting was positively medieval. Dogs limped through the streets; thick smoke, tasting of rough tobacco and hot wax, plumed out of carved wooden windows. Clusters of pan-spitting twelve-year-old boys sat in some of the doorways, chain-smoking Yak filter cigarettes and laying into half-finished Buddhas, Taras, and Manjushris with primitive carving tools.

Our shopkeeper's house was a tall white structure that leaned imposingly into the narrow, brick-paved alley. I knocked at the rickety wooden door. No answer. Damnation! The guy wasn't even home! At last the *sowji*'s little son answered the door and bade us wait inside.

"Where is your father?"

"Gone away. He come back soon, I think."

"How soon?

The wagged his head noncommittally. I snorted. Time was a wastin'. Our appointment had been for two; it was already a quarter to four. Soon the shops down on New Road would be closed – their new shipments of Buddhas spoken for by affluent collectors. Who could say what golden opportunities were slipping away as we bided our time in Patan? Finally it was too much to stand.

"Tell your father I couldn't wait any longer," I said, "and that his rudeness has cost him a very important sale. I was genuinely interested in that little Chenrezig."

"You must please come back tomorrow."

"No chance. One wasted day is enough."

The moment we stood up to leave I heard the tympanic thrum of a motorcycle approaching down the alley. Sure enough, it was Tashi, the proprietor of the shop. He parked the cycle, glanced guiltily at me, and pulled off his helmet. He looked surprisingly pale.

"I'm sorry to be so late..."

"I'm sorry too," I snapped.

"... but right after you called, my sister-in-law came running over to give me some terrible news. My brother was hit by a taxi, and they had to rush him to Patan Hospital."

"I see." We stood there in silence for a long moment. "Gee, I'm really sorry." More silence; it was still my move. "Well," I said, "do you feel like taking a walk down to your shop? I'd still like to see that Chenrezig."

The shopkeeper nodded, and we strolled in silence to his store. He opened the lock and threw back the shutters. There it was – the statue that I'd had such grand memories of – that I had essentially made up my mind to buy.

But wait! Something was wrong! Something was terribly, terribly wrong! The Chenrezig, which in my memory had been smooth and clean, seemed to be covered all over with black, rancid butter!

"What's all this gook?" I cried, setting the statue down and wiping my hands compulsively on my jeans. I turned to Nancy, embarrassed and apologetic. "It wasn't like this before!"

"Oh, yes," Tashi muttered. "Same, same, same..."

"No it was *not* the same! What have you done? You've smeared all this butter oil all over it! Oh, why, why, why?"

"Same as before. Nothing is change."

I heaved a sigh of disappointment and shook my head. Was he right? No – couldn't be – I would definitely have remembered something like this! Wouldn't I?

"Well, listen. There must be some way to clean all this stuff off, isn't there? Some chemical? Look, I could do it myself."

The shopkeeper picked his keys up off the glass counter. I won't describe the look he gave me.

"There is no way. Everything is same. You see the bell shape? Same. So. Do you want to buy?"

"No. No. No. No."

I trudged from the shop into the dusty dry air, avoiding the sight of my reflection in the snack shop windowpanes.

—Jeff Greenwald. *Shopping for Buddhas.* San Francisco: Harper & Row, 1990.

This scene below works because the author is in the apartment in which two mad Russian geniuses have built a supercomputer out of scrap parts in order to try to calculate the value of *pi*. His first-person retelling gives him credibility.

Gregory said, "Our knowledge of pi was barely in the millions of digits ..."

"We need many billions of digits," David said. "Even a billion digits is a drop in the bucket. Would you like a Coca-Cola?" He went into the kitchen and there was a horrible crash. "Never mind, I broke a glass," he called. "Look, it's not a problem." He came out of the kitchen carrying a glass of Coca-Cola on a tray, with a paper napkin under the glass, and as he handed it to me he urged me to hold it tightly, because if a Coca-Cola spilled into it – he didn't want to think about it; it would set back the project by months.

—Richard Preston. "The Mountains of Pi." *New Yorker*, March 2, 1992.

Here's a scene written by John Updike about the last at-bat of Ted Williams, reminding us that the quality of sports writing is inversely proportional to the size of the ball. The passage illustrates a classic Nancy Reagan by asking the question, "will he hit a home run?" Bonus: the iconic phrase at the end.

The afternoon grew so glowering that in the sixth inning the arc lights were turned on – always a wan sight in the daytime, like the burning headlights of a funeral procession. Aided by the gloom, Fisher was slicing through the Sox rookies, and Williams did not come to bat in the seventh. He was second up in the eighth. This was almost certainly his last time to come to the plate in Fenway Park, and instead of merely cheering, as we had at his three previous appearances, we stood, all of us – stood and applauded. Have you ever heard applause in a ballpark? Just applause – no calling, no whistling, just an ocean of handclaps, minute after minute, burst after burst, crowding and running together in continuous succession like the pushes of surf at the edge of the sand. It was a sombre and considered tumult. There was not a boo in it. It seemed to renew itself out of a shifting set of memories as the kid, the Marine, the veteran of feuds and failures and injuries, the friend of children, and the enduring old pro evolved down the bright tunnel of twenty-one summers toward this moment. At last, the umpire signaled for Fisher to pitch; with the other players, he had been frozen in position. Only Williams had moved during the ovation, switching his bat impatiently, ignoring everything except his cherished task. Fisher wound up, and the applause sank into a hush.

Understand that we were a crowd of rational people. We knew that a home run cannot be produced at will; the right pitch must be perfectly met and luck must ride with the ball. Three innings before, we had seen a brave effort fail. The air was soggy; the season was exhausted. Nevertheless, there will always lurk, around a corner in a pocket of our knowledge of the odds, an indefensible hope, and this was one of the times, which you now and then find in sports, when a density of expectation hangs in the air and plucks an event out of the future.

Fisher, after his unsettling wait, was wide with the first pitch. He put the second one over, and Williams swung mightily and missed. The crowd grunted, seeing that classic swing, so long and smooth and quick, exposed, naked in its failure. Fisher threw the third time, Williams swung again, and there it was. The ball climbed on a diagonal line into the vast volume of air over center field. From my angle, behind third base, the ball seemed less an object in flight than the tip of a towering, motionless construct, like the Eiffel Tower or the Tappan Zee Bridge. It was in the books while it was still in the sky. Brandt ran back to the deepest corner of the outfield grass; the ball descended beyond his reach and struck in the crotch where the bullpen met the wall, bounced chunkily, and, as far as I could see, vanished.

Like a feather caught in a vortex, Williams ran around the square of bases at the center of our beseeching screaming. He ran as he always ran out home runs – hurriedly, unsmiling, head down, as if our praise were a storm of rain to get out of. He didn't tip his cap. Though we thumped, wept, and chanted "We want Ted" for minutes after he hid in the dugout, he did not come back. Our noise for some seconds passed beyond excitement into a kind of immense open anguish, a wailing, a cry to be saved. But immortality is nontransferable. The papers said that the other players, and even the umpires on the field, begged him to come out and acknowledge us in some way, but he never had and did not now. Gods do not answer letters.

—John Updike. "Hub Fans Bid Kid Adieu." *New Yorker*, October 22, 1960.

SCENES KEEP THE STORY MOVING

Here's a personal essay that gives the reader the sense of being there. Helene Dillman writes scenes with characters, dialogue, conflict, setting, and a few Scheherazade Scenarios, and her son Roscoe as a running thread.

"I want the Lego ATTE." "I want the I-Touch." "I need a new computer." "I want fun things in my stocking." My children were chanting their Christmas wishes. I was waiting in vain for the moment when I would hear, "I want to help the poor."

We were able to give our children the gingerbread cookies and turkey and heaps of store-bought presents, but my husband and I felt it was time to give them a lesson in the spirit of giving. Our four smart, comfortable children agreed with our wild idea that we should do something for those who are less fortunate for Christmas. We were living in Bangkok and there are many opportunities for helping others.

The Human Development Foundation, which is run by the pragmatic Father Joe Maier, an Irish priest from Boston, quickly came to mind as a group we might help. They build schools, protect street children and offer shelter to orphans and people with AIDS. They believe that simple but progressive solutions can impact the lives of those living in the slums of Bangkok.

The simple solution Father Joe proposed is that our children take his children shopping. Surprisingly, my gang all agreed to give up $72 of their Christmas cash to treat the 24 orphans to a shopping spree. "I'm giving up 72 songs on iTunes" said Victoria, 14. "That's a lot of nail polish and earrings" lamented Alison, 13. "My

American Girl Doll," whined Catherine, 7. "That's a lot of money" thought Roscoe, 10. He loves everything about money and hordes his cash in a secret hiding spots.

After a reconnaissance, we agreed to shop at Carrefour, a hypermarket with the best prices on Barbie Dolls, games and plastic planes. Each orphan would have 400 baht (roughly US$14), ample money for a new toy and some candy. Introductions were quickly made. We were overwhelmed. How would we ever remember all of the names: Noy, Lek, Lem, SomChit? How could we keep them all straight when they were all wearing identical yellow golf shirts, blue shorts and the same bobbed hair cut?

My family decided to divide and conquer. My older daughters tried to get the younger girls to go with them to the toy section. Roscoe, grumbling about the lack of boys, followed a group of slightly older girls, muttering about the great dart set he had previously scouted. Catherine and I chased in vain after the identical triplets whose carts moved in perfect synchronization.

These kids had a plan. They led us to the epicenter of the store. A huge table piled with a rainbow selection of all sizes and shape of knickers. They were gleeful choosing colors and holding them up for size. Roscoe was mortified. He went to the toy section and came with some games sets and cans of silly string. The girls brushed him off like his own sisters did, with a look and a shrug.

He wasn't about to give up. Any candy was better than knickers. He approached the girls again with the jumbo bag of jellies. He saw the look and backed away. Our older daughters stood off to the side a bit, embarrassed over the colorful selection of thongs and hipsters. They pursed their lips and looked down at their shoes. Catherine was right in there asking for some new ones too. We reminded her it wasn't her day.

After a good twenty minutes of going through every pair on the table, decisions were made. Some of the girls had a cart full of lacy colors and some had empty carts. Like a swarm of birds startled by a cat, they all grabbed for their carts and rushed off in different directions. We had missed the secret signal.

We soon realized the next prearranged meeting point was for flip flops. Again we were met with the big bargain bin. Forty-eight feet were simultaneously trying them on for size. Then as quickly as at the knickers, it was over. Everything was back in place and now most of the carts were sporting Pepto Bismol-pink sandals.

I started chasing after the triplets again. They lost me in toothbrushes. Nat, 12, was looking to buy her brother, who was back at the orphanage, some new shorts, and a gift for her mother, who was in jail. Another two girls were pooling their extra money together to buy something for Ploy, who was too sick to come out today.

The older girls reined in the triplets and helped them find pajamas, new toothbrushes with mini tubes of toothpaste and their own bottles of shampoo.

The shopping spree was ending. Roscoe was getting excited and was running out of time. He tried in vain to get the girls to follow him down the candy aisle. They turned one aisle too soon. They wanted lip balm. Yes, thought my older daughters. They could help them choose the perfect shade of lip gloss. They held up all of their favorite colors. No, the girls wanted something for chapped lips and the camphor inhalers, for stuffed up noses. My daughters sighed.

The children lined up at the checkout counter. Not one asked for more than their 400 baht budget. Most children were under the amount; 399, 397. They maximized the opportunity. Catherine decided she would help out as the bagger. Roscoe was not touching all of those knickers.

While Roscoe and Catherine were frustrated with the purchases made, the older girls were more introspective. It was the first time they realized how much more they had than many others. "I felt proud to help, but was embarrassed that I thought they would want material things. It inspires me to be better," explained Victoria. "The kids had fun, but it feels sad that now we go to our very different homes," continued Alison. "It felt like I gave something real."

Part of me likes to think I gave the children an uplifting lesson. But I have a feeling my real Christmas gift to my children was much more basic: Catholic guilt, something they would keep their whole life.

—J. Helene Dillman. Participant in my writing workshop.

Think of the scene as a brick, the building block of your story. A man in twelfth-century Paris stopped by a construction site and asked two masons what they were doing. The first replied, "I'm making a brick, as you can plainly see, you silly old fool." The second replied, "I'm building a cathedral to be named Notre Dame to honor the glory of God." (And under his breath muttered, "silly old fool.")

ONCE IN A WHILE, TAKE AS MUCH TIME AS YOU NEED

In writing, as in sex, the winner isn't necessarily the one who finishes first.

Here's a 1,300-word scene in *Eat, Pray, Love*, in which Elizabeth Gilbert weaves the five scenic elements: characters, dialogue, problem/conflict, setting, movement in the story.

I won't get into the question of whether this scene is too neat to be real, but it certainly works as literature.

The first few paragraphs introduce the problem, setting up a Scheherazade Scenario – will she get the divorce?

> Going through a difficult and excruciatingly painful divorce, I'd been living in a giant trash compactor of non-stop anxiety. My relationship with my husband now thoroughly ruined, with even civility destroyed between us, all I wanted anymore was the door.
>
> The question was – would he sign the divorce papers? More weeks passed as he contested more details. If he didn't agree to this settlement, we'd have to go to trial. A trial would almost certainly mean that every remaining dime would be lost in legal fees. Worst of all, a trial would mean another year – at least – of all this mess.
>
> I had lines in my face, no, permanent incisions dug between my eyebrows, from crying and from worry.

But the above problems are floating without an anchor. Here Gilbert introduces a sidekick (with her own conflict-laden backstory) and a setting (a long car ride) that works as a crucible.

> And in the middle of all that, a book that I'd written a few years earlier was being published in paperback and I had to go on a small publicity tour. I took my friend Iva with me for company. Iva is my age but grew up in Beirut, Lebanon. Which means that, while I was playing sports and auditioning for musicals in a Connecticut middle school, she was cowering in a bomb shelter five nights out of seven, trying not to die. I'm not sure how all this early exposure to violence created somebody who's so steady now, but Iva is one of the calmest souls I know. Moreover, she's got what I call "The Bat Phone to the Universe", some kind of Iva-only, open-round-the-clock special channel to the divine.

Having two characters gives Gilbert the chance to use dialogue, often expressed as questions.

> So we were driving across Kansas, and I was in my normal state of sweaty disarray over this divorce deal – will he sign, will he not sign? – and I said to Iva, "I don't think I can endure another year in court. I wish I could get some divine intervention here. I wish I could write a petition to God, asking for this thing to end."
>
> "So why don't you?"
>
> I explained to Iva my personal opinions about prayer. Namely, that I don't feel comfortable petitioning for specific things from God, because that feels to me like a kind of weakness of faith. I don't like asking, "Will you change this or that thing in my life that's difficult for me?" Because – who knows? – God might want me to be facing that particular challenge for a reason. Instead, I feel more comfortable praying for the courage to face whatever occurs in my life with equanimity, no matter how things turn out.
>
> Iva listened politely, then asked, "Where'd you get that stupid idea?"
>
> "What do you mean?"
>
> "Where did you get the idea you aren't allowed to petition the universe with prayer? You are part of this universe, Liz. You're a constituent – you have every entitlement to participate in the actions of the universe, and to let your feelings be known. So put your opinion out there. Make your case. Believe me – it will at least be taken into consideration."
>
> "Really?" All this was news to me.
>
> "Really! Listen – if you were to write a petition to God right now, what would it say?"
>
> I thought for a while, then pulled out a notebook and wrote this petition:

> Dear God.
>
> Please intervene and help end this divorce. My husband and I have failed at our marriage and now we are failing at our divorce. This poisonous process is bringing suffering to us and to everyone who cares about us.
>
> I recognize that you are busy with wars and tragedies and much larger conflicts than the ongoing dispute of one dysfunctional couple. But it is my understanding that the health of the planet is affected by the health of every individual on it. As long as even two souls are locked in conflict, the

whole of the world is contaminated by it. Similarly, if even one or two souls can be free from discord, this will increase the general health of the whole world, the way a few healthy cells in a body can increase the general health of that body.

It is my most humble request, then, that you help us end this conflict, so that two more people can have the chance to become free and healthy, and so there will be just a little bit less animosity and bitterness in a world that is already far too troubled by suffering.

I thank you for your kind attention.
Respectfully, Elizabeth M. Gilbert

I read it to Iva, and she nodded her approval.

"I would sign that," she said.

I handed the petition over to her with a pen, but she was too busy driving, so she said, "No, let's say that I did just sign it. I signed it in my heart."

"Thank you, Iva. I appreciate your support."

"Now, who else would sign it?" she asked.

"My family. My mother and father. My sister."

"OK," she said. "They just did. Consider their names added. I actually felt them sign it. They're on the list now. OK – who else would sign it? Start naming names."

Here Gilbert starts to write music – read the next few paragraphs out loud to see how she dances.

So I started naming names of all the people who I thought would sign this petition. I named all my close friends, then some family members and some people I worked with. After each name, Iva would say with assurance, "Yep. He just signed it," or "She just signed it." Sometimes she would pop in with her own signatories, like: "My parents just signed it. They raised their children during a war. They hate useless conflict. They'd be happy to see your divorce end."

I closed my eyes and waited for more names to come to me.

"I think Bill and Hilary Clinton just signed it," I said.

"I don't doubt it," she said. "Listen, Liz – anybody can sign this petition. Do you understand that? Call on anyone, living or dead, and start collecting signatures."

"Saint Francis of Assisi just signed it!"

"Of course he did!" Iva smacked her hand against the steering wheel with certainty.

Now I was cooking:

"Abraham Lincoln just signed it! And Gandhi, and Mandela and all the peacemakers. Eleanor Roosevelt, Mother Teresa, Bono, Jimmy Carter, Muhammad Ali, Jackie Robinson and the Dalai Lama ... and my grandmother who died in 1984 and my grandmother who's still alive ... and my Italian teacher, and my therapist, and my agent ... and Martin Luther King Jr. and Katharine Hepburn ... and Martin Scorsese (which you wouldn't necessarily expect, but it's still nice of him) ... and my Guru, of course ... and Joanne Woodward, and Joan of Arc, and Ms. Carpenter, my fourth grade teacher, and Jim Henson ..."

The names spilled from me. They didn't stop spilling for almost an hour, as we drove across Kansas and my petition for peace stretched into page after invisible page of supporters. Iva kept confirming – yes, he signed it, yes, she signed it – and I became filled with a grand sense of protection, surrounded by the collective goodwill of so many mighty souls.

The list finally wound down, and my anxiety wound down with it. I was sleepy. Iva said, "Take a nap. I'll drive." I closed my eyes. One last name appeared. "Michael J. Fox just signed it," I murmured, then drifted into sleep. I don't know how long I slept, maybe only for ten minutes, but it was deep. When I woke up, Iva was still driving. She was humming a little song to herself. I yawned.

And she ends with a circular structure (Too contrived? You decide.), completing the Scheherezade Scenario.

My cell phone rang.

I looked at that crazy little *telefonino* vibrating with excitement in the ashtray of the rental car. I felt disoriented, kind of stoned from my nap, suddenly unable to remember how a telephone works.

"Go ahead," Iva said, already knowing. "Answer the thing."

I picked up the phone, whispered hello.

"Great news!" my lawyer announced from distant New York City. "He just signed it!"

—Elizabeth Gilbert. *Eat, Pray, Love.* New York: Viking. 2006.

Kids, Try This at Home

· · · · · · · · · WRITE A JOKE · · · · · · · · ·

∽

Think of a favorite joke. Write it. This is surprisingly hard; it forces you to consider structure, rhythm, dialogue, how much detail to put in. If it hangs together, bravo – you've just written a scene.

ANOTHER TERRIFIC SCENE

It's my summary of the end of the first act of Puccini's *Turandot.*

Turandot, the beautiful but nasty Chinese Ice Princess, insists that her suitors answer three riddles. If they fail, she orders them killed.

Enter a stranger, a prince incognito, named Calaf. Through the magic of contrived Italian opera, he runs into the slave girl Liù, who used to work in his palace and who has had a crush on him since forever – in her famous aria she tells Calaf that her motivation to continue living is "because you once smiled at me." Calaf watches enchanted as Turandot orders that her most recently unsuccessful suitor change his Facebook status from hapless to headless. Calaf says, "that's the girl for me," and prepares to bang the royal gong that signifies "a suicidal suitor is in the house."

Liù begs him not to.

Ping, Pang, and Pong, royal jesters who fill the niche of Commedia dell'Arte-like clowns, beg him not to.

Calaf's own father, the King of Tartary (it's complicated) begs him not to.

The chorus swells in warning.

Calaf says, "By golly, Turandot is the princess of my dreams."

He bangs the gong three times.

Liù is dismayed.

Calaf's father is terrified.

Ping, Pang, and Pong laugh cynically.

Curtain of first act.

Music: Giacomo Puccini. Libretto: Giuseppe Adami and Renato Simoni.

HOW TO RECOGNIZE (AND FIX) A NARRATIVE IN DESPERATE NEED OF A SCENE

Here's an article that is informative but feels flat because the writer has not written in scenes. Rene Sepul's lead is as cold as Wikipedia and does nothing to get us into the story.

> Luang Prabang, the former royal capital of Laos, is situated by the Mekong river in the mountainous north of the country. It is easy to understand why this peaceful city of exquisite charm and beauty was appointed "the best preserved city of Indochina" and official "Heritage of Culture" by UNESCO last year. Its origins go back to very ancient times.

And then Sepul *tells* us about interesting events and observations but does not *show* us. He needs to write in scenes, to speak with Laotians. He introduces important and interesting concepts, like "nirvana" and "stupa" without explaining their meanings. The story has no Nancy Reagan conflicts, no human beings, no blood and guts, and the result is flat, like this passage:

> The following morning there is a market where parents go with their children to buy all sorts of animals – small birds, parrots, turtles, lizards and a multitude of fish – and set them free.
>
> The parents believe that by doing this good deed their children can attain *nirvana*. Another important item that is for sale at the market is the zodiac flag. The flags come in use later in the afternoon when most people catch a boat to an island on the Mekong where they build sand stupas on the beach.
>
> This is an act of personal purification since each grain of sand that is incorporated in the *stupa* signifies a sin that one is getting rid of.

> —Rene Sepul. "Pi May in Luang Prabang." *SilkWinds.*

Each writer would have his own way of creating a scene out of such a passage; here's one way Sepul could have crafted a scene to increase reader intimacy – I've made up details, but you get the idea:

> One hardly needs to "escape" from Luang Prabang, but I nevertheless sought a respite from the town's charm. I paid twenty cents to board a simple ferry one afternoon to join several family groups, carrying picnic baskets and child-sized pails and shovels, heading for Paradise Island, not much more than a large sandbar in the middle of the Mekong. Scattered along the beach were groups of people building what looked like mound-shaped sand castles. I looked closer and saw that the constructions were actually sand *stupas*, and when one of these knee-high structures was completed, the architects of the divine made a small offering and placed a market-bought zodiac flag alongside.
>
> Seeing my interest, and perhaps sensing my confusion, an elderly gentleman approached me and asked, in serviceable French, if he could be of service. In my bad French I asked what was going on. "They are getting rid of their sins," he said in English, but using the French word *péché*." I must have looked bewildered and he continued. "The stupa represents a holy place that contains relics of Lord Buddha. Each grain of sand signifies a sin that the person wants to get rid of." My immediate thought was that, judging from the size of these constructions, these folks must have a lot of sins for which they wish to atone, but for once I kept my peace and strolled with the old man along the shore.

DON'T CONFUSE A SITUATION WITH A SCENE

Here's a situation – note that it is static. I have deliberately used present tense and the verb "to be," which tends to freeze action as quickly as a Minnesota winter will ice a shallow lake.

> My wife and I are trekking in northern Laos, without a guide, without a map. We are tired, hungry, and lost.

Here's a possible evolution of the situation above, written in simple past tense, which is the default tense for most personal stories. It uses the five scenic elements: characters, dialogue, problem/conflict, setting, and movement.

Night was falling quickly in the forest and it started to rain. Our last meal had been toast and coffee some ten hours earlier. My wife had twisted her ankle sometime around noon, but gimped along gamely. "We'll walk another fifteen minutes and if we don't see a village we'll camp rough," I said.

We stumbled in the dark. I could see my wife couldn't go much further.

"Time to stop?" she said softly.

"Let's just climb this hill."

"I'm not sure I can make it."

"Come on, lean on me."

It took us twenty minutes to reach the crest of the hill.

"Is that a lantern over there?" I asked.

"It's too far away," my wife said. "Let's camp here."

But I insisted and an hour later we half-crawled, mud-caked, into the tiny village.

A scrawny man approached.

"Can we sleep here please?" I asked as politely as I could.

He nodded. "Come," and pointed to a thatched-roof hut.

I smelled the opium even as we approached the bamboo-walled shelter. But we were guests, I explained to my wife, and exhausted, and anyway we didn't plan on smoking any of the stuff.

Which is exactly what I explained to the policeman who shook me awake just after dawn and snapped handcuffs on my wrists.

Writing good dialogue can be tricky. Usually less is more.

DIALOGUE AND PITHY QUOTES BRING A SCENE TO LIFE

Dialogue, and dialogue's first cousin the pithy quote, is a key ingredient in a scene. Just think of "Oh Grandma, what big eyes you have!"

∞

Consider the dialogue in this story about how high school girls in New York discovered that many of the city's expensive sushi restaurants were serving cheap freshwater tilapia instead of luxury white tuna.

Their field technique was simple, Kate Stoeckle said. "We ate a lot of sushi."

Or, as Mark Stoeckle [Kate's father] put it, "It involved shopping and eating, in which they were already fluent."

—John Schwartz. "Sushi Sellers Flunk DNA Test in High School Project."
International Herald Tribune, August 23, 2008.

∞

In a 2008 story about a controversial election in Myanmar.

"If you believe in gnomes, trolls and elves, you can believe in this democratic process in Myanmar," the chief human rights investigator for the UN, Paulo Sergio Pinheiro, said late last year.

—Seth Mydans. "Myanmar Leaders Focused on Election."
International Herald Tribune, May 10–11, 2008.

∞

On Mike Tyson working again with promoter Don King:

Why would anyone expect him to come out smarter? He went to prison for three years, not Princeton.

—Dan Duva, boxing promoter.

∞

An interview with Mike Nichols:

"American society to me and my brother was thrilling because, first of all, the food made noise," recalled Nichols. "We were so excited about Rice Krispies and Coca-Cola. We had only silent food in the old country, and we loved listening to our lunch and breakfast."

—Sam Kashner. "Who's Afraid of Nichols & May?" *Vanity Fair*, January 2013.

∞

Let people speak in their own voices:

You guys line up alphabetically by height.

—Bill Peterson, a Florida State football coach.

∞

Nobody in football should be called a genius. A genius is a guy like Norman Einstein.

—Joe Theismann, former player turned football commentator.

∞

An expert's quote can bring a description to life better than simple narrative. (Providing the expert speaks elegantly and the writer can figure out how to extract a single quote from an interview lasting perhaps a couple of hours.)

"The thing about Coke and Pepsi is that they are absolutely gorgeous," Judy Heylmun, a vice-president of Sensory Spectrum, Inc., in Chatham, New Jersey, says. "They have beautiful notes – all flavors are in balance. It's very hard to do that well. Usually, when you taste a store cola it's" – and here she made a series of pik! pik! pik! sounds – "all the notes are kind of spiky, and usually the citrus is the first thing to spike out. And then the cinnamon. Citrus and brown spice notes are top notes and very volatile, as opposed to vanilla, which is very dark and deep. A really cheap store brand will have a big, fat cinnamon note sitting on top of everything."

—Malcolm Gladwell. "The Ketchup Conundrum." *New Yorker*, September 6, 2004.

∞

Helen Eisenbach interviewed former Playboy model Rebekka Armstrong about her battle with HIV. The writer included a description of getting up at the crack of dawn for the next eight months for four a.m. shoots that captured "the early morning apricot light" on the roof of the Playboy building.

When she asked why so many pictures had yet to yield a winning spread, Armstrong was told, "The pubic hair on the left side wasn't fluffed as much as on the right."

—Helen Eisenbach. "Ms. June." *POZ*, June 1998.

 Pro Tip

You Have a Choice as to How You Structure Dialogue

The default way to present dialogue is the "he said/she said" structure:

"I love you more than I love beer and pizza," he said.

"That's so sweet," she replied. "I'm going to go wash my hair."

But sometimes you can present indirect dialogue without the quotation marks:

> When trying to "dress well" some form of altercation usually ensues between the man and woman about where "the good tie" might be, and whose responsibility is it anyway to keep track of such a thing, and it's your tie, so obviously it's your responsibility, but of course I wouldn't have this responsibility or tie at all for that matter were it not because you insist I own it and put it on when we go to parties that involve your parents, and OK, maybe that's true, but don't you think – given your conduct last time with my parents – you'd be well advised to make a good impression this time by dressing well …
>
> —Derek B. Miller. "Marrying Into the Tribe." *Financial Times Magazine.* February 16–17, 2013.

WRITING TIP #3

The Nancy Reagan Principle - Conflict

Remember Nancy Reagan's solution to the drug problem in America?

"Just say no."

The concept of "no," or put another way, the Nancy Reagan Principle, is the loco-motive that drives every story.

The term Nancy Reagan Principle is a mnemonic device to help you remember that conflict, or "no," is essential in every personal essay. Without a problem (which I call a Nancy Reagan) you don't have a story.

Conflict is the single most important concept in storytelling.

TWO TEENAGE KIDS IN LOVE

Listen to these two stories (the second adapted from one of the most famous tragedies ever written). Pay attention to the Nancy Reaganesque use of active verbs in the second example.

Version I
Boring, No Nancy Reagan Conflicts

Two teenage kids love each other very much.

Their parents belong to the same country club and throw them a big, high-society wedding.

He graduates from Brown Summa Cum Laude and becomes a famous tax attorney.

She graduates from Stanford and becomes a famous brain surgeon.

They have four lovely, smart, courteous children.

They die senseless and tragic deaths.

Version II
Interesting, Full of Nancy Reagan Conflicts

Two teenage kids love each other very much.

Their families hate each other.

The brothers and cousins fight and kill each other.

They secretly get married.

A meddling cleric concocts an ill-advised sleeping potion.

When they are barely post-pubescent they die horrible, disillusioned deaths.

Without a problem (villain), you have no solution (hero).
The bigger the problem, the bigger the stakes, the more heroic the hero.

NANCY REAGAN DRIVES THE NARRATIVE OF ALL STORIES

Wars, revolutions, sports rivalries, murder mysteries are based on the Nancy Reagan Principle of conflict. A story without a problem is like playing a football game without keeping score. The most intriguing rivalries have the most interesting opponents. Muhammad Ali is a bigger hero because Joe Frazier is a big opponent. Problems force the questions: "Who will win?" "At what cost?" "What happens next?"

Yankees   Red Sox   Republicans Democrats

Muhammad Ali & Joe Frazier   The Crusades

French   English   Hannibal Lecter   Clarice Starling

Kids, Try This at Home

·········· FOUR MAGIC NANCY REAGAN WORDS ··········

These words are guaranteed to create conflict in any sentence.

- **but**
- **however**
- **in spite of**
- **nevertheless**

These words force you to consider another opinion, another point of view. By using these words you create internal conflict and tension – which is a bad thing in a marriage but just what you want in an article.

NANCY REAGAN WORDS IN ACTION

By introducing a Nancy Reagan word, you introduce a conflict.

Illustration: Sarah Steenland

Here's a hypothetical example of how the Nancy Reagan words work to indicate conflict and involve the reader. I've added italics to highlight the four Nancy Reagan words – but, however, in spite of, nevertheless.

"The United States economy is rebounding and I predict a rosy future," noted President Barack Obama today at a campaign rally in St. Louis.

But not everyone shares Obama's optimism. Hal Rubenstein, a University of Pennsylvania economics professor, believes that "the economy is sitting in a miasmic swamp of stagnant financial sewage and is not likely to break free for several years, if then."

However, the most recent statistics released last week by the Department of Commerce show that manufacturing jobs have increased by fifteen percent over the same period last year.

In spite of these promising numbers, a *Wall Street Journal* poll showed that CEO confidence in the strength of the U.S. economy was at twenty-eight percent, the lowest in some twenty years.

Nevertheless the stock market continues to show strength.

So, is the economy getting better, worse, or staying flat? Shirley Riche, an investment analyst with Merrill Lynch in New York, observes: "Who the hell knows what's going to happen? It's a crap shoot out there."

Here's how one writer uses two Nancy Reagan words to shift the viewpoint:

"It's a small study, so I'd want to see it repeated. *But* I have no reason to doubt the result," said Susan Roberts, a professor of nutrition and psychiatry at Tufts University in Boston.

However, University of Minnesota nutrition professor Joanne Slavin said that though the calorie-burning differences could work to people's advantage, she worried that dieters would flock to low-carb diets that might be unhealthful. [italics added]

—Eryn Brown. "It's Not Just How Many Calories, but What Kind, Study Finds."
Los Angeles Times, June 27, 2012.

Nancy Reagan words like "but" are useful when you want to point out contradictions, as this review of the premiere of Beethoven's Eroica Symphony shows:

> There are many beautiful things in the symphony *but* the continuity often appears to be completely confused and the endless duration ... is tiring even for the expert; for a mere amateur it is unbearable. [italics added]
>
> —*Der Fremüthige*. February 1805.

And a Nancy Reagan word, following a provocative-statement lead (note the Triple Whammy).

> The Battle of the Tennis Court hardly has the resonance of Waterloo, the Somme or Stalingrad. *Yet* this was the fiercest episode of one of the most important battles of the Second World War, Kohima, which came to be known as the Stalingrad of the East. [italics added]
>
> —Jonathan Glancey. *Nagaland*. London: Faber and Faber, 2011.

Journalists are taught to be objective.
(That concept is impossible to achieve, but it remains part of the myth.)
What is true is that journalists are taught to show both sides of the argument,
often by using Nancy Reagan words. Think of it as a ping-pong match.

Pro Tip

Practice Ping-Pong Journalism

In Thomas Kamm's news story about the Paris-Dakar rally he bounces back and forth between contradictory ideas and statements: Danger vs safety. Poverty vs luxury. He uses power words like "rags," "picking bones," "controversy," "colonialism." And one Nancy Reagan word, "but."

Ping-pong journalism works particularly well with the Nancy Reagan words: but, however, in spite of, nevertheless.

Here's an example in which the opening contains major conflicts – death, poverty, luxury.

> Night is falling at this makeshift campsite in the Sahara desert, and the participants in the grueling Paris-Dakar rally are ready to rest. They have driven 688 kilometers through sand dunes and canyons this day ... during the day's leg, one participant died in an accident and another three were critically injured ... Several Europeans are dining on roast lamb ... washed down with an excellent 1982 Saint-Émilion ... unseen, a small boy dressed in rags runs from the darkness and begins picking bones from their plates. The scene cuts to the heart of a controversy that has haunted the race since its inception 10 years ago.

> "Paris-Dakar is the most bewitching adventure of modern times," says Jean Todt, the head of French carmaker Peugeot SA's racing team. "I don't see anything comparable in the world today."

> But to its critics, the race is a tasteless flaunting of money and power in the Sahel, one of the world's poorest regions ... moreover the rally smacks of colonialism.

> "It's an insult to Africa," charges Jeanne Gouba, an aid worker from the West African nation of Burkina Faso ... "It's like a western (movie) in which Africans play the role of Indians."

> —Thomas Kamm. "Controversy Travels Along with the Drivers in Paris-Dakar Rally." *Wall Street Journal*, January 1, 1988.

A Nancy Reagan conflict forces the reader to make a choice.

WHAT ARE THE STAKES?

A Nancy Reagan problem always indicates that something is at stake.

The stakes are what the hero stands to gain or lose.

A quest without stakes is like a boxing match without a winner.

Here's a possible increasing progression of stakes:

I want to write a book.

I keep the idea to myself, working quietly at home each night.

I tell a few friends.

I go to a writing group and make a promise to write a chapter a week.

By staying up late each night, my work suffers; I am told to improve my performance or I'll be fired.

I light the candle at both ends; I get fired.

I have no other income. I have enough savings to last five months.

I look for other jobs but can't find any.

I must complete and sell my book.

A friend knows an agent.

My daughter gets sick and requires an operation.

I borrow money from a Mafia loanshark.

To pay him back I go gambling in Atlantic City.

I lose everything at blackjack.

My daughter needs the surgery in two months.

I have to complete the book.

My agent fires me ("No market for an erotic novel about a teenaged lesbian vampire who invents a cure for halitosis," she says. The fool.)

I get writers block.

My daughter's condition worsens and she needs the surgery in three days.

The Mafia guy comes to collect his money.

And so on.

USING NANCY REAGAN WORDS IN A PERSONAL ESSAY

I like this piece for its honesty and use of scenes, the strong lead, the use of Nancy Reagans (what would you do if a stranger touched your breast and made a statement about something so intimate that you hadn't even told your husband?), the use of questions (what test?), the use of dialogue (with a subtle Nancy Reagan – in the staid German portion of Switzerland, an adult never addresses a stranger using the informal *Du*). Lisa Sennhauser-Kelly uses the bystanders as a curious but silent chorus, and she deals with awkward and unwelcome questions in a language she hadn't yet mastered. Still more – she asks questions and uses a circular structure. Quite a lot of technique and heart for three hundred words.

Smiling, she reached out instinctively, unexpectedly, and stroked my breast with her right hand. I was mortified, as were the others on the train platform. This woman had appeared before me from nowhere.

My gut reaction was to run, or scream or hit out at her, but a sense of dignity and restraint told me to try and understand first. Something wasn't right. Besides, surely someone would help me if necessary? I glanced around. They had noticed, definitely; they were all as equally restrained.

"*Wie heisst Du?*" she asked my name, as if I was only a child. OK I can deal with this, I thought. A simple enough question. Her face was beautiful, with rosy cheeks, yet somehow distorted. Had she been in an accident? Or had it happened at birth?

"Lisa," I stammered, only too aware that the others on the platform were all solemnly pretending not to be watching or listening to this scene. "*und Du?*" I asked, still dumbfounded. A glimpse of disappointment in her eyes. Should I know?

"Connie," the answer came, and she smiled again like a flirtatious four-year-old. "How old is your baby?"

I freeze. What were the other people thinking? "I don't have any children, Connie," I answered quickly. Confusion and dismay swept through her eyes and features; something was wrong. Then her eyes brightened again. "But you're pregnant," she squealed with delight.

How could she know? Barely pregnant with my first child, I hadn't even told my husband yet. Only my doctor knew, asking me just that morning if I wanted the test.

I had told nobody. I observe this woman, or perhaps just a girl, with admiration. Naïve, sweet, innocent and yet so aware. Her hand inexplicably pulled my blouse back as she looked inside. "Connie! You know you shouldn't do that!" I admonished in my very best, dreadful Swiss-German. I felt the others on the platform look discreetly away. "Will you breastfeed?" she persevered, "*Wotsch stille?*"

Suddenly I knew. I understood. Everything was clear to me. "Yes, I hope to be able to," I replied clearly, and with strength. Connie's elderly carer arrived, perhaps her mother. She led Connie to the approaching train and chatted quietly to her. Connie waved goodbye with animation. I sensed the collective relief of my fellow commuters that this unpredictable being was being removed from our ordered day.

I called my doctor and gave him my answer. "No thanks, despite my age, I won't do the amnio test. Yes, I can accept a child with Down Syndrome." A sunny, happy, blissfully innocent and yet miraculously aware child, like Connie.

—Lisa Sennhauser-Kelly. "An Angel Like Connie." Participant in my writing workshop.

Kids, Try This at Home

········· FOUR MAGIC NANCY REAGAN WORDS ·········

Next time you read a story that doesn't work, check whether there are enough Nancy Reagans to create tension.

Or, if you like to think musically, consider these two musical mnemonics:

- "(I Can't Get No) Satisfaction." Rolling Stones.
- "You Can't Always Get What You Want." Rolling Stones.

"HOW ABOUT SOMETHING WITH A LITTLE MORE ACTION, DAD? THIS ONE IS PUTTING ME TO SLEEP."

Want more action? Increase the conflict.
No Nancy Reagan = no reason to keep reading.

Don't Open That Door!

Here's a classic Nancy Reagan in a suspense film context. If the situation is truthful, you can use this kind of structure to build up the tension in a nonfiction piece.

A teenage girl is home alone. (Helps if she's pretty and wearing cut-off shorts and a tight T-shirt.)

She hears a noise in the basement.

She isn't scared; after all, she's a big girl.

She hears the noise again.

She is scared.

She tries to call her best friend. No answer.

She dials 911, but then hangs up. What would she tell them? She'd look foolish if it is nothing, which surely it is.

She hears the noise again.

She calls 911. As the 911 operator answers, the girl's cell phone battery dies.

She shouldn't be scared; she's a varsity cheerleader and vice-president of the Chastity Club, for Pete's sake.

She heads to the kitchen, from where there is access to the basement.

The lights go out.

She grabs the emergency flashlight hanging next to the basement door.

She opens the door and shines the light down.

Her mind is going back and forth – go down and check it out; don't go down there.

The reader is saying, "don't go down there."

She goes down a step.

A noise.

Just the cat.

Another step.

She shines the flashlight all around the basement.

Nobody's there. She's breathes a sigh of relief.

Everything's ok.

And then, OMG, all hell breaks loose.

NANCY REAGAN CAN (AND SHOULD) POP UP EVERYWHERE

Here's the problem-studded intro to a profile on American politician Michael Huffington.

> Drop $30 million on a campaign.
> Lose the race.
> Search your soul.
> Divorce Arianna.
> Decide you're gay.
>
> —David Brock. "The Strange Odyssey of Michael Huffington." *Esquire*, January 1999.

∞

And here's a whole bunch of Nancy Reagans in a book about Abraham Lincoln, with barely a hint of Nancy Reagan words (*but, however, in spite of, nevertheless*). Interesting how he creates conflicts with just semicolons:

> The marriage was a curious one, and in countless ways, the two couldn't have been more different. He loved humor; she had none at all. He grew up on dirt floors; she was served by slaves and attended finishing school. She was neat and fastidious; he was rumpled and disorganized, both at home and at the office. She insisted upon servants; he often did not file and would not keep a clerk ... Yet there was a deep root of tenderness in their marriage, and over time, she came both to understand his awkwardness and to respect his righteousness. In turn, he relied on her, far more than is often credited by history.
>
> —Jay Winik. *April 1865: The Month That Saved America.* New York: HarperCollins, 2001.

∞

Here's how I used a Nancy Reagan contrast in a lead:

In Jakarta, Indonesia, several years ago, President Soeharto signed into law a bill authorizing that schools, medical clinics and agricultural support be made available to thousands of isolated communities.

Just a hundred and fifty kilometers to the west of the capital, a reclusive tribe of 400, called the Baduy, ignored the edict. They had survived for more than four hundred years without schools, without modern agricultural methods, without western medicine. They would continue to do so. Let the government build their schools elsewhere.

—Paul Spencer Wachtel. "Touch not the dirty hands of civilization."
Silver Kris, May 1979.

Useful Advice from Someone Who Wrote Pretty Well

Usually, when people get to the end of a chapter, they close the book and go to sleep. I deliberately write a book so when the reader gets to the end of the chapter, he or she must turn one more page. When people tell me I've kept them up all night, I feel like I've succeeded.

—Sidney Sheldon

YOU MAY RECALL THE SCHEHERAZADE STORY

Think of the Scheherazade Scenario as Literati Interruptus.

A playboy Persian prince named Shahryar had a harem filled with beautiful young women. Each night he would summon one maiden to his chambers and, after making love, would become bored and have her killed before sunrise. It was some kind of royal custom (or royal curse, depending on your point of view), which Shahryar was advised never to try to alter.

One evening Shahryar entered the harem, scanned the room, and his eyes fell on teenaged Scheherazade, known by her nickname Sheri (she signed her name with a cute little ♥ dotting the i). "This is your lucky night, babe," he told her. "Come around nine."

Scheherazade, a demure lass with chestnut hair who was in the harem because her father had failed to pay a gambling debt to the prince's horse trainer, turned to Agnes, her BFF in the harem, and said, "Oh dear! What can I do to survive?"

"You're toast, girlfriend," said Agnes, a prediction that took a lot of the bounce out of Sheri's naturally bubbly personality.

But Sheri was a lateral thinker.

She went to the prince's chambers; he deflowered her in great style and then said: "It's been great Sheri, but be gone and be beheaded."

"Hold on a sec, Great Prince of the Persians, Shahryar. Before you have me killed, and God knows I deserve it for screaming so loudly, I'd like to give you a gift."

"What could you, a poor farmer's daughter, offer me, a great prince?"

"I'd like to tell you a story."

And she did. She told him of heroic journeys, of great quests, sprinkled with curious characters, unexpected plot twists, and plenty of Nancy Reagans.

The time went by so quickly that before Shahryar knew it, the roosters were crowing and the sun was just beginning to rise. He had only a few seconds left to fulfill his royal obligations and have Sheri killed. But she hadn't finished the story. "What happened then?" he asked her.

"Well, look at that, oh Great Prince of the Persians. The sun's risen. See you around the harem sometime."

"Wait, you've got to tell me how the story finishes," Shahryar begged.

"See you later, Royal Alligator," Sheri said.

And Shahryar had no choice but to invite Sheri back that night, and Sheri once again made the post-coital story so interesting that she was able to stop the tale at dawn, right at the key moment in the action.

This went on the night thereafter, and the night thereafter. For 1001 nights. What happened after 1001 nights is unclear. One historian speculates that Sheri started to repeat herself and Shahryar said, "I said no reruns!" and banished her to live with his scheming younger brother, the smirky Harold, Lesser Great Prince of the Persians. Another version is that Shahryar began to fancy himself a storyteller and started to tell Sheri tales of his own. Sheri found these fables wooden and plodding, with unsympathetic characters and little pizazz. She begged him to stop, to let her tell the stories, but Shahryar refused. Ultimately, Sheri couldn't take it any longer and snuck out of the harem one morning with a cute, but goat-scented, shepherd.

The Scheherazade Scenario works because the brain dislikes ambiguity – it tries to complete partially presented images, thoughts, and concepts.

SCHEHERAZADE SCENARIO. LITERATI INTERRUPTUS. KEEP 'EM HANGING ON. CLIFFHANGERS.

Here's the Scheherazade Scenario in action.

For example, you're at home watching CNN and the newsreader says:

> "Is Paris Hilton carrying Dick Cheney's love child? The answer after a short commercial break – don't touch that dial!"

Or you're reading a page-turning, stay-up-all-night thriller. Chances are that the writer keeps you hanging at the end of a chapter, and might not come back to the cliffhanger until a few chapters later.

This is called an open loop, or the Scheherazade Scenario. Think of the Supremes's song "You keep me hangin' on." The Scheherazade Scenario relates to Gestalt psychology, the idea that our brain is uncomfortable with missing pieces and will try to complete an incomplete piece of information.

∽

Adventure writers love to use the open loop at the end of chapters. They leave you hanging and might not conclude the action until several chapters later, and then will likely throw in another open loop to keep you reading all night.

James Rollins (nobody could accuse him of being an elegant writer, but he uses devices like the Scheherazade Scenario to keep the reader turning the page) used an open loop (in this case the same device – a suddenly cut emergency phone call) in two almost-adjacent chapters.

> Before he could respond, his cell phone rang. He pulled it out. It was his personal BlackBerry, unencrypted.
>
> *Must be Lisa checking about the barbecue party.*
>
> He put the phone to his ear, needing to hear her voice.
>
> But it wasn't Lisa. The caller's words came rushed, breathless. "Uncle Crowe ... I need your help."
>
> Shock choked him.
>
> "I'm in trouble. So much trouble. I don't know –"
>
> The words suddenly died. In the background, he heard the growl of a large animal, followed by a sharp, terrified scream.
>
> Painter gripped the phone harder. "Kai!"
>
> The line cut off.

And a few chapters later:

> Gray shook his head. "Any answers – or at least clues to the truth – may lie in further correspondence between Franklin and Fortescue. We need to start searching.
>
> The jangle of Gray's cell phone cut him off. It was loud in the quiet space. He slipped the phone from his coat pocket and checked the caller ID. He sighed softly.
>
> "I have to take this." He stood and turned away.

As he answered the call, the frantic voice of his mother trembled out, distraught and full of fear. "Gray, I … I need your help!" A loud crash sounded in the background, followed by a bullish bellow.

Then the line went dead.

—James Rollins. *The Devil Colony*. New York: HarperCollins, 2011.

DON'T MAKE THE READER WAIT FOR GODOT

If your story is boring, it might well be because nothing is happening. There's not enough movement. It's like watching an Andy Warhol movie.

 Pro Tip

"It Don't Come Easy."

Think of Ringo Starr's song.

What does "It don't come easy" mean in practice? You will notice in much fiction (and nonfiction based on fiction storytelling techniques) the use of the Double No often precedes the Final Yes.

How does this work?

Let's say Character A wants to convince Character B to do something (go out on a date, give him a loan, kidnap his mother-in-law).

Character B should refuse two times, and only at the third time should he agree. Like the Triple Whammy – see Writing Tip #7 – this tripartite structure is comforting to readers.

For example, in your personal story you want to buy a third-class ticket on a train from Delhi to Chennai. The lady at the ticket window refuses to sell it to you. This is a Nancy Reagan – "Yes, I will, No, you won't."

The train is leaving in ten minutes. This is a ticking clock.

There's a woman you met only once but who you really like waiting for your train to arrive. This is the stake – what you stand to lose if you don't get on that train.

If the ticket seller simply accepts your handful of greasy rupee notes, then there isn't much of a story.

But if she refuses two times, and you are getting increasingly desperate (and increasingly creative about finding a solution), and she finally, grudgingly makes the transaction two minutes before the train is to depart, and you run like hell to make the train, scattering beggars, chickens, and policemen in your wake, then you've got a more interesting scene.

The magic number is three. Two refusals, then success.

Why three? It seems to provide us with neural comfort. I don't know why, but it works, and you'll see it everywhere, now that you know what to look for.

 ## Kids, Try This at Home

· · · · · · · · · CONFLICT DOESN'T HAVE TO BE LOUD · · · · · · · ·

Isolate yourself from distractions and listen to the second movement of Beethoven's Fourth Piano Concerto. Listen to the piano's hesitant voice in conflict with the orchestra's confident voice. Listen to the dance between the piano and orchestra, how the piano gains assurance until, at the end of the movement, the two are in parity, having a dialogue of equals.

Pro Tip

Ticking Clock

To make a story hotter, personalize (Story of One and use of "I"), introduce conflict, use details.

Judith the Conscientious has an eleven a.m. appointment for a job interview.

She's already had to cancel the previous job interview with this company when her kid was sick.

She has a record (soft drugs). This is the only company that seems to be willing to even give her a chance.

But this is the last chance.

She's unemployed and has no money.

She has to pay the nursing home bill for her mother or else the old lady is out on the street.

It's ten a.m. The office where the interview will take place is a twenty-minute drive. No problem.

She can't find her car keys.

Judith's baby spits up on her dress; she has to change.

The babysitter comes late.

The car won't start.

No neighbors are home.

She tries to call for a taxi, but her cell phone is dead.

She thinks she's getting her period.

Judith the Conscientious considers running to the main road, hoping to find a taxi.

Or maybe she can hitchhike.

RECOGNIZING YOUR HERO'S JOURNEY

Or maybe she can flag down a car.

It starts to rain. She doesn't have an umbrella or raincoat.

Some idiot kid in a Jeep drives past and throws a green Slushee at her.

She passes the unkempt lawn of Patrick the Creepy Plumber, a smelly, fat, tattooed giant who has propositioned her many times and grabbed her ass during a neighborhood block party.

Patrick the Creepy Plumber is sitting on his porch on an ancient lawn chair, drinking beer, picking his nose.

"Hey Sweetie Pie, where's the fire?" he calls out to her.

Judith the Conscientious pretends to ignore him.

"You too good to talk to me?"

The rain is heavier.

Judith has thirty minutes before her last-chance interview.

She has a decision to make.

Judith the Conscientious asks Patrick the Creepy Plumber: "Does that rusty truck of yours work?"

VISUAL NANCY REAGANS CAN SUPPORT
WRITTEN NANCY REAGANS

I wrote a story about the potential for establishing a peace park on the wilderness border between Poland and Belarus. Although one ecosystem supporting the largest remaining population of European bison, the land is separated by a three-meter-tall fence and rusting guard towers. There was little enthusiasm from Polish authorities, who feared an invasion of freedom-seeking Belarusians. The Belarus authorities, however, were all for the idea. The photographer, Lynda Richardson, came up with the idea of photographing the director of the Polish Bialowieza National Park, Czeslaw Okolow, leaning against a four-hundred-year-old oak tree and the deputy director of the Belovezhskaya Pushcha National Park, Viacheslav Semakov, with similar body language, leaning against a similarly old tree in his park on the Belarus side. The art director ran the headline "Across a divide" vertically in the gutter.

Paul Spencer Sochaczewski. "Across a Divide."
International Wildlife. *July/August 1999.*
Photos: Lynda Richardson. Design director: Dan Smith.
Photo editor: John Nuhn.

∾

In a *National Geographic* article, Peter Theroux writes: "Battles lines have yielded to tan lines at the yacht club adjoining the war-scarred Hotel St. Georges – symbol of Beirut's glamorous past and ground zero in Lebanon's 15-year civil war." This Nancy Reagan-rich photo puts it all in perspective.

Few cities exhibit as much contrast as Beirut. This photo shows socialites getting a tan at the yacht club adjacent to the battle-scarred luxury Hotel St. Georges. Note the details – the gold chains, the designer sunglasses, Ambre Solaire suntanning lotion, cigarette holder, perfectly manicured nails, and French gossip magazine, all in contrast with the bombed-out hotel in the background.

Photo: Ed Kashi / VII.

WRITING TIP #4

Start with a Bang

Think of the lead (if you want to be pompous, use the classic journalist's term "lede") as getting your foot in the door, the smile you give a girl/guy when you first meet, the movie trailer that makes you say, "I'm gonna spend fifteen bucks to see this thing."

HOW MANY WAYS TO LEAD?

How many different leads are there? That's like asking: How many species of beetles exist? How many people live in Shanghai? How many husbands did Liz Taylor have? The answer in each case is plenty.

I've counted one hundred and fourteen different types of leads, give or take a few dozen. But basically there are just six categories of good leads (and they are often combined).

1. **Ask a question**
2. **Anecdote/scene**
3. **Provocative statement**
4. **Dialogue**
5. **List**
6. **Current news, historical, celebrity, cultural, or literary reference**

Here is a selection:

1. Ask a Question

How do you solve a problem like "Camilla?"

If you are Andrew Motion, Britain's poet laureate and the man charged with producing a cheerful commemorative poem about Prince Charles's impending marriage to Camilla Parker Bowles, none of the obvious rhymes – vanilla, flotilla, Godzilla – seems appropriate, somehow.

—Sarah Lyall. "For British Laureate, Every Rhyme Has a Reason." *The New York Times*, April 7, 2005.

∽

How much is a bird's song worth?

—Paul Spencer Sochaczewski. "Putting a Value on Nature Means Special Sort of Arithmetic. Try $33 Trillion a Year." *Earth Times*, August 10, 1997.

∽

Women often ask, "what do men REALLY want, deep in their souls?"

The best answer – based on in-depth analysis of the complex and subtle interplay of thought, instinct and emotion that constitute the male psyche – is that deep in their souls, men want to watch stuff go "bang."

—Dave Barry. "A Male Goal: The Big Boom." Knight-Ridder Newspapers. *International Herald Tribune*, October 8, 1994.

∽

What was God saying to you and me when he came up with sexually transmitted diseases? Perhaps he was trying to curb our appetites. Enforce a period of contemplation. Maybe he was trying to avoid the seventies. It is possible that, as he is wont to do, he was just introducing a paradox – killing us by the same fleshly means by which he creates us. Or, just maybe, he was testing our ingenuity.

—Rene Chun. "The Goo that Saved the World." *Esquire*, January 1998.

∽

Could a single molecule – one chemical substance – lie at the very center of our moral lives?

> —Paul J. Zak. "The Trust Molecule." *Wall Street Journal*, Apr 27, 2012.

∞

The philosophical question for the day is, if a Blonde is lost in the forest, will she know it?

I know the answer. Not for a real long time.

> "Me, Myself, and I." Participant in my writing workshop.

∞

Feel good that you've switched to dolphin-free tuna? Now there's another creature that can give consumers an attack of eco-gastro guilt: the shrimp.

> —Paul Spencer Sochaczewski and Biksham Gujja. "The Tiny Shrimp Causes Big Ecological Worries." *International Herald Tribune*, April 11, 1997.

∞

Who gets credit, and who takes credit, for changing the world?

> —Paul Sochaczewski. "Survival of the Fittest." *International Herald Tribune*. Reprinted in *An Inordinate Fondness for Beetles*, 2012.

∞

A young girl wanders in and out of the Pat Pong go-go bars in Bangkok selling flowers to foreigners on holiday. Where did she come from? Who takes care of her? What will become of her?

Four-year-old identical triplet girls are sold for two cases of whiskey. Who buys them? Will they ever go to school? Do they have any chance in life?

A disabled trash-picker stakes her living, along with her hopes and dreams, on her "almost magical" walking cane. Will she make enough today for a few bowls of rice?

> —John Padorr, writing the introduction to Father Joseph Maier's *The Open Gate of Mercy: Stories from Bangkok's Klong Toey Slum*. Bangkok: Heaven Lake Press, 2012.

∞

Normally when I play golf, I clutter my head with an excess of swing thoughts – turn, extend the arm, hit towards two o'clock.

But standing on the first tee of the Manaus Golf Club outside the Brazilian city of Manaus, I complicated my life even more by posing a historical conundrum – if Manaus, and the surrounding Amazonian forest, had never existed, would we still be playing golf with featheries?

—Paul Spencer Sochaczewski. "Rubber Soul." *Travel and Leisure Golf*. September–October 2004. Reprinted in *Distant Greens*. Singapore: Editions Didier Millet, 2010.

∞

Answer this: if vampires can't see themselves in mirrors, how do they manage to look so good?

—Peter Gutierrez. "Sharp Looks." *Financial Times*, May 12, 2012.

∞

Should European farmers pay for pollination provided by bees? Should city dwellers in Brazil pay for the abundant rain generated over the Amazonian forest? And if mangroves are a shield against tsunamis, shouldn't seaside resorts in Thailand be paying for them?

These are the kinds of questions being asked at the world's top biodiversity conference in India, where policymakers are desperately seeking ways to preserve the world's dwindling plant and animal resources.

"Counting Cost of Nature." AFP, October 17, 2012.

∞

Are you a rainforest half-destroyed sort of person? Or do you prefer to think that the rainforest is half-saved?

—Simon Barnes. "Saving the Orangutan." *The Times Magazine*, September 10, 2013.

2. Anecdote/Scene

It was the second time in her young life Miss Mingkwan really screamed.

Blood running down her face, she picked up a stick. Got in one good lick, cracked the old woman on her gimp knee. Then she ran. Crawled through a hole in the Lumpini Park fence and ran for her life. Mrs. Rungtip had just beat her, had drawn blood. Plus the cursing hurt a lot, even more than her bloody head.[1]

—Father Joe Maier. "Thailand's Lost Generations." *Bangkok Post*, March 8, 2008.

On an evening some time ago, as young Yor Saeng left her home in Issan to catch the overnight bus to Bangkok, a *jing-jok* (small lizard) made its "tak-tak" sound at her. Her Momma shuddered: "Girl, that creature is warning you. Make a "ta-tak" sound back to thank the *jing-jok* and change your clothes so the naughty mischievous spirits won't recognize you.

But Yor Saeng only laughed. Her name means something like "the beauty of a temple with a grove of sacred trees under a Northeast pre-dawn sky." And she's a Star. No doubt about that ... Stars are tough survivors with a beauty about them. Also warts, wrinkles thrown in, with mud from the rice fields between their toes.[2]

—Father Joe Maier. "The Warning of the Jing-Jok." *Bangkok Post*, October 3, 2010.

I was eleven months old when my parents awoke one morning to find my crib empty. After a frantic search through the house – under beds and into closets – they say they discovered me behind a couch in the living room, sitting happily on top of the Sunday edition of the newspaper, eating the front page. I had consumed half a story on the Germans invading Poland and an entire column on the physical dangers of swing dancing. Certain that the impromptu breakfast would make me sick, my mother stuck her finger down my throat. My father held me upside down and shook me. Nothing worked; I devoured the news and digested it – ink and paper seethed into my bones and blood and skin. And for the rest of my life I wanted to be a journalist.

—Toni Polancy. "The Last Sob Sister." Participant in my writing workshop.

---

[1] Father Joe, who runs the Mercy Center (www.mercycentre.org) notes that Miss Mingkwan was sponsored by a Canadian hockey team from Tokyo and won a scholarship to United World College in Norway.

[2] Miss Yor Saeng is on antivirals and spends her days visiting HIV-AIDS patients in the slum communities. Her two sons are in third grade, have dyed their hair red – "totally normal boys except for the meds," Father Joe advises. Her husband still "does his gangster thing" but thus far has managed to stay out of jail.

Listen to the music of the lead – short, sharp sentences when describing the fight, longer, complex sentences for the reflective passage.

Her elbow cut into my forehead. I felt blood streaming from my left eyebrow, I could barely see. I was the white underdog, a curiosity, and the crowd at the Sanam Luang Thai boxing stadium in Bangkok roared enthusiastically with every punch, kick and jab from Jomyutying, the Thai champion. Our shins clashed – bone on bone. To protect my head from further injury, I clinched her neck and threw several knees towards her midriff. I heard her gasp in pain. I continued to kick.

During the fight I had no time for reflection; but later, having my battered thighs massaged in the dimly lit changing room, infused with the smells of liniment and sweat, I smiled to myself. My non-athletic, socially inhibited former self would never have imagined that I would be exchanging body blows in front of a live audience of 10,000, and countless more on Thai national television.

I was not born a warrior.

—Melissa Ray. "Blood, Sweat and Fears." Participant in my writing workshop.

Haunted by want, depleted from hunger, Akhtar Mohammed sold off his few farm animals and then, as the months passed, bartered away the family's threadbare rugs and metal cooking utensils and even some of the wooden beams that held up the hard-packed roof of his overcrowded hovel. But always the hunger outlasted the money. And finally, six weeks ago, Mohammed did something that has become ruefully unremarkable in this desperate country. He took two of his 10 children to the bazaar of the nearest city and traded them for bags of wheat.

—Barry Bearak. "Afghans Trade Sons for Wheat."
International Herald Tribune, March 9, 2002.

"Aaeeoghh!" A mind-searing scream. "I'll kill you – I'll KILL you for this. I swear I will!"

"Take her away," the orderly snapped, securing another strap on the strait-jacket that held her captive after her desperate attempt to escape by leaping through the second floor window of the hospital's admission wing.

Weighing only 81 pounds for all 5'2" of her, Jane [not her real name], my 17-year-old daughter and only child, was, despite her screams and struggles, virtually invisible within the contorted convolutions of white canvas.

"Catharsis." Participant in my writing workshop.

∾

I watched the dead float down a river in Tanzania. Of all the gut-wrenching emotions I wrestled with during three years of covering famine, war and misery around Africa, no feeling so gripped me as the one I felt that scorching hot day last April, standing on the Rusomo Falls bridge, in a remote corner of Tanzania, watching dozens of discolored, bloated bodies floating downstream, floating from the insanity that was Rwanda.

—Keith B. Richburg. "A Black American Confronts a Cold Reality." Washington Post Service. *International Herald Tribune*, March 27, 1995.

∾

This scene has conflict (illustrated by her frustration), characters, dialogue, setting, and an iconic quote that sets the tone for the rest of her book.

"George Orwell," I said slowly. "G-E-O-R-G-E-O-R-W-E-L-L." But the old Burmese man just kept shaking his head.

We were sitting in the baking-hot front room of his house in a sleepy port town in Lower Burma. The air was oppressive and muggy. I could hear mosquitoes whining impatiently around my head, and I was about to give up. The man was a well-known scholar in Burma, and I knew he was familiar with Orwell. But he was elderly; cataracts had turned his eyes an oystery blue, and his hands trembled as he readjusted his sarong. I wondered if he was losing his memory but, after several failed attempts, I made one final stab.

"George Orwell," I repeated. "The author of Nineteen-Eighty-Four." The old man's eyes suddenly lit up. He looked at me with a brilliant flash of recognition, slapped his forehead gleefully, and said, "You mean the prophet!"

—Emma Larkin. *Secret Histories: Finding George Orwell in a Burmese Teashop.* London: John Murray. 2004.

A young Chinese man, maybe 20, walked up to me as I studied the details of an intricate roof overhang at a Buddhist temple in Kunming. He hesitated, then asked, in English.

"May I ask you a word?"

I smiled. Our encounter took place at the Yuantong Zen Buddhist Temple, built 1,200 years ago. A place of worship, yes, but historically also a university, a seat of learning. An appropriate venue for a student to ask a question of a teacher.

"I forget how to spell a word."

"What word?"

"Negotiate." He pronounced it correctly, but carefully, as if he had fragile eggshells in his mouth.

I took out a slip of paper and printed, neatly – NEGOTIATE – and handed it to him. I neglected to ask him why that word.

"Yes. That's it." He thanked me and left.

Negotiate. A harmless word, with a straightforward meaning. It was my first full day in China. I rolled the word around in my mind, already becoming saturated with ornamental cornices and statues of demons and frenzied markets. Negotiate. The nine letters changed from a word wearing a suit and tie at a business meeting to one wandering the world in the cloak of a koan.

—Judy Halbakken. "Two Hands Clapping: Meditations in Southwestern China."
Participant in my writing workshop.

It was 18 years ago that I sat in a makeshift bar on the side of Sukhumvit Road in Bang Na with my morose Thai friend Vichien. We were onto our second bottle of Hong Tong whisky. Still in my teens, I was able to drink a small bottle or two of Hong Tong. Those days are long gone. These days I find Hong Tong good for polishing bronze cutlery and poisoning rats, but that is off the track.

Poor Vichien. Poor lovesick young Thai man shaking his head as ice cubes clinked in his drink.

"I don't know what to do about Rojana," he said. "We've been going out for three years now."

Another few embarrassed clinks.

"And she's two months pregnant."

I downed my drink and said: "I know this may sound radical to you, Vichien, but ... why not marry her for God's sake?"

—Andrew Biggs. "Cash and Marry?" *Bangkok Post*, November 27, 2011.

∽

Note how Barbarisi handles Ahmad's quotes – sometimes a paraphrase is better than a direct quote; this device leaves more room for Cashman's direct quote.

The Yankees were still out on the field, in the final moments of losing a game early Sunday in front of a funereal crowd, when a small group gathered in the athletic trainer's office deep inside Yankee Stadium.

Dr. Christopher Ahmad, the Yankees' team physician, was flanked by general manager Brian Cashman, the team's trainer, Steve Donahue, and the revered former Yankee manager, Joe Torre.

And then there was Yankee captain Derek Jeter, his ankle immobilized. The other men were all there to tell Jeter something he didn't want to hear.

Ahmad told Jeter quickly, succinctly. His ankle was broken. His season was over. He emphasized to Jeter that this was something he couldn't play through, no matter how much toughness or grit or will he had.

Jeter said nothing, Cashman recalled. "He had no response."

—Daniel Barbarisi. "Injured Jeter Out for Season in Loss to Detroit."
Wall Street Journal, Oct 14, 2012.

∽

Windows are broken and paths half paved in the ramshackle little town of Dharamsala, India, where the Dalai Lama lives. The absolute spiritual and temporal ruler of Tibet still has to drive 10 hours over roads crazy with scooters and cows every time he needs to take a flight (from New Delhi, 300 miles to the south). And when you call his tiny office, you usually hear that "all circuits are busy" – or the five-digit number changed yesterday, or, amid a blizzard of static, you get cut off in mid-sentence, the only small consolation being that you are put on hold to the tune of *London Bridge Is Falling Down*.

—Pico Iyer. "The God in Exile." *Time*, December 22, 1997.

It usually stars an hour after I eat: a burning sensation that hovers somewhere behind my breastbone. If I have an antacid on hand, the burning subsides. If not, it builds until I'm in fiery agony.

—Michael Lemonick. "Fire in the Belly." *Time*, April 26, 1999.

One early evening in February 2006, John Edwards, the former North Carolina senator then gearing up to launch his second presidential campaign, was hanging out in the bar of the Regency Hotel on Park Avenue with one of his donors and his young traveling aide, Josh Brumberger. A woman sitting at a nearby table with some friends walked over and introduced herself.

"My friends insist you're John Edwards," Rielle Hunter said. "I tell them no way – you're way too handsome."

"No, ma'am. I'm John Edwards," the candidate replied.

"No way! I don't believe you!"

Brumberger saw this kind of thing all the time. Women were always hitting on his boss. He and Edwards had a well-oiled system in place for dealing with these situations tactfully and politely.

"He is John Edwards,"Brumberger interjected, "and I'm sorry, but we're in the middle of something. Thank you."

—John Heilemann and Mark Halperin. "Saint Elizabeth and the Ego Monster."
Game Change. New York: HarperCollins. 2010.

Look at yourself. Really clever. Locked in the bathroom. Naked. Why did you have to play with the lock, opening and closing it, just to see if it worked? Well, it sure does work. Were you worried that someone would barge in and interrupt your shower? Come on. This isn't the Bates Motel. It's the Chateau de Lucens, a user-friendly restored medieval Swiss castle. And the guest rooms next to the shower are deserted. Everyone else is up in the tapestry room having dinner.

—Monique Filsnoël. "Flaubert, The Ghost and the Naked Writer."
Participant in my writing workshop.

∽

The six-word quote sets the tone for the rest of the story.

This was supposed to be the weekend I put my garden to bed for wintertime to clip the lilac suckers, mulch some perennials and tuck in a few last bulbs – but instead I'm on a train to Philadelphia to say goodbye to a friend who is dying. I had planned for my hands to be happily immersed in dirt, but then I got the call asking, "Will you come hold my hand?" She never asked me to hold her hand before. I'm thinking about her, and my garden, and suddenly I'm confirming my resolve to specialize in perennials, plants that only pretend to die. They surprise you each spring with a resurrection you never really expect, but then there it is.

—Jeanne Marie Laskas. "The Garden in Winter." *The Washington Post Magazine*. Reprinted in: Lee Gutkind. *The Art of Creative Nonfiction*. New York: John Wiley & Sons, Inc., 1997.

3. Provocative Statement

The problem with the past year is that you stopped breathing and I went on. Yours was, I suspect, the easier path. You don't have to worry about a thing any more, whereas breathing can be damn difficult at times.

"To Vincent." Participant in my writing workshop.

∽

Two things guaranteed to ruin a trip are dysentery and bad traveling companions, and I frankly prefer the former, because dysentery at least ensures some quality private time.

—Randy Wayne White. "He's With Me." *Outside*, August 1996.

∽

I'm not a helicopter parent and my children would tell you I don't bake cupcakes for their birthday parties. But I'd readily cut off my breasts for them – and recently, I did.

—Alison Gilbert. CNN, October 18, 2012.

∽

Driving down Route 89 south from Montpelier toward White River Junction, I tried to remember exactly how long it had been since I'd had sex. Although we didn't actually separate and agree to divorce until February of 1993, the last time my husband and I had made love – and the last time I'd had sex – was in late May of 1992, and here it was, the Fourth of July, 1994. Two years and one month later. One hundred and nine weeks. Seven hundred and sixty five days.

—Joan Goldfeder. "Nurturing Body and Mind." *Writer's Digest*, June 1996.

∽

After four years on dialysis, with no sign that he was nearing the top of the transplant waiting list, Moshe Tati decided to buy a kidney.

—Michael Finkel. "For Sale, Used Kidneys: Buyer Beware."
International Herald Tribune, May 31, 2001.

∽

My gym could beat up your gym. No, seriously. My gym could take your gym, pull its underpants over its head, and stuff it in a locker. My gym is Old School."

—Chris Connolly. "Old-School Training." *Men's Fitness*, May 2008.

∽

I am not the sort of woman who wants to go back to nature. I am the sort of woman who wants to go back to the hotel.

—Val McQueen. "Against Nature." *Silver Kris*, September 1994.

∽

Southeast Asia's mega-cities are drowning in a sea of trash.

—David Lamb. "In Southeast Asian Capitals, Sanitation Becomes Dirty Word."
Los Angeles Times, August 13, 1999.

∽

The Lingerie Football League is hanging up its garters for the 2012 season.

—Chris Chase. *Yahoo! Sports*, April 13, 2012.

∞

The World Cup begins here on Friday with excitement at so elevated a level that even many of the unhappy are happy.

—Barry Bearak. "South Africa's Hopes Extend Beyond Field."
The New York Times, June 10, 2010.

∞

If you think having a boyfriend can ruin your sex life, try surgery.

—River Huston. "River Runs Dry." *POZ*, July 1998.

∞

Here's what it takes to catch a dragon.

—Jennifer S. Holland. "Once Upon a Dragon." *National Geographic*, January 2014.

∞

I knew I was in trouble when it took 40 minutes to chop a garlic clove.

—Steve Friedman. "Cook and Tell Confessions of a Kitchen Romeo."
The New York Times, February 9, 2005.

∞

The numbers/letters combo 804c, 803c and 802c might not have a particularly familiar ring, but they're playing an increasingly important, and occasionally annoying, role in your daily life.

—Tyler Brûlé. "Blame Is a High-Vis Business." *Financial Times*, April 28, 2012.

∞

The country which owns the trademark to "Gross National Happiness" is also home to a minor, but nevertheless irritating cause of despair – the deepest bunker I've seen on a golf course.

—Paul Spencer Sochaczewski. "The Flying Phallus and the Monster Drive."
Distant Greens. Singapore: Editions Didier Millet, 2008.

∞

Everything I hear and read about the possible impeachment of Bill Clinton starts out with a sentence like "Nobody denies that what the president did was wrong." Here comes Nobody. I deny that what the president did was wrong.

—Larry Beinhart. "Who Says Clinton Did Wrong?" *Los Angeles Times*, October 27, 1998.

∞

One of the first and most embarrassing things I have to admit is that I had to let my characters get to know one another for fourteen full pages before I would let them jump into the sack.

—Pam Houston. "Confessions of a First-Time Pornographer."
Nerve.com, October 12, 2000.

∞

God sat before me on the sofa, clad in a poorly fitting sweatsuit, puffing down a cigarette.

—Jonah Blank. *Arrow of the Blue-Skinned God.* New York: Simon & Schuster. 1992.

∞

Swedish botanist Carl Linnaeus was to taxonomy what Brigitte Bardot was to the bikini.

—Paul Spencer Sochaczewski. *An Inordinate Fondness for Beetles.*
Singapore: Editions Didier Millet. 2008.

∞

Oysters. Termites. Mushrooms. Snake blood. Brains. Broccoli.

On the long list of strange things that people voluntarily ingest, one might add civet coffee.

Civet coffee, called *café chon* in Vietnam and *kopi luwak* in Indonesia, is probably the only popular foodstuff which is consumed by people simply because it has passed through the digestive system of a wild animal.

—Paul Spencer Sochaczewski. "Do You Know Where That Coffee's Been?"
Curious Encounters of the Human Kind: Southeast Asia. Geneva: Explorer's Eye Press, 2016.

∞

Sometimes a lead defies categorization. Is this a Provocative Statement lead or an Anecdote Lead or a Cultural/Literary Lead? It lives happily in several categories.

I am lost. For a long time I have been mentally and physically lost, and now, because of you, there is a pistol aimed at me.

It is a carbon-gray 9 mm and the driver of the station wagon is pointing the muzzle at my chest. In between his legs sloshes a half-empty beer can.

Like a black hole the gun creates a space that sucks everything around it inside. The driver shouts at me in Black Sea Turkish. He tells me to give him 100 lira or he will shoot me.

I blame you for this, Jack, because when I was 16 in Oklahoma and the wish to be somewhere else was on me, I discovered, as an unusually dreamy teenager, *On the Road*.

—David Joshua Jennings. "Dear Jack Kerouac." *The Writer*, July 2012.

4. Dialogue

You've heard the one about the old man who was dying? He smelled cherry pie baking, so he roused himself from bed and staggered in to the kitchen. He was reaching for the pie when his wife swatted his wrist away. "No!" she barked. "That's for the funeral."

—Judith Woodburn. "A Time in a Life for Pie and Beer." *The New York Times*, June 16, 2009.

∞

"Postcards, mister?"

I explained to the teenaged boy outside a luxury hotel in Hanoi that I didn't need any more postcards.

"Please mister."

So I bought a few more postcards, hoping my dollar would buy the young man a meal or two.

—Paul Spencer Sochaczewski. "Into the Frying Pan." *The Sultan and the Mermaid Queen*. Singapore: Editions Didier Millet, 2008.

∽

And all along I had thought golf was a cause of anxiety.

"No, just the opposite. Golf relieves stress," Eisa Eshagi, president of the Iranian Golf Federation, said. "And that's what we need, since we're a nation that has suffered wars and hardships."

—Paul Spencer Sochaczewski. "Golf, an Antidote to War and Hardship." *Travel and Leisure Golf*. Reprinted in *Distant Greens*. Singapore: Editions Didier Millet. 2010.

∽

"Cancer humbled Lance," the mammographer says as she squeezes my tender left breast between the vise. "Up a little closer. Angle in there. You're small-boned. This is going to come in tight against your frame. Raise your arm and grab the rail. Now drop it. Now relax."

—Susan Pollack. "Lance Armstrong Leads the Pack Against Cancer." *The Boston Globe*, July 16, 2004.

∽

"I can make you a new phallus, no problem."

"But we're leaving in the morning."

"Trust me."

Figuring that we could always use a bit more protection against demons in our house in Bangkok, I was ordering a flying phallus sculpture from Karma, a village artist in central Bhutan.

This seemed to be a practical, and economical, form of Asian homeowners' insurance. Of course there was no guarantee that the wooden phallus, once imported to Thailand, would have the same anti-demon properties that it provides in this landlocked, traditional country, but I figured it was worth a ten dollar investment.

—Paul Spencer Sochaczewski. "Flying Phallus Fights Forces of Evil." *Distant Greens*. Singapore: Editions Didier Millet, 2010.

∽

"So, you want to know about my love life?" said Sophie Silverman, 85 years old and twice a widow, climbing out of the pool and settling into a lounge chair at her retirement community, On Top of the World. She pushed her oversized purple sunglasses halfway down her nose. "It stinks."

—Sara Rimer. "At Eightysomething, a Good (preferably younger) Man Is Hard to Find." The New York Times Service. *International Herald Tribune*. December 24–25, 1998.

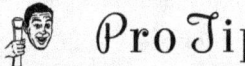

"Don't go that way, there's nuclear!" shouted the eight-year-old Brummie girl, hopping from rockpool to rockpool. "Nuclear what?" I asked, breaking my stride. "Bombs and bullets and things," she replied, darkly. "My dad said."

—Chris Moss. "Footprints of Wales." *Financial Times,* April 28, 2012.

Pro Tip

Paraphrase Dialogue

Dialogue can be suggested, and doesn't have to use quotation marks.

Daddy, did you ever feel we lived in the Land of Point?

I used to listen to Harry Nilsson's album, and his song about poor Oblio.

In our ever-industrious household, on any given weekend, each member of our family was alone and purposeful and self-improving – reading, gardening, building castles out of Lego. We drifted in proximity, but on our own.

Daddy, do you remember how I used to listen to LP records on our gramophone in Alyth? The gramophone stood on the heavy wooden bookshelf in the living room outside your study.

While you were nearby, behind your closed study door, writing your books, I would choose an LP to listen to, for 45 minutes of daydreaming.

—Alexandra Lamont. "This Is a Long-Playing Record." Participant in my writing workshop.

5 . List

He proposed to Karen. He proposed to Yana. He proposed to Monica.

He proposed to Kathy. He proposed to Sarah. He proposed to Susan. He proposed to Vicki. He proposed to Colette.

You get the idea.

—N.R. Kleinfield. "One U.S. Colonel, 49 Broken Hearts." *The New York Times*, June 11, 2003.

∾

And, with a similar theme, read this list-like lead aloud, just for the pleasure of the music:

This happens in Russia to a man I know named Spencer, who travels there to find a wife. He meets Elvira. He meets Tamara. He meets Alla and Eva and Ksenia and Irina and Ekaterina Lebedeva, who chose these words to describe herself: faithful, kind, bright, and honest. He meets Marina and he meets Galina and he meets many, many Natashas. He meets twenty-three-year-old Olga Dionisieva, with chestnut hair and periwinkle eyes and a smile that reads as forced, crimped by anxiety or boredom or collapsing desire, it's awfully hard to tell.

He meets Nadia. He meets Valavia and Julia. Through a simple scheduling error he manages to meet Maria Chergsheva at the same moment he meets another woman, and Maria's voice turns dark and her eyes glitter and as the scene becomes farce he pleads a foreigner's confusion and calls for forgiveness, just a mistake, they can meet again of course, maybe a drink, anything she likes. He meets Anna and Victoria and he meets Tatiana, just beginning her eighteenth year, still coltish, who folded her schoolgirl frame into a wooden seat aboard a local train for nine numbing hours, all the way from Moscow Station, coming to see the American.

—John Tayman. "Project Wife." *Men's Journal*, December 2000.

∾

These are some of the weapons in the arsenal of the Tamil Tigers, the guerrilla army waging a war for an independent state on the island nation of Sri Lanka: surface-to-air missiles from Cambodia, assault rifles from Afghanistan, mortar shells from the former Yugoslavia and Zimbabwe, and 60 tons of explosives from Ukraine.

—Raymond Bonner. "A Tamil Tiger Primer on International Arms Bazaar." *The New York Times*, March 10, 1998.

President Clinton once bought a small bronze frog. A German collector recently examined antique adding machines. Two soldiers eyed a case of silver coins. It is hard to define just what is on sale on Surabaya Street, where artisans squat at the curb carving wooden Buddha statues and polishing brass diving helmets. For tribal masks, silver cigarette cases, worry beads, grandfather clocks, ivory miniatures, sextants, samurai swords, xylophones and telephone switchboards, you've come to the right place.

—Seth Mydans. "Streets of Dreams." *The New York Times*, September 28, 2009.

Like many good leads, this one combines two elements, in this case a list and a question.

Mike Ditka mangled it. Bea Arthur smoked it. Mel Gibson risked his life trying to do it. *NSync asked to do it. Oprah refuses to do it. On a 90-degree day Joe Frazier *froze* in the middle of it.

What is *it*?

It's Singin' the Stretch at Wrigley Field – standing in the broadcast booth after the top of the seventh inning and leading more than 35,000 people in Take Me out to the Ball Game.

—Rick Reilly. "Seventh-Inning Stress." *Sports Illustrated*, September 2, 2003.

And another list (note the Triple Whammy – the Rule of Three).

My favorite golf course in Vietnam owes its existence to a puppet king, a French architect who restored Roman ruins, and a rich American who craved virgins.

—Paul Spencer Sochaczewski. "Napalm Be Gone: That Boom You Hear in Vietnam Is an Explosion of Golf Courses." *Distant Greens*. Singapore: Editions Didier Millet, 2010.

6. Current News, Historical, Celebrity, Cultural, or Literary Reference

John Tierney's lead starts with a historical citation with dialogue, and then brings us back to his own contemporary story.

Peary became aware of a wooden feeling in his feet. When Henson ripped off the sealskin boots he saw that the explorer's legs were bloodless white to the knee. As he tore off the undershoes, two or three toes from each foot clung to the hide and snapped off at the joint.

"My god, Lieutenant!" he cried. "Why didn't you tell me your feet were frozen?"

"There's no time to pamper sick men on the trail," Peary told him, and added, "besides, a few toes aren't much to give to achieve the Pole."

I spent much of my first night on Ellesmere Island thinking about Robert Peary's toes.

—John Tierney. "Going Where a Lot of Other Dudes with Really Great Equipment Have Gone Before." *The New York Times*, July 26, 1998.
Tierney began the lead by quoting Pierre Berton in *The Arctic Grail*, describing the outcome of a dog-sled trip on Ellesmere Island in 1898.

In announcing that he had prostate cancer, Mayor Rudolph Giuliani of New York paused to make a pitch that all men have the test that revealed the early signs of his disease.

—Kenneth Chang. "Findings Fuel Debate Over Prostate Test."
The New York Times, May 6, 2000.

Sartre was wrong. Hell isn't other people. Hell is tourists – specifically, other tourists.

—Parul Sehgal. "A World on the Page: Five Great Travel Memoirs." NPR, July 31, 2012.

This mountain is to cycling what St. Andrews is to golf, what La Scala is to opera. More than a mountain, it is a shrine, where hundreds of thousands of cycling fans gather each year that the Tour de France ends a stage here.

—Edward Wyatt. "In Cycling, a Mountain That's More Like a Mecca."
The New York Times, July 24, 2008.

Summertime, and the living ain't easy. It is hot, wells dry up and the water quality plunges, leaving Indian children especially vulnerable to diarrhea.

—Miriam Jordan. "Setting Up Business for Good Cause."
International Herald Tribune, June 6–7, 1998.

In ancient Greek mythology, Hercules had to slay the multiheaded serpent-like Hydra, guardian of the underworld, although each time a head was cut off, two others would grow in its place.

In modern sports, it can seem that the authorities face a similar and equally herculean task in the global fight against illegal sports betting and match-fixing.

—Rob Hughes. "Fighting to Keep World Sports a Fair Game."
International Herald Tribune, April 24, 2012.

Here's a cultural/literary lead that Hayes combines with a list lead.

If only I had read Plato.

That's what I thought when I saw my MRI: 28 images, impossible to deny, of a torn rotator cuff muscle – a consequence of years of weightlifting. And that's just my shoulder. May I present C4, C5 and C6 (my herniated discs), my plantar fasciitis, my patellar tendinitis – residual damage done to a body, now 51, in the name of exercise, in pursuit of being buff.

Plato could have warned me. In *The Republic*, he advises "temperance" in physical training, likening it to learning music and poetry.

—Bill Hayes. "Plato's Body, and Mine." *The New York Times*, April 21, 2012.

The recent capture of the Kurdish guerrilla leader Abdullah Ocalan has focused new attention on the war he has waged against the Turkish Army for 14 years ... Lurking behind [all the arguments] however, is water.

—Stephen Kinzer. "A Fierce Struggle for Water Drives All the Players in the Kurdish Conflict." *International Herald Tribune*, March 2, 1999.

"How dare you stand up and talk about something when you've never been there. Shame on you."

So said Representative Don Young, Republican of Alaska, speaking in Congress last week in favor of Arctic oil drilling.

Well, I've been there. For two summers, short, soaring, bittersweet summers. I worked there.

—John Balzar. "The American Wilderness Is Fragile as a Snowflake."
Los Angeles Times, August 9, 2001.

I hate cruelty of any kind ... So what was I doing, on Saturday night, sitting on my sofa in my dressing gown with a glass of wine in my hand, heart pounding with excitement as two big blokes, Nigel Benn and Gerald McClellan, slogged the living daylights out of each other?

—Virginia Ironside. "The Guilty Thrill of Watching Men Behaving Badly."
The Independent, February 27, 1995.

In one of the best examples of bad judgment since General Custer declared "let's head out to Little Big Horn and teach those renegade Sioux a lesson they'll never forget," Sharon Stone's husband, Phil Bronstein, was induced to enter the Los Angeles Zoo cage of a hungry Komodo dragon.

—Paul Spencer Sochaczewski. "Dragon's Breath." *The Sultan and the Mermaid Queen.*
Singapore: Editions Didier Millet, 2008.

 Kids, Try This at Home

After you've figured out your inciting incident or key scene, write six new leads based on that particular scene, using the six lead formats.

    1. Ask a question

    2. Anecdote/scene

    3. Provocative statement

    4. Dialogue

    5. List

    6. Current news, historical, celebrity, cultural, or literary reference

---

IN MEDIAS RES

Remember your Latin?

In medias res means "in the middle of things."

This advice is attributed to the Roman poet Horace, who wrote in *Ars Poetica* that an epic poem ought to begin in the middle of the action rather than at the beginning.

Just as Côtes du Rhône goes with aged Camembert, *in medias res* goes particularly well with the Scheherazade Scenario in which you start a scene but don't finish it until the end.

In writing, the term *in medias res* generally refers to "the middle of the action." Put another way, it can also mean "start at the defining moment." Obviously it's not always easy to define such a plot point (there may be several), but perhaps it helps to think of your story as a painting. A painter has to choose one moment to illustrate. That's what Leonardo da Vinci did with the "Last Supper."

The following two examples illustrate *in medias res*.

Here's how it works. In the William Tell story a satisfying place to start is the moment the father pulls back his crossbow, takes aim at the apple on his son's head, and is about to squeeze the trigger. Then you can go back and tell the story of how father and son arrived at this dramatic juncture.

Later, at the end, you can tell us whether he pulls the trigger. And if he does, whether he hits the apple or – "damn, should have aimed a bit higher."

Or, let's say you're writing about your first (and only) bungee jump, a dare from your fourteen-year-old daughter. You might want to start the story with you standing on the edge of the bridge, saying "I can't do this, I can't do this," while the jumpmaster counts down "Three, two, one ..." Then tell the story of how you got there. End the story with the leap (or the un-leap).

MAYBE NOW IS A GOOD TIME TO MOVE.

Don't start with this guy having his breakfast. Start the story in medias res,
when he's about to be flattened by the 10:05 Zephyr Express.

CRASH AND BURN

Here's what happens when you ignore *in medias res* and start with a weak lead.

An Air Zimbabwe pilot spent his 1994 vacation flying a 35-year-old Cessna around southern Africa, accompanied by his unnamed girlfriend.

Hidden in the article, published in the Air Zimbabwe in-flight magazine, are several adventures, any one of which would have made a good *in media res*-lead for the article.

Instead, he starts with an info dump.

First, let me introduce the aircraft, which was built in the USA in 1969 as Cessna's smallest two-seat production single. Designed primarily as a basic trainer, with a standard range of some 400 miles, it has a cruising speed of 105 miles an hour. It has very little instrumentation and just a compass for navigation.

I purchased Tango-Tango, as she is nicknamed from her registration, as a wreck in 1989, by which time she had already completed over 1 million miles of air training. For the purposes of the trip I was about to undertake, Tango-Tango was slightly modified with a Cessna ferry tank, giving her a range of up to 1,000 miles.

—Chris Brittlebank. "West to the Cape." *Skyhost*. Volume 2, Number 4.

How *might* Brittlebank have started his story? Here are a few options, loosely based on clues he has given us in the story.

Ask a Question:

I've been a commercial pilot for twenty-eight years. I've flown all over the world for British Airways; I've flown jet fighters and cargo planes. So what was I doing in a tiny Cessna, flying over the Skeleton Coast of Namibia, with no fuel, smoke in the cabin, visibility at zero, with a whimpering girlfriend at my side?

Anecdote/Scene:

The cockpit of my 35-year-old Cessna was cramped at the best of times, but now it was unbearable. Yet claustrophobia was the least of my problems. "You smell something?" Janet asked. Indeed, the electrical system was on fire, producing an acrid burn I can still remember a year later. Janet was trying hard to be calm and reassuring. I glanced over at her, sitting in the co-pilot's seat, and saw that her calm was all a sham. She was pale as a ghost on the Skeleton Coast we were flying over. Brave girl, I thought. If we get out of this I'll buy you a big dinner. It was a big "if." We were flying in a thunderstorm. Our navigation system was kaput. And the cockpit was filling with smoke. "I think the airstrip is three miles ahead," I said with more confidence than I felt. The gas gauge read zero. Janet just smiled, retreating into the the zen-like countenance she uses when I tell her I'm going off to play rugby with the boys. The compass started to spin wildly, like an Alice in Wonderland gadget. I glanced over at Janet, trying to offer a reassuring smile. She isn't religious, but I sensed she was in conversation with some higher power. If we get out of this, I thought, I'll buy you a big dinner with an engagement ring for dessert.

Provocative Statement:

I thought I was a pretty good pilot until the cockpit started filling with smoke. I'll be the best dead "good" pilot if I don't sort this out fast, I thought, as we started to dive.

Dialogue:

"Are the seats in this miserable little plane waterproof?" my girlfriend Janet asked.

I didn't have time for her inane questions. We were running out of fuel, flying through a thunderstorm without navigation. There was smoke in the cabin and I had no idea whether we were over the Atlantic Ocean, over the sand dunes of the Skeleton Coast, or heading toward the Outiniqua mountain range. "Huh?" was all I could manage.

"I just wet my pants," Janet said. "I thought you should know."

List:

No fuel. Check. Fire in the instrument panel. Check. Smoke in the cockpit. Check. Visibility zero. Check. Nearest airstrip ten miles away. Check. My girlfriend Janet sitting next to me, our unborn son in her belly. Check. Check. Check.

News:

I'm a commercial pilot and we are sent sometimes-obscure reports of news from the aviation industry. I recalled that in southern Africa last year some two thousand small-plane pilots were killed through mechanical failure coupled with their own stupidity. *Next year they can add me as a case history*, I thought, as the cockpit filled with smoke and the altitude gauge went into a frenzy.

DAM AND BE DAMNED

Here's the tepid lead from a published article about a major conservation issue – how dams are creating environmental havoc along the Mekong River.

For Thais, Laos and Cambodians, the brownish river that snakes along the borders is called the "Mekong". Yet the river is known by other names as well. Trickling down from its source on the eastern Tibetan plateau, it is called the Dza Chu (River of Rocks) or Lancang Jiang (Turbulent River) as it runs through China.

—Anchalee Kongrut. *Bangkok Post.* March 28, 2010.

The writer misses several opportunities to get the reader involved with a catchy lead. For example, she could have started with any of these hypothetical leads. You'll note I've invented details, characters, and situations for the sake of this exercise:

Ask a Question:

Are the Laotians selling their country down the river by allowing the Chinese to build dozens of dams along the Mekong?

Anecdote/Scene (Option I):

Boun Somsy's life has never been easy, but it's about to become a lot tougher. He's a fisherman eking out a living by casting his circular fishing net into the Mekong River, outside Luang Prabang, where, if he's lucky he might catch a modest basketful of small, bony fish his wife can sell at the market. But today he comes up with just two spindly river fish. "It's the dams," he says despondently, as if that explains everything. And in a way, it does.

Anecdote/Scene (Option II):

Kaysone Thongvin is a businessman who runs a small garment factory in the Lao capital of Vientiane. He uses a modest amount of electricity to power the lights, and to operate the ceiling fans, sewing machines, and computers he needs to run his business. But the supply of even that small amount of power is irregular and he has lost track of how many times a day his sewing machine operators have to take an unexpected coffee break while waiting for the power to come back on.

Siri Phomvihane is a farmer who lives outside of Champasak, in the south of Laos. The only electricity he has comes from a kerosene-powered generator owned communally by the village. It's useful to power small light bulbs by which his two children can do their homework, but not much more.

Both men have heard of the massive dam building projects on the Mekong, which are designed to provide electricity. Both men wonder when that fabled electricity is going to make their own lives better.

Provocative Statement:

The Laotians dither between welcoming the cash and being concerned. The Cambodians are increasingly angry. The Vietnamese are furious. The focus of this vitriol: the Chinese, specifically Chinese government-supported entrepreneurs who have built dams all along the Mekong River, which starts in China and then flows through Thailand, Laos, Cambodia, and Vietnam. "When the Chinese dam the river upcountry, in their own territory, they are showing blatant arrogance and disregard for the downriver states like Vietnam," says Tran Anh Tuan, Vietnam's deputy minister of environment. "It's a Middle Kingdom form of environmental piracy."

Dialogue:

"Laos is a poor country," Hartmut Helvetia, a Swiss development expert with the World Bank, says. "It needs electricity to grow, and hydroelectricity is the best option."

"Laos is a poor country," agrees Khammoune Latsamay, head of Laotian environmental group Friends of the River. "But these mega-dams are devastating for both people and nature. We're selling our future," she says, and predicts "in ten years, if the trends continue, we'll be poorer, our wildlife will be gone, and the only people who get rich will be the already-rich people who made these horrid deals with foreign countries to dam our waterways."

List (with a question):

Here are the things that could go wrong if Laos continues building dams on the Mekong: The fishing industry will be devastated. The country will be, de facto, owned by the Chinese. Biodiversity of global importance will be destroyed. Downstream countries like Vietnam will be furious and possibly take military action. Thailand will laugh all the way to the bank (again) at the gullibility of the Laotians in selling their natural resources cheaply. World Bank experts will pocket their huge consulting fees and take a vacation in the Maldives.

One might reasonably ask, "Why then, do they continue?"

News:

The prime ministers of Thailand and China will meet this weekend. High on the agenda is the question of which country gets to build, and which country gets to benefit from, hydroelectric dams along the Mekong River. Not on the agenda: the environmental damage that will result.

THINK CIRCULAR - THE BEST STRUCTURE ISN'T LINEAR

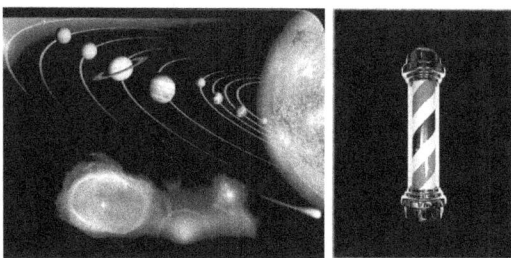

Most beginning writers make a basic mistake of thinking a story should be chronological and linear – I went here, I did this, then I went there and did that. But a circular structure is more satisfying to the reader; as in the examples that follow. Pick a metaphor – a planet revolving around the sun, or stripes on a barber pole. In a circular structure the story revolves around a central incident, a core theme. Sometimes it's in close orbit, sometimes it wanders. The key is that the story always ends not too far from the original incident.

Put another way:

A linear structure tends to be sequential.

A circular structure, described as follows, tends to be more interesting; it's a satisfying structure for the reader.

CIRCULAR STRUCTURES IN ACTION

Here's a circular structure in a personal essay by Julie Myerson. A few points to consider. She finishes near where she started. She writes in short (but complete) scenes (which I've lettered A to F), with lots of details (black rubber dagger, beige room, dahlias, Jaws, pink juice), interesting dialogue ("Purple's coming in") and memorable characters ("the Jack Nicholson of the dental profession.") She doesn't take herself too seriously and we like her for it. She does a nice job of introducing various themes – a woman's desire to be attractive (her teeth and the Hennes advertising poster) and her desire to have a "normal" family life ("It is one of those days.") versus the realization that lots of families have it much worse. And, with the abrupt transition from the department store scene [D] to the (second) Tube scene [E], she gives the story a disquieting edge. She could have written an adequate, publishable personal essay focusing just on her quest for perfect teeth, but by adding the homeless girl and her baby, Myerson has put her own quest into perspective.

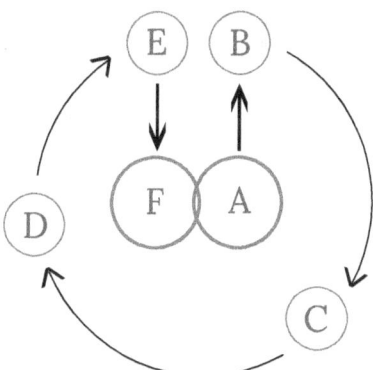

[**A – at home**] Right from the start it is one of those days. We wake to a steady black downpour and in the hour it takes to get everyone breakfasted and coaxed into garments for school and nursery, the downstairs lights have fused and I have inadvertently poured my youngest's cereal into the wrong bowl and provoked a screaming tantrum. "Remember you're premenstrual," my partner chants with horrible calm. "Relax."

As a child dabs a black rubber dagger into my ribs, I do a silent calculation. He's right, though I refrain from admitting it. I ought to batten down the hatches and stay at home but hell, I have a life. I have an orthodontist to see.

[**B – the Tube**] The streets are windy, distressed, vacant. Soiled newspapers roar around the mouth of the Tube. I negotiate my way underground. I stand dead centre on the platform so as not to be pushed under a train. A cleaner with pink rubber gloves is washing the Clapham Common sign and singing a hymn. I smile at her, but she looks straight through me.

[**C – orthodontist's office**] In the clean grey heart of W1, I find the orthodontist's surgery and am led to a beige room. I sit by a bowl of dahlias, alone for the first time today. I stare at a print of a mountain range until my name is called.

The orthodontist has receding black hair and a troubling, anarchic light in his eye. Jack Nicholson of the dental profession. He doesn't hang about. "Your problem," he says after a quick look, "is that your jaw is V-shaped, not U-shaped." I can't argue with that. "That's why your teeth protrude; your lips just can't accommodate them."

As he levers me back upright, I notice bitterly that his own jaw is perfectly, relentlessly U-shaped. "An appliance," he continues, "could be fixed to the upper and lower jaw. We're talking 18 months."

I flinch. "A brace? I don't think I could go around with one at my age. What about a nighttime one?"

He chuckles fiendishly, "They'd spring back during the day, with a vengeance." He jumps up. "Let me show you a picture. It's maybe not as invasive as you're imagining." He flips open a laminated album. A red-haired boy grins out with a totally unfounded confidence. His teeth are hugged by a dark metal grid. Think Jaws in the Bond movie.

"What does it cost?"

"You could have that for three thousand." I open my Roger Rabbit mouth. "Unless you decide to go for the deluxe option," he mutters. "For people in the public eye, you put the appliance discreetly inside the top teeth. The only drawbacks are a sore tongue and a temporary lisp. It's roughly double the cost."

"Double?"

"Well, that particular appliance has to be flown from America." He grins demonically and I slip from his chair. "Pity you weren't done as a child, really," is his parting shot.

[**D – department store**] It's still pouring with rain. I go immediately into John Lewis and buy a purple Clinique eyeshadow. "Purple's coming in," the assistant soothes as she strokes it on my inner wrist. "All those heathers and mulberries." I notice that it contrasts interestingly with my cobalt veins. Fingering the delicious silver compact, I head for the Tube. So, where could I hide for 18 months?

[**E – back to the Tube**] As I rush down the windy tunnel, I pass a young girl and a baby slumped against the wall. A piece of cardboard at their feet says, "Feed Us." Like everyone, I walk straight past and only when I reach the platform do I realise what I've seen. I don't know why, but it's a shock when the tears come. Embarrassed to be crying in public, I keep my head down. My train comes and goes. Finally, I walk back to her.

She's 15 or 16, long brown hair, a chubby, freckly face. The baby's wearing a shrunken acrylic jumper and lies asleep across her knee. She has a feeding bottle with pink juice in it and a can of Coke for herself. Behind her head, a wolfishly startled model pouts from a Hennes poster.

I give her £5 (yes, the eyeshadow cost more) and she grins and nods. I can't walk away. "How old is the baby?" I ask.

"One."

"What's his name?"

"Tom."

"Are you alright? Where do you sleep at night?"

She looks at me warily. "The shelter."

"Well, good luck," I say and move away; I've run out of reasons to stay.

[**F – and finally back home, where she started**] At home, I burst properly into tears. I've been waiting to do so all day. I'm crying because I've achieved nothing, failed to change either my teeth or the world.

Partner suggests I ring the London Connection – a day centre for the homeless – about the girl. They promise to look out for her that evening. "Now tell me about your teeth," he says.

"I have a V-shaped jaw," I say absolutely without humour, and relate the options. He roars.

"I'm not spending 18 months with a metal mouth." I'm let off the hook. The cost suddenly seems both ludicrous and repulsive. "Anyway, I'm used to you as a rabbit."

Upstairs, I take out the purple eyeshadow and wonder at the hormonally challenged mess I've become. The face in the mirror is blotchy with crying, a pathetic casualty of my day. I apply the eyeshadow.

—Julie Myerson. "Cosmetic Comfort for a Kick in the Teeth."
The Independent. February 27, 1995.

Look at the circular structure in the 900-word article I wrote about a conservation program in Vrindavan, northern India, birthplace of the Hindu god Krishna. It starts with the Scheherazade-Scenario tree planting [A], wanders and revolves around that incident [B, C, D, → L] and finishes the circular structure [M] just about where it started, completing the loop.

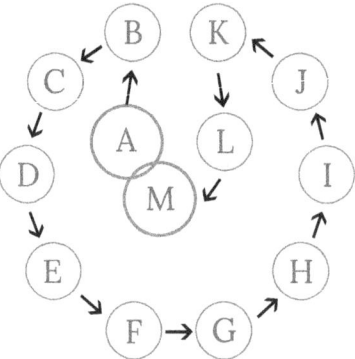

[A] When I visited Vrindavan in north India, birthplace of Lord Krishna and site of a city-wide re-greening effort, I was asked if I wanted to plant a tree. I arrived at the designated site and found that the hole had already been dug. For me, digging my own hole and getting dirty is part of the ritual, a point I politely explained as I took up the spade.

[B] I was reminded of the observations of Richard St. Barbe Baker, who led a movement he called Men of the Trees. "Planting a tree is a symbol of a looking-forward kind of action," he said, "looking forward, yet not too distantly."

[C] Vrindavan clearly needs quick environmental action. During the 1960s Vrindavan was among the cleanest towns in India, with streets washed twice a day and clean water available to all. Today, during the monsoon season, cholera threatens. Monkeys destroy vegetable gardens. There are few public toilets. Politicians get rich while public services are reduced. People are fed up.

[D] Vrindavan is a one-business town: Krishna. Every year the town of 70,000 swells by some 2.5 million pilgrims; more people visit Vrindavan's 5,000 temples than gaze at the Taj Mahal, just 70 kilometers south.

[E] The irony is that in their search for spiritual blessings, people have destroyed the natural beauty that made Vrindavan special in the first place.

The Yamuna River, where Krishna playfully hid the clothes of bathing maidens, is today brown with sewage and industrial wastes. Most of the 36 forests of Krishna's mythological time have been cut. The greatest scar is the condition of the holy parikrama, an 11-kilometer pilgrimage route. In some parts it is lined with newly constructed ashrams and shops. Pilgrims on this route, who are instructed to touch their feet to Vrindavan soil, are forced to walk for several kilometers on burning asphalt while dodging traffic. In other places they risk parasites of a most diverse kind as they tread on a rainbow of excrements.

[F] However, in the midst of these very real environmental problems in a very holy setting, there are a few signs that Krishna's ideal vacation site might just get restored.

The renewal effort in Vrindavan is an interesting combination of logic and belief.

People are complex, and make decisions and assimilate information with their left brains (logic, statistics, facts) in combination with their right brains (emotions, religions).

In Vrindavan the left-brain facts are clear – the place is a mess and something has to be done to maintain basic hygiene.

But the soft, fuzzy right-brain side of the argument might be even more persuasive.

[G] Swami Rathadas Ji Maharaji offers his temple's land and services for a tree nursery.

"Plants are revered," he explains. "We felt we should contribute to the community. And we're not alone; many ashrams are eager to take part." He explains that trees are more than trees in this part of India. "They're monks who haven't finished praying and who requested to be reincarnated in a forest."

[**H**] Swami Raman Das, a forest monk, shows me an ancient ax scar on a centuries-old *jamun* tree. "See this cut?" I'm skeptical of his religious-storybook tales, but he explains how, long ago, a woodcutter started to chop this tree. In order to save itself, the tree turned into a woman wearing a green sari, who complained to the resident sadhus: "Tell this guy to stop hacking away at my body. I haven't finished praying yet." And the saints spoke to the woodcutter and he apologized to the tree.

[**I**] The massive tree-planting program has catalyzed a burgeoning social movement.

In one corner of Vrindavan two toddlers join forces to lug a half-filled bucket of water to care for "their" tree in a tennis-court-sized park built on the site of a former dump. "We encouraged the government to put in a water pipe and provided saplings," notes Sanjay Rattan, the WWF coordinator of the re-greening effort. "But as you can see, the people themselves take responsibility for keeping it alive."

[**J**] In another part of town, religious leader Pran Gopal Mishra presides over a meeting of religious leaders. Their decision: seek help to regreen Gyan Gudari, one of the city's holiest sites. "The trees spoke to Krishna," Pran Gopal Mishra says. "If we learn how to listen to the voice of the earth, things will come right. The real solution to Vrindavan's problems will come from trees. Social problems, environmental problems, they're all linked."

[**K**] Another leader, Swami Raman Das, dug deep into his treasury of metaphors-to-live-by. "The ancient scholars said that the story of Krishna demonstrates what all human beings are capable of," the monk said. "Krishna shows that a two-armed, flesh-and-blood mortal, when energized by the spirit of the highest god Vishnu, can stand up to myriads of multi-armed demons. Every human being can perform miracles."

[**L**] In spite of modest success and soaring philosophy, some monks are very frustrated. Sadhu Tyagi Baba has travelled the world, but has chosen to settle in a simple ashram along one of the prettier parts of the *parikrama*. "It's not easy to stop this destruction, to stop the search for money," he says. "But we'll gather the religious leaders together. The environmental problem is as political as Sarajevo. We must force a cease-fire to all tree cutting, a cease-fire to all new construction."

[M] After planting the seedling in Vrindavan I realized that after I left India the tree would become orphaned, with no one having responsibility for it. So I asked Rajni, the ten-year-old son of the chief gardener, if he would do me the honor of watering and caring for my tree in my absence. Together we painted on a metal plaque: 'Planted by Paul.' And in Hindi: 'Looked after by Rajni.' We both signed it. To further cement the agreement I promised Rajni that I would plant a tree in his honor on my return to Switzerland.

Both trees are flourishing.

—Paul Spencer Sochaczewski. "Spiritual Leaders Help to Re-Green Krishna's Birthplace." *Earth Times*, May 1997.

∞

And another example of circular structure:

In a *New York Times* story about how Russian immigrants have taken on the job of counting people in Times Square, the writer starts by asking a question:

How many people pass through Times Square each day?

She ends 700 words later by giving the answer:

As for the Times Square tally? In April, during Mr. Habib's last count, there were about half a million people who passed through Times Square in a single day; 356,000 pedestrians, 15,000 bus passengers and 128,000 in other vehicles. December, he expects, should be even busier.

—Jennifer 8 Lee. "How Russians Count New York Crowds." *The New York Times*, December 25, 2008.

∞

I appreciate the circular structure in this personal essay:

I met a woman who had a stroke and lost her ability to speak. She had only one word left, and that word was "love." I liked to watch her say it. She would roll that word around in her mouth like a raspberry, eyes lit with pleasure, and say it slowly, as though tasting every letter.

Here Brunette examines the conflict:

So much loss for her: to lose language, to have her thoughts trapped inside with no way out. And yet, even though she was doing speech therapy to regain what words she could, she seemed strangely satisfied with the word that had not abandoned her, as though she would be fine if this were all she ever got.

As I spent time with her, I came to see that she had earned that word. I could tell by the way she said it – and by the way she listened. When I spoke to her, she had no reason to plan how she would answer me. I had her full attention, and I could see the comprehension in her intelligent eyes, but no matter what I said, her response was always the same: "Love."

A monogamous relationship with one word – and she got to have "love."

Two powerful questions:

I couldn't help theorize: Did she get that word because it was the one she had said the most – because it was the baseline of her communication and of her stance in the world? I suspected this was the case and wondered about myself. If I were to lose all but one word, which one would stay with me?

This question has haunted me for years now – given me the incentive to watch my thoughts and communications closely, to keep track of what word would best describe the essence of what I just said to myself or another. It helps me stay alert: I don't want to have all words fall away and be left with only "fear."

A bit of an info enhancement, done gently and philosophically.

In the Vajrayana tradition of Tibetan Buddhism, each aspect of the fully awakened mind has its meditational deity, and each deity is said to arise from a specific sound. They call this sound the "seed syllable" – a vibrational seed out of which a particular kind of awakened energy arises and takes form. A similar notion exists in Christianity. "In the beginning was the word. And the word was made flesh."

Words become flesh – they create something real and tangible in the material world. The habitual words we use serve as seeds for what we embody now and in the future, individually and collectively. We become what we intend, consciously or unconsciously, and language is the vehicle of our intention. Why not use this power by choosing our seed syllable – choosing the word we want to make flesh?

And she finishes as a changed person, but not too far from where she began.

With this one word, we make the world – not just for ourselves, but for everyone. Thanks to the woman who married "love," I've become vigilant: What word will I be tethered to when all else drops away?

—Jane Brunette. "Can a Word Change Your Life?" *Huffington Post*. June 11, 2011.

At the beginning of this personal essay, Andrew Biggs alerts the reader that he will introduce a circular structure. He then completes the circle at the end.

We call them "soap operas". The Thais call 'em "stinky water" and believe me, the water doesn't get much stinkier than in the melodramatic storylines of this TV drama.

Early on in the story the pretty female lead is captured, tortured and raped by the leading male character. So what does she do? Call the cops? Purchase some garden shears then go on a rampage that leaves the guy a lifetime member of the castrati?

Nothing of the sort. With violins rising in the background, and the actress gazing out into the night sky, she resolves to work hard to change him. Make him a better man.

At this early point in my column we must leave Prisoner of Love, but fear not. We shall return to it by the last paragraph, because I am sure you are dying to know what happened in the end.

I am writing this from Krabi in the south of Thailand where the Andaman Festival, the official start of peak season, kicked off last Tuesday night.

Amid the fireworks and grilled chicken stands, however, a cloud has descended upon the Krabi tourism industry in the form of the alleged rape of a 19-year-old Dutch tourist in July.

If you thought the futsal stadium was bad for Thailand's reputation, wait till you hear this.

The woman was celebrating her birthday at the Chang Beer Bar at Ao Nang with her boyfriend and a Thai man. The boyfriend went home early. The Thai man offered to drive her back.

The woman ended up in a local hospital saying she'd been raped. The Thai man fled the scene, as Thai men are wont to do when they do something wrong. He finally showed up and was charged, went to court and was released on bail.

This release enraged the girl's father, who made a music video called *Evil Man From Krabi*. In it, he stomps around the countryside in trench coat, rifle and hat to a reggae beat. His fury is as manic as it is understandable.

Krabi police counteracted with their own video called *The Truth From Krabi*. To date *Evil Man From Krabi* has garnered nearly 500,000 hits on YouTube. *The Truth From Krabi* has clocked up 984. The father is winning.

What followed was, to many, as shocking as the crime itself.

Tourism Minister Chumpol Silpa-archa made an outrageous comment that ricocheted around the world.

There was more to this crime than met the eye, he said knowingly. This girl knew the guy and even had dinner with him on the night of the attack. It couldn't, therefore, be rape.

How can somebody make such an official comment? Is Mr. Chumpol in chauvinistic dreamland? Or is something else going on here?

In the West we have "consensual sex" and "rape". You either agree to it or you don't. If only things were so black and white in Thai culture. Because somewhere in the middle of those two is *plum*, pronounced like the fruit.

I first heard this word 15 years ago as a work colleague explained the story of a soap opera to me, though not Prisoner of Love.

Just about every TV drama in Thailand has a *plum* scene, since it contains all the ingredients necessary to a soap – shock, violence, screaming, glimpses of naked flesh and, of course, sex.

"The man wants to set up a business with the woman, so he *plums* her," I was told.

I had no idea what my work colleague was taking about.

"*Plum*," he reiterated, frowning a little. "It means, like, like he takes the girl and sleeps with her."

"It means having sex?" I asked.

"Well yes and no. But *plum* ... it's more than that. He forces her to have sex with him."

"So it's rape?"

"'Oh no, that's *khom kheun*," he replied with a smile. "But this is ... well, *plum* and *plum* is, well ...""

"Stop repeating the word. You're telling me he forces her to sleep with him, yet it's not rape? Is he offering her money?"

"Oh no, that's prostitution," he answered sternly.

"Of course, and we can't have that. And what happens after he *plums* her?"

"Well, she's tied to him, isn't she?"

"She is?"

"Now that she has slept with him, she has to do business with him. She is bound to the guy."

It took me a while to figure out that *plum* is forceful seduction. A woman makes it known she likes a guy, but social mores make it difficult for her to take it a step further.

A romantic Thai man thus takes the only recourse possible – he forces himself on the woman. The deed having been done, they can get on with having a relationship.

So is it consensual? Now that's a hard question. The woman may not be consenting, but once it is over, she has a bond or relationship with that man, which is something she may have wanted from the start.

Thus we have the outrageous soap opera situation of a woman being forced to do business with the man who raped – *plummed*? – her for the sake of saving face.

Oh, did you hear that just then? That was the echoing sound of the gaping chasm between Thai and Western culture creaking, as the two cliffs shift even further apart, and the chasm plunges deeper.

To summarise: There are two separate verbs in the Thai language – if you know the guy, then he will *plum* you. If he is a total stranger, then he will *khom kheun* you.

That second word has a dark, foreboding meaning as nasty as "rape" in English. It is an all-out assault on a helpless woman, often ending in murder in this country in order for the man to escape detection.

There's nothing cute about rape, and the act is rarely seen in Thai soapies. In the eyes of Thais, this is the deranged sex fiend jumping out from behind the bushes.

This is why Chumpol Silpa-archa and others can make comments like: "She went to dinner with him so it can't be rape."

He's not being a total fool. As odious as that line of thinking may appear, he is making it from the context of a society that separates the act based on familiarity of the assailant.

I'm not even touching the logical progression of this line of thought, that it's OK for a man to force his way onto a woman who flutters her eyelashes at him. This is an age-old patriarchal culture where a flirtatious woman can still pay a terrible price.

Thais are getting educated, though, and it won't be long before the concept of *plum* goes the way of other Thai customs such as slavery, torture devices outside parliament and a wife praying to her husband each night before getting into bed with him.

Here Biggs closes the loop.

And what of that poor woman in Prisoner of Love? The one who resolved to change the man for the better after she had been *plummed* (the past participle of *plum* for all you grammar aficionados)?

She did change him. He realised the error of his ways. He realised what a good woman she was and fell in love. And they lived happily ever after.

And he even manages to repeat the "stink" image.

I was right. Water doesn't stink much more than that.

—Andrew Biggs. "'Evil Man from Krabi' and the Culture That Created Him." *Bangkok Post*. November 18, 2012.

Here's my personal essay about my name change; it finishes not too far from where it started, but with movement.

I filled out the forms and wished my ancestors had been Burmese or Chinese. I was changing my name to my grandfather's original, and Win or Wong would have been a lot easier to put on a new credit card than Sochaczewski.

I introduce the backstory.

But we have little control over whose descendants we are. My grandfather, Josef Sochaczewski, came to America from Kalisz, Poland, then part of Russia, in 1912, part of a great wave of European immigration. His family – my grandmother Esther, my father Samuel, and my aunt, whom I always called Syd – followed in 1913. I have an old family portrait which I treasure. My mustached grandfather looks like a Polish Pavarotti; my grandmother, pregnant with my uncle Bill, resembles a weary but very wise Madonna. Apparently she had tuberculosis when the photo was taken and died a year later.

A few years after passing the Statue of Liberty and arriving on Ellis Island, it came time for little Syd to go to school. Her Aunt Lena, the only relative who spoke good English, accompanied the girl. But the school official, apparently aghast at such an odd and difficult name as Sochaczewski, refused to register the girl and told Lena to come back with a simpler moniker. Today, the school official's politically incorrect action would be grounds for dismissal (if not a lawsuit); around 1915 he had simply made my family an offer they couldn't refuse. Aunt Lena, thinking quickly, suggested that Syd Sochaczewski be registered instead as Wachtel, which was Lena's married name.

My grandfather thought this was fine, since, to him, Wachtel sounded more American than Sochaczewski. And, like most immigrants of that period, he wanted to jump into the American melting pot as quickly as possible. He legally changed the family name to Wachtel.

I divert into a short info enhancement.

Americans change their names for many reasons. Some are motivated by show business glitter (Norma Jeane Mortenson later Baker, to Marilyn Monroe), some by religious conviction (Cassius Marcellus Clay Jr. to Muhammad Ali), and some by a personal vision of how a commercially successful name is constructed (John Paul "Jack" Rosenberg to Werner Erhard).

But most name-changers of the early twentieth century, like my grandfather, never made the limelight. Thousands of people during that period strove to de-link themselves from their pasts. It seems this desire to become American (and by definition un-become Italian or Russian or Polish) was part of a ritual cleansing, a symbolic burning of old vêtements, as if to say "I can't, I won't go home again."

And here's the nut graph.

As I grew older I realized that home is comprised of many nests. My life was in transition. For me, the way forward lay in a desire to return to roots. I wanted to change my name, and while I had known the story of my family's name change for years, several factors had prevented me from reverting to the original.

I offer four distinct Nancy Reagans.

The first was concern that my modest writing career would be hindered, the second was that I dreaded having to change all my records, and the third was that, as an American expatriate in Switzerland I had to wait until I returned to the United States long enough to meet an arcane legal requirement of residence.

The fourth problem, however, was the most daunting and problematic. No one in our family knew how to spell the original name.

I played with different spellings, even going so far as to send some ortho-graphic variants to a numerologist friend in India who calculated the relative impact of different phonetic spellings of what I thought my name might be.

And here I try to solve some of the dilemmas suggested by the Nancy Reagan problems.

I eventually went to the Ellis Island Museum and saw an exhibit of belongings immigrants had brought with them to America. The handmade doll in a display case was probably not much different from a similar doll I imagine Aunt Syd cuddling; the stuffed bear similar, perhaps, to one my father might have embraced. I saw women's jewelry and men's watches and photos and mementos of home that were lightweight enough to fit into a steamer trunk but heavy enough to provide solace during the uncertain future. I admired the courage these people had to leave for a place where they neither spoke the language nor had any guarantee of success. I have lived overseas for more than half my life, but my adventures seem smaller than those of my daring relatives.

Officials at Ellis Island put me in touch with the National Archives and Records Administration in Bayonne, New Jersey, and I told them roughly what I had been told about the family's arrival in America. Several weeks later they sent me photocopies as long as my arm of the original folio pages from passengers arriving in Ellis Island aboard the S.S. Kaiserin Auguste Victoria, sailing from Hamburg. It was the best use of taxpayers' money that I've come across. SOCHACZEWSKI, the folio said. I called up some Polish friends to learn how to pronounce it (say: soh-kha-CHEV-ski). I practised my signature a few times (it still hurts my hand to write, and I'm not comfortable enough with it yet to scrawl it). I spelled it on the phone to friends, first in English, then in French. It felt like I had been dealt a Scrabble hand with no vowels.

The climax accompanies a geographical shift, linked to the "melting pot" metaphor.

I took a sabbatical at the East-West Center in Honolulu, and the office of the (Philippines origin) Lieutenant Governor, Benjamin Cayetano, was helpful in walking me through the paperwork. Most Americans are immigrants, of course, but it felt somehow suitable to go back to my Polish roots in the Hawaiian melting pot. Fannie, the Chinese woman in the East West Center in charge of aloha (that's her real job description), organized a quasi-Chinese ceremony – in politically correct Hawaii we substituted bursting balloons for firecrackers.

Another info enhancement (I can't help myself).

I changed my name, not so much because I feel Polish (I don't speak a word) but because I don't feel German (and I certainly don't feel like a quail, which is how Wachtel translates). Somehow it feels right. The 19th-century Scottish philosopher, Thomas Carlyle, recognized that a name can shape a life, reflecting "What mystic influence does it not send inwards, even to the centre."

Details, signs from the heavens.

Almost as cosmic proof that I chose rightly, odd and pleasant things began to occur. Strangers see my complicated name in a publication and write to me, asking if, just possibly, we might be related. A newly found cousin in Montreal, Ari Sochaczewski, invited me to his son's Bar Mitzvah. I told a friend in Basel, Switzerland, about the name change and she explained that she had a friend, Simon

Sochaczewski, also in Basel, with a similar name. We couldn't possibly be related, I thought, but she spelled his name and it had the same odd concurrence of Slavic consonants. I called him, learned about his service in the Résistance in France. He mentioned a relative who had moved to Brooklyn. "I'm from Brooklyn!" I said, and immediately called Aunt Syd. "Sure, Jack Sachs," she remembered, explaining that Simon's/Jack's branch of the family Anglicized the name rather than changing it completely, as ours had done. "Jack died about twenty years ago." I called Simon back and we figured out that we are second cousins, I think (I'm not very good at figuring out these family trees). Right here in Switzerland.

And complete the circle.

When I first decided to make the name change I called my aunt, who started all this trouble by wanting to go to school some fourscore years ago.

She calls herself Syd, and I asked her why. "My name was Sadie," she explained, "but I never liked that name so I changed it to Syd."

"But your name isn't Sadie," I said. "It's Sarah. Says so right here on the immigration documents they filled out when you got off the boat at Ellis Island. Sarah. Four years old. Nationality: Russia. Race: Jewish. Final destination: Brooklyn. It says here you were 'illiterate.'"

"Oh my," my eightysomething Aunt Syd/Sarah replied. "If I had known that I never would have changed my name. I rather like the name Sarah, don't you?"

—Paul Spencer Sochaczewski. "Aunt Sarah Rather Liked Her Original Name." *International Herald Tribune*, March 24, 1994.

Useful Advice from Someone Who Wrote Pretty Well

We shall not cease from exploration
And the end of all our exploring
Will be to arrive where we started
And know the place for the first time.

—T.S. Eliot. *Four Quartets.*

Circular Structure in Presentations

At a scientific conference in Indonesia, a friend closed his presentation with this photo and the remark, "we have to work to conserve marine life and people."

Photo: James Morgan

It would have been more effective if he had *started* his (rather technical) presentation with this photo (perhaps with a large question mark superimposed). By doing this he would have used the Story of One to tell the Story of Many, along the lines of:

> This is a photo of a ten-year-old boy named Enal. He's a sea gypsy and lives near my home in south Sulawesi, in the middle of the world's greatest coral reef diversity. The shark he is playing with is a young tawny nurse shark that lives on the coral reefs.
>
> How much longer will Enal be able to fish and play in the reefs? How much longer will tawny sharks still swim in these warm waters? What can we do to benefit both people and nature?

And my friend could have *concluded* his presentation by closing the circular structure with the same picture, and the comment:

> Let us hope that the steps I've outlined – establishing protected areas and no-take zones, community control of the reefs, a ban on shark fishing throughout Indonesia – can help Enal and the shark continue to swim free.

DON'T EVER DO THIS

(EXCEPT IF YOU'RE REALLY CONFIDENT)

❧

There's a variation on the circular structure: the surprise ending. Done poorly this can be as hokey as the "and then I woke up, it was all a dream" kind of ending that you must avoid. It's tricky, but done with style it can be effective.

He couldn't stop thinking about the thong underwear. He couldn't believe Monica had pulled up her jacket to show it off. It so inflamed his imagination. At meetings, at briefings, at the most unlikely times, his mind suddenly reverted to the image of those straps, quickening his pulse, making him catch his breath.

But it was the cigar that undid him. He was driven by the thought of what had been done with it. Suddenly the capital became a city of cigars. He saw them wherever he went. They ignited his desire. When he was alone or talking to other people, he took secret pleasure in letting smoke rings drift through his mind.

There were times when he worried that he might be a sex addict. He couldn't stop thinking of Monica: what she wore, when she wore it, where she wore it, or didn't wear it. Her little letters were so brazen, promising such wild pleasure. Everything she scribbled, every gift she gave, mesmerized him.

And then there was the power of her voice over him. He knew that he was entering the dangerous territory of obsession. No matter how much he heard Monica talk about sex, it was never enough.

He was a busy man. A powerful man. A serious man. But there were times when all he could remember were the sizzling phone conversations. They filled his head like a drug. People warned him that he was endangering his legacy. Friends and strangers tried to pull him back from the brink of his single-mindedness. But it was too late.

He had become the helpless victim of his cravings for ecstasy ...

He wanted to think about her eating cherry chocolates. He imagined her wrapped up like Cleopatra in the Rockettes blanket or panting in that Black Dog T-shirt. He kept seeing her in that blue Gap dress. It was too tight, and he was glad. Again and again he was visited by images of a man's roving lips. He knew it was wrong. But he liked to dip into sin. He needed a release from all the pressure, from the extraordinary responsibilities of a very public man.

When he went to church on Sundays, he wrestled with his conscience. He even wondered if he needed professional help.

Sometimes he worried that he was abusing his power and hurting the country. He even fretted that the Constitution itself might be damaged by his obsession.

And sometimes it wasn't easy to behold all the human damage that he already had caused: ruining a young woman's life, dragging all sorts of people through the muck, wounding reputations and bankrupting those who came near him. Would the Presidency survive his lust? It didn't matter ...

He had his own definition of sex. Still, he was drawn to the endless discussion of the existential meaning of sex – its forms, its uses. He was a lawyer, but this was not just tortured legalism. This was tortured eroticism. He liked to parse the lurid definition over and over and over again, gaining pleasure from repetition: "breasts," "genitalia," "inserted," "stain."

His acolytes and subordinates became agents of shamelessness. It seemed that everyone around him, everyone in the city, everyone in the country, was talking about what he wanted to hear. All of them had become his collaborators in perversity. He was spending millions and millions of dollars to drag an entire nation down to his twisted level.

He knew how strong he was. He was the most powerful man in the land. He could reach into every recess of the Government to satisfy himself. And the prospect of impeachment didn't frighten him.

In fact, the more he fixated on the strap of that thong, the more certain he was that he could hang Bill Clinton with it. And, of all those naughty words he loved to hear, none filled him with more pleasure than "impeachment."

After all, nobody could impeach him. He was Ken Starr.

—Maureen Dowd. "When It Came to Monica, He Simply Lost Control."
International Herald Tribune, September 24, 1998.

 ### Kids, Try This at Home

· · · · · · · · · IMAGINE THE MUSIC · · · · · · · ·

If your personal essay or travel story is like a two-minute song, then the lead is like the opening bars of the song. The first few bars of "Satisfaction" are iconic and give you a sense of what's to come. Same for the short piano riff and opening line of Jerry Lee Lewis's "Great balls of fire" ("You shake my nerves and you rattle my brain") or the iconic opening notes of Beethoven's Fifth Symphony.

If a musician were to put your story into a song, who would you choose? Verdi? Carole King? Muddy Waters? What tempo would the songwriter use? Soft and dreamy or loud and raucous? And using the lead you've written, what would the opening chords sound like?

LEAD PLUS NUT PARAGRAPH

The nut paragraph refers to the paragraph that contains the "nut," the kernel, the essence of the story. If you want to be a touch pretentious, you can refer it as the "nut graph."

The nut paragraph is generally straightforward and unadorned. It is a statement of fact.

In a cold story the nut paragraph can be the lead.

But in a hot story the nut paragraph usually comes right *after* an opening anecdote – often an anecdote that reflects the Story of One.

A number of examples follow.

⸾

Here's a news feature that starts with an anecdote lead, a Story of One that represents the Story of Many:

> Irina takes a deep pull on a cigarette to calm her nerves, but her hands still shake slightly. Her short brown hair is damp from the first hot shower she has had in days, and she is finally wearing clean clothes. But she cannot hide her swollen eyes, the bruise on her left cheek, or her blackened nails, and so she fidgets uneasily while describing the horrors through which she has passed.
>
> She speaks a few hours after being rescued from two months of rape, prostitution, and furtive border crossings. Her story is hers alone, but in broad outline it matches those of tens of thousands of young women from Eastern Europe, whom criminal gangs lure each year from poverty at home into a heinous underground of modern-day enslavement in foreign countries.

And then the nut paragraph.

> According to the International Organization for Migration, 300,000 women from Eastern Europe work as prostitutes in Western Europe, 35,000 in Italy alone. The United Nations estimates the worldwide profit to be $7 billion a year, while other sources place it at $12 billion. The number of prostitutes from the Balkans, where close to a decade of war has wiped out many ordinary jobs, "has tripled if not quadrupled in the last three to four years," says Peter von Behtlemfalvy [sic, his correct name: Peter von Bethlenfalvy], the migration organization's top representative to the EU.
>
> —R. Jeffrey Smith. "Sex Trade Enslaving East Europeans: A Survivor's Brutal Tale." Washington Post Service. *International Herald Tribune*, July 26, 2000.

And another example (note the details, the rhythm):

Begin on the sixth floor, third room from the end, swathed in fluorescence: a 60-year-old woman was having two toes sawed off. One floor up, corner room, a middle-aged man sprawled, recuperating from a kidney transplant. Next door: nerve damage. Eighth floor, first room to the left: stroke. Two doors down: more toes being removed ...

As always, the beds at Montefiore Medical Center in the Bronx were filled with a universe of afflictions. In truth, these assorted burdens were all the work of a single illness: diabetes. Room after room, floor after floor, diabetes. On any given day, hospital officials say, nearly half the patients are there for some trouble precipitated by the disease.

And here comes the nut paragraph.

An estimated 800,000 adult New Yorkers – more than one in every eight – now have diabetes, and city health officials describe the problem as a bona fide epidemic. Diabetes is the only major disease in the city that is growing, both in the number of new cases and the number of people it kills. And it is growing quickly, even as other scourges like heart disease and cancers are stable or in decline.

—N.R. Kleinfield. "Diabetes and Its Awful Toll Quietly Emerge as a Crisis." *The New York Times*. January 9, 2006.

This example starts with a "cultural" lead:

In the classic film, *The African Queen*, Humphrey Bogart emerges from a swamp and is horrified to find slimy bloodsucking creatures clinging to his skin. "I hate leeches," he shouts.

Most of us share Bogie's revulsion. We shudder at the thought of finding leeches' shapeless forms clinging to our toes; we are also thankful for having escaped the medical Dark Ages In the eighteenth and nineteenth centuries, when doctors prescribed the animals for virtually every ailment.

And here comes the nut paragraph:

> Yet after a century of neglect, the lowly and vilified bloodsucker is making a remarkable comeback in science and medicine. Surgeons in modern hospitals use the physical sucking and anti-clotting agents in the leech's saliva to increase blood flow following micro-surgery. And scientists have discovered that the leech is also a veritable pharmacopeia, supplying at least nine unusual chemicals that are useful both for medical research and for treating diseases.
>
> —Paul Spencer Wachtel. "The Medicinal Leech: An Unlikely Superstar."
> *International Wildlife*, September 1987.

Look at how much information the writer puts into this anecdotal lead, including a pithy quote that leads nicely into the nut paragraph:

There are elephant footprints all over Jacqueline Mwaviswa's farm. But she doesn't think they are cute or even interesting. Love of the floppy-eared, six-ton elephant is something for tourists and wildlife conservationists, says this grandmother of 15.

She is upset because an overnight elephant rampage around her village last week left her entire food supply for the next two months – her cashew nuts, her cassava and banana trees, her mangos and corn – trampled or devoured by the world's largest living land mammals.

In Voi and the other poor rural villages that ring Tsavo National Park in southern Kenya, elephants – with their nimble trunks and wide, padded feet – have not only destroyed $30,000 worth of food, but have also killed four people since April, causing schools in the area to close and local leaders to urge villagers to arm themselves against marauding wildlife.

"The elephants have spoiled everything," Mwaviswa said as she walked through her shredded fields. "Why can't we get rid of some of them?"

Here are the two nut paragraphs:

> Her question is the focus on an emotional and complex debate halfway around the world this week as 160 countries meet in Santiago under the UN Convention on International Trade in Endangered Species of Wild Fauna and Flora.

The southern African countries of Botswana, Namibia, South Africa, Zambia and Zimbabwe are pushing for revision of a 13-year-old global ban on the sale of ivory that would allow them to sell stockpiles of elephant tusks worth millions of dollars.

—Emily Wax. "Five African Countries Push for End of Ivory Ban." *International Herald Tribune*, November 11, 2002.

❧

The nut graph follows an anecdote lead in this article about the uproar that occurred in Europe when processed products labeled "pure beef" were found to contain horse meat. Extra delicious: the memorable quote.

Outside the village of Rasnov in Transylvania, two cousins unload manure from a rickety wooden cart. Stela, the scrubby six-year-old mare pulling it across the field stretching away towards the snow-capped Bucegi mountains, tosses her head wearily.

Properly cared for, says Florin, 32, the mare may be good for another decade of farm work. After that, "she goes to the abattoir," says Niculai, 17.

"And then she's salami."

The writers then head into their nut graphs:

As recent events have shown, Stela and her kin may also become frozen lasagna, ultra-cheap beefburgers or the sort of meatballs harassed, cost-conscious parents feed their children.

The appearance of horsemeat in food purporting to be beef across Europe has sparked an outcry and triggered a blame game among politicians, the food industry and supermarkets. Tonnes of ready meals and burgers have been junked; shoppers are switching over to less processed foodstuffs and vegetarian options.

—Louise Lucas and Neil Buckley. "Demand for Cheap Food Drives Hard Bargaining in Global Supply Chain." *Financial Times*, February 16–17, 2013.

❧

And one more, which starts with a double Story of One.

Mary Multhoni Gakahu has spent all day in Nakuru, the third largest city in Kenya, selling a few greens from her drought-ravaged garden in order to buy food for the nightly meal. In the lengthening shadows of evening she enjoys a happy, noisy reunion with her husband and 11 children. Later the family will have to mount an all-night vigil: their cinderblock hut and scores like it are clustered along the boundary fence of Lake Nakuru National Park, and warthogs and baboons are likely to raid the few precious rows of maize growing in the family's cramped garden plot.

Meanwhile, Manuel Elotlan Fuentes sits with his pregnant wife and four children in their crumbling, stucco-walled home in Mexico City. The afternoon rains have leaked through the seams in the corrugated-metal roof to pool on the rough concrete floor. Absentmindedly running his foot along the puddles' edges in their eight-foot by ten-foot room, he explains how he left the country to find a better life for himself and his family here in the city.

Here's the nut paragraph:

Theirs are faces behind the frightening arithmetic of world population growth. In a little more than 10 years, our planet has added the equivalent of a new India to its human numbers. By the year 2000, there will be 22 cities with more than 10 million people each. In all, there will be more than 6 billion people on Earth by the end of this century, an increase of 4.5 billion since 1900. The result is a brewing crisis, as our species increases far faster than the ability of the land to sustain such numbers.

—Introduction to the article written by the editors. Following story of the Gakahu family by Mike McRae, following story of Elotlan family by Mark J. Kurlansky. "A Tale of Two Families." *International Wildlife*, January 1986.

Interesting dialogue, using *in medias res*, to start:

"Off, off. OFF," she said and pointed to my panties. When I did nothing, she tugged at them. The underwear would be coming off, along with my expectations of a "spa experience" in India.

And then a nut paragraph to explain what's going on. (Tip: the use of "had" in the past perfect tense is a standard device to suggest a passage is a flashback.)

My friend Sholeh and I had just arrived at the Jagat Palace in Pushkar, a marble-domed hotel overlooking the Thar Desert, Snake Mountain and the scattering of tents in the field where the drivers stayed. I looked out the window of my marble palace, knowing our driver Sharma was out there somewhere. As I squinted through the looking glass of my privilege, I let the guilt slide in, but part of me knew that I was using that guilt as a way to make myself feel better. I feel guilty, so I must be a good person. So it's not without shame that I tell you I turned from that window and made our appointments for Ayurvedic massage.

—Suzanne Roberts. "Across the World and Standing Naked in a Cold Broom Closet." *Matador.* March 20, 2013.

 ## Kids, Try This at Home

· · · · · · · · WRITE A NEW LEAD FOR A NEW YORK TIMES · · · · · · · ·
TRAVEL STORY

Here's part of a long personal travel story published in The New York Times. After sharing it with my workshop participants many times, I've come to several conclusions: First, Karen Swenson took the trip of a lifetime. Second, she wrote a flat article that lacks personality, conflict, insight, and heart. Third, the editors published it, which tells you something about the state of journalism today. Fourth, she incorrectly uses the term Sherpa. Sherpas are not porters (porters are correctly called porters). Sherpas are members of a Tibetan-origin ethnic group living in Nepal who are high mountain guides and expedition leaders. Fifth, she misspells the name Parvati. Sixth, and most important, she missed about a dozen opportunities to start with a bang.

So, why take up space with this piece?

Here's your challenge. Imagine you are the author, having taken this trip. Write three new leads based on descriptions/incidents/situations Swenson uses in her story. And, since this is just an exercise, you can fudge a bit – it's ok to make up traveling companions, dialogue, and experiences as long as they reflect the essence of Swenson's narrative.

Bonus points: Send me your revised leads; I might use them in future editions of this book.

Mount Kailas, a white pyramidal mountain in western Tibet, is a mystical locus of four religious groups of Asia: Buddhists, Jains, Hindus and Bonpos, who practice the shamanistic, pre-Buddhist religion of Tibet. Pilgrims from all four come to the scruffy little town of Darchen to perform the 33-mile circum-ambulation of the mountain.

Kailas, also known as Kailash, is a 22,028-foot mountain in the Himalayas. It is the throne of the Hindu deity Shiva; "the navel of the world" for Hindus and Buddhists; the earthly image of Meru, the mountain whose roots reach to the seventh hell of Buddhist belief and tower to the highest heavens. Buddhists, who call the mountain Kang Rinpoche, associate it with the meditation deity Demchog and the guru-poet Milarepa, who claimed the mountain from the Bonpo practitioner Naro Bonchung in a series of magical competitions. To Jains, it is the place where the first of their founding saints, Rishabha, achieved enlightenment. To Hindus, it is the home of Shiva and Paravati. To Bonpos, it is where the founder of their faith, Tonpa Shenrab, came down to earth.

Four of us, all but one with previous Tibet experience, arrived in Darchen by Land Cruiser after a five-day drive from Lhasa. Like many towns associated with the spiritual in both East and West, Darchen is a squalid hustlers' heaven, particularly in mid-May, the high pilgrimage season, which is when we visited.

Visitors can stay in rooms in spartan hotels, which provide a thermos of hot water and a cot. There are also permanently standing tents on concrete platforms; these are favored by Hindu pilgrims from India – during our stay, long-bearded sadhus in orange dhotis, their hair in top knots, were in residence. That area, where Westerners are also allowed to pitch their tents, was cordoned off from a separate Tibetan campground by a concrete-block wall.

As was once true of the Russians, the Chinese believe in segregating residents from foreigners. A Chinese official assigned us a campsite that we named Cholera Corner, because once a day a man with a spade would appear, dig a trench from the public lavatory on the other side of the wall, wend it between our four tents and then sluice out the day's accumulation. (We had our own toilet tent, as well as a separate dining tent.) Despite our pleading, we were not allowed to camp anywhere else.

Even though Westerners can't pitch their tents in the Tibetan camping area, they are welcome to spend money there; there were numerous informal shops set up in tents in which you could buy everything from mandarin oranges in glass jars to silver-studded saddles. I saw two women admiring a dainty belt adorned with little bells that draped another woman's waist and hips.

There was also a tent in which Buddhist services and blessings occur; several other tents housed card games.

In Darchen you can ask your guide to hire local porters to carry your tents and equipment if you have not, as we had, arrived with Sherpas; they carried our loads, set up our tents and prepared our food – plain but filling meals of meat, vegetables, bread, rice and pasta. We had hired five Sherpas and an English-speaking Tibetan guide from an agency in Katmandu.

The circuit of the mountain, which Tibetan Buddhists call the kora, starts at about 15,000 feet. Some Tibetans do its 33 miles in one day. Westerners often do it in three; we took four. This was the year of the Horse in the Tibetan calendar, which recurs every 12 years, and, therefore, there was a religious bargain going on. If you complete one circumambulation, you not only are forgiven all sins up to this point in your life but you also receive credit for 12 circumambulations. We had been passing pilgrims in our Land Cruiser as we approached Darchen, sitting on their bundles in the back of trucks and waving gaily.

There was little increase in altitude on the first day of our kora – from 15,000 feet to 16,000 feet – but the huge rock formations, barren peaks and views of Mount Kailas were magnificent. After a couple miles' walk we came to the official beginning of the kora, marked by a cairn of stones. Along the path we would come across more cairns, yak skulls and a spider web of prayer flags in primary colors marking the way.

After adding our flags to one tangent of the sizable web, we walked on to Tarboche. There, a huge wooden sort of flagpole (which is known as a tarboche and gives the place its name) was cocooned in prayer flags and khatas, the white scarves that Tibetans present to holy images. It had been raised at the Saga Dawa festival, which celebrates the date of the Buddha's enlightenment, usually in May or June, depending on the lunar calendar. A group of pilgrims were singing and dancing by the pole. Nearby, there is a walk-through chorten, a small stupa-like structure, called Kangnyi. It was hung with ram's heads and tails laced together rather like braided garlic in a Western kitchen. This, we decided, was probably a contribution from the Bonpos, who walk around the kora counter-clockwise, the opposite direction from everyone else, including us. From there we walked up to the "sky burial" site.

Tibetans cannot bury their dead because the ground is often frozen, nor can they burn them because there are no trees to build a pyre. Therefore, they cut them up, feed them to carrion-eating birds and retrieve the bones to be taken home and scattered; in the case of an important person, the bones might be mixed into the mud with which a chorten is built. At festival time, the site was simply strewn with clothing discarded by pilgrims – a gesture symbolic of their desire for rebirth through walking the kora. Among the clothes was a stretcher on which a body had been brought up.

Across the river called the Lha Chu, we ascended a path and stairs to the Choku Gompa, one of three ancient monasteries on the kora destroyed during the Cultural Revolution, but later rebuilt. In its inner chapel, there is an alabaster statue of a squat figure known as Choku Rinpoche, and a pair of elephant tusks. Two women having butter tea in an empty room invited me to join them. In the distance, the white peak of Mount Kailas, surrounded by fluttering flags, rose up above the barren mountains.

The rest of the trail that day was along a valley walled in on the left by stark mountains in wind-turned shapes adorned with snow. I didn't find the hike strenuous in general, but I moved slowly to preserve my breath because of the altitude.

That afternoon, we camped beside the Lha Chu. A caravan of yaks with fine carpets over their saddles passed. Across the river a waterfall cascaded in sun, but in the morning it was a frozen braid. Nets of pink flowers clutched the earth around our tents.

Our second day was laced with views of the northwest, of the slightly concave face of Kailas and more fantastical peaks along the left side of the path. We crossed the river to the second monastery, Dryra Phuk, which contains a cave with an imprint in the shape of the dri, a female yak, which is said to have guided the first circumambulator, the master Gotshangpa, to this cave.

The third day of the circumambulation is the killer. Rising in the dark, we started at 8 a.m. Already pilgrims were streaming up toward Drolma La, a pass at 18,600 feet. The path goes through, over and around big glacier-dropped boulders. We were adopted by a little girl who danced around us, imitating our labored breathing, but after a while she left us to join her relatives. From time to time we saw a woman or man lie down by the side of the path to nap. On our right, Kailas slowly disappeared from view. People greeted us as they passed. On one ridge a Bonpo practitioner sat, looking out to the mountains, chanting and playing his drums.

Finally, balancing our way across boulders, we reached the great rock at the top of Drolma La, totally enveloped in prayer flags and khatas. Here sins are forgiven and pilgrims are considered reborn. Tibetans sat among the boulders, drinking tea and exchanging food. I handed out apricots; one of my companions distributed postcards; another gave away his lunch. One pilgrim threw cigarettes into the web of prayer flags as an offering. A woman cut off a hank of her hair. Here is where the 21 Drolmas, who had led Gotshangpa to the pass, are believed by Tibetan Buddhists to have changed into wolves and dissolved into the rock.

The wild cries and singing of elated pilgrims on their way down echoed on the slopes as we descended the boulder-strewn path from the pass. Reaching the Melung Chu, we walked along marshy banks to our campsite on a midriver island.

The next morning the mountains were wreathed with cold mist. We arrived at Zutrul Phuk monastery. It was undergoing renovations, but we could see a sacred statue of Milarepa and the imprint of his hand left on the ceiling when he raised the roof during a contest with Bonchung the Bonpo priest. Their final contest, however, concerned who could reach the top of Kailas first. Bonchung mounted his drum before sunrise and slowly rose while Milarepa, despite his followers' urgings, seemed unconcerned. When the first beam of sunlight arrived, Milarepa threw his leg over it, rising instantly to the top of Kailas and making it a Buddhist mountain.

Our path wound along the top of the gorge of the Melung Chu. Despite the lower altitude I was just able to keep up with an elderly woman wearing tattered sneakers and carrying a cane and a prayer wheel she kept in constant motion. We arrived at a line of prayer flags, strung high across the chasm of the river. From there we drove to Darchen, marking the end of the kora.

—Karen Swenson. "A Sacred Circuit." The New York Times, March 16, 2003.

DON'T EVER DO THIS

NEVER START A STORY WITH A DEFINITION.

❦

And try not to lead with the weather (no matter how much we love Edward Bulwer-Lytton's lead in Paul Clifford: "It was a dark and stormy night …")

End Your Story/Chapters with a Good Lead

The lead isn't just the beginning of the story or the beginning of a chapter. In longer pieces the *end* of each chapter benefits from a gripping lead (should it be called an un-lead?).

∞

Francesca Borri's personal essay about the life of a freelance journalist in war-torn Syria starts with a strong lead.

> He finally wrote to me. After more than a year of freelancing for him, during which I contracted typhoid fever and was shot in the knee, my editor watched the news, thought I was among the Italian journalists who'd been kidnapped, and sent me an email that said: "Should you get a connection, could you tweet your detention?"
>
> That same day, I returned in the evening to a rebel base where I was staying in the middle of the hell that is Aleppo, and amid the dust and the hunger and the fear, I hoped to find a friend, a kind word, a hug. Instead, I found only another email from Clara, who's spending her holidays at my home in Italy. She's already sent me eight "Urgent!" messages. Today she's looking for my spa badge, so she can enter for free. The rest of the messages in my inbox were like this one: "Brilliant piece today; brilliant like your book on Iraq." Unfortunately, my book wasn't on Iraq, but on Kosovo.

And Borri finishes a few hundred words later with a moral call to arms that resonates with her opening. Note the subtle repetition of "hug."

> Had I really understood something of war, I wouldn't have gotten sidetracked trying to write about rebels and loyalists, Sunnis and Shia. Because really the only story to tell in war is how to live without fear. It all could be over in an instant. If I knew that, then I wouldn't have been so afraid to love, to dare, in my life; instead of being here, now, hugging myself in this dark, rancid corner, desperately regretting all I didn't do, all I didn't say. You who tomorrow are still alive, what are you waiting for? Why don't you love enough? You who have everything, why you are so afraid?
>
> —Francesca Borri. "Woman's Work." *Columbia Journalism Review*, July 16, 2013.

WRITING TIP #5

The Easiest Way to Create Reader Intimacy?

What's the single easiest way to generate intimacy with a reader or audience?

Ask a question.

Everybody loves to be asked their opinion. Questions demand answers. They insist on the reader's involvement.

The narratives of our lives run on questions: "What should I wear?" "Should I have married the accountant instead of the waste management guy?" "What do women want?"

By asking a question you invoke a mystery. "What happened to Amelia Earhart?" "Why did the dinosaurs die out?" "Was there a conspiracy in JFK's assassination?"

The technique of asking a question is a valuable corollary of the Nancy Reagan Principle. A question implies conflict. It's as essential a tool in writing as olive oil is in cooking Italian food.

Consider this piece by Nicholas D. Kristof. It ran in the business section. At its heart it's a piece about the 1997 Asian financial crisis and the impact the crisis had on people in rural Thailand. He *could* have written a simple cold lead along the lines of: "The Thai economy has crashed because of the Asian financial crisis, resulting in hardship for many people."

Instead he uses an anecdote lead with a big question to heat up the article and his Story of One involves the reader. To strengthen the Story of One, the editors included Kristof's photo of Bangon Phailak – a sad-looking, simple woman and a cute, trusting daughter.

Photo: Nicholas D. Kristof/The New York Times

Sitting on the ground beside her hut, Bangon Phailak chopped up wild plants for lunch and pondered a wrenching question: What does her 4-year-old daughter need more, food or a mother?

Mrs. Bangon, a gentle woman whose soft face is framed by thick black hair, explained that the family cannot afford both. As a result of the Asian financial crisis, her husband has lost his job as a construction worker, so the family earns only a trickle of cash through odd jobs in this village in northeast Thailand.

That money can be used to buy rice and milk for the little girl, Saiyamon, who has become anemic and malnourished. Or Mrs. Bangon can try to save the tattered small-denomination bills to pay for a stomach operation that she needs to save her own life.

—Nicholas D. Kristof. "As Seen Up Close, the Crisis Is This: For a Child to Eat, Her Mother Dies." The New York Times Service. *International Herald Tribune*, June 8, 1998.

Ask a question and people will live for your answers.

QUESTION EVERYONE AND EVERYTHING

Ask yourself questions: Why are you writing this story? What's it really about? Why should anyone bother to read it? Why should an editor pay you money to publish it? Does it have your voice? Are you deliriously happy with it?

Ask your characters questions. With live people you must ask detailed questions in order to get detailed answers. A good writer must be a good interviewer. Most interviewees will leave out illuminating details; they may not recount a story in clear terms or understand what you're looking for. Interviewing well is an essential skill. And it's easier to get what you need by meeting the interviewee in person. Next best is phone. Worst is by email.

And dead characters? Ask people who knew them. Look at published articles. Then you have to speculate. I don't mean invent dialogue or situations, but it's reasonable for you to say, "Then it's plausible that the following scenario played out..."

"He's like, 'To be or not to be,' and I'm like, 'Get a life.'"

Questions provoke responses.

ASKING QUESTIONS CREATES INTIMACY

Jay Winik, in his book about Abraham Lincoln, asks multiple questions.

Note the use of quotes that add verisimilitude. And note the repetitive use of the Triple Whammy – Rule of Three, which I've [numbered] for easy reference.

> Now the great question would be, was Lincoln equal to the task? [1] Was he equal to the approaching Civil War? [2] Or for that matter, it could well be asked, was he even ready for the presidency? [3] Many thought not. He was widely dismissed as a "gorilla," [1] regarded as a "third rate lawyer," [2] considered a "nullity," [3] and mocked as a "duffer," [1] a "rough farmer," [2] and " a man in the habit of making coarse and clumsy jokes." [3] Members of his own cabinet derided him behind his back: Stanton called him "the original baboon," [1] "a western hick," [2] and that "giraffe ..." [3]
>
> —Jay Winik. *April 1865: The Month That Saved America*. New York: HarperCollins, 2001.

Here's how I started one of my articles about golf and environment. My entire article is 1,800 words. I used twenty-two question marks and Nancy Reagan words (which you recall are *but, however, nevertheless, in spite of.*)

> The world has no shortage of argument-generating themes. Politics. Religion. Football. But there seems to be surprising unanimity about one point. Golf is bad for the environment.
>
> Or is it?
>
> —Paul Sochaczewski. "Golf and Nature. Happy Bedfellows?" *Travel and Leisure*. September, 2009. Reprinted in *Distant Greens*. Singapore: Editions Didier Millet, 2010.

SAVE A FLAT ARTICLE

I once wrote a personal essay about my Uncle Joe. The lead paragraph was okay:

How could I not love an uncle who, when he babysat for me, let me stay up well past my bedtime to watch wrestling (Antonio Rocca was my favorite) and horror movies (*The Mummy* was the scariest). How could I not love an uncle who lived in the middle of Greenwich Village, who took me to my first Broadway show (*Li'l Abner*), who tried to disprove Einstein's General Theory. How could I not love an uncle who invented a slew of useless gadgets, and who chastised major corporations for their lousy ad campaigns – and then offered them new campaigns which were hardly better. How could I not love an uncle who married a minor Romanian princess and bought a farm in the middle of the Adirondack mountains because it resembled her native Transylvania.

But the rest of it was as flat as Twiggy's bosom. I related what I knew of his life: he went there, he did this.

In the rewrite I asked a question (a question about a question, actually), and the article generated a new dynamic, an inner tension. Here are my second and third paragraphs.

Uncle Joe Rubin died of cancer when I was twelve. I was at an age when I was particularly incurious about life's complexities, and more than a little spooked by having a close family member wither away in our spare room.

Why is it that we neglect to ask the good questions when the opportunities arise?

It's not as dramatic as if Uncle Joe were secretly a spy, or had leaped onto the subway tracks to rescue a fallen toddler. But by asking a question, I created an internal dynamic that I used throughout the story, filling the piece with questions: How did he meet Anisoara, his Romanian wife? What did they see in each other? What was the reaction of their respective families to the marriage between an intellectual and dreamy Jew from Greenwich Village and a royal, conservative Eastern Orthodox woman from a distant and exotic country? Why did they buy the farm in upper New York State? Was he right about Einstein being wrong? Did watching *The Mummy* instill in me a deep passion for zombies or treasure-hunting archeologists?

WRITING TIP #6

$E^2 = 0$ – Chop Fluff like Michelangelo

$E^2 = 0$

Is this Einstein's first attempt at the Special Theory of Relativity?

Actually, it's cribbed from Herschell Gordon Lewis, the godfather of direct marketing, who said, "If you try to do everything (E^2) you wind up achieving nothing (zero).

In writing terms it means focus, cut, clarify, condense.

COMMIT AX MURDER

The hardest thing about writing? Editing.

If you came to my long workshop, I'd ask you to bring in a 3,000–5,000 word manuscript. Then the pain begins.

"Cut it down to 1,000 words," I would say, and you would scream.

"Cut it down to 500 words," I would command, and you would want to karate kick me.

"Cut it down to 100 words," I would command and you would stick pins in my effigy.

"Cut it down to five words, max." You've given up by now. You cut.

"Put those five words on a Post-It on your computer screen."

"OK, now write three leads for a new story."

"Finally (big sigh of relief from students), write an 800-word article, using one of your three leads."

By going through this distilling exercise, you would see that your 3,000-word manuscript was rambling. It had no central theme, no purpose. It was like the story of Morgan Spurlock, who ate only at McDonald's for thirty days. Sure, he was alive, but he was in lousy shape.

In writing terms the editing process is called "murdering the 'lil darlins." But I feel your pain. "I can't cut one word – these are the greatest words ever written in the English language," you will argue. Maybe, but if they don't move the story, then they are fluff. And fluff is like french fries. Fills you up but doesn't provide nutrition. You need vitamins and protein, not greasy carbohydrates.

Ax Murder and Liposuction

There are two ways to achieve focus: ax murder and liposuction.

Ax Murder

Take a sharp weapon. Ruthlessly excise whole paragraphs, subplots, everything that doesn't move your story. Amputate a limb.

Liposuction

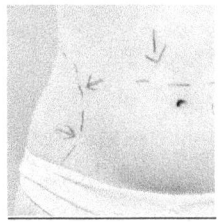

This technique is like removing barnacles from a ship, like de-junking your computer's hard drive, like getting a tummy tuck. Trim away the fat – underneath that flabby stomach lies a six-pack.

It's not one or the other – you'll need both. But the goal is the same: achieve target and focus.

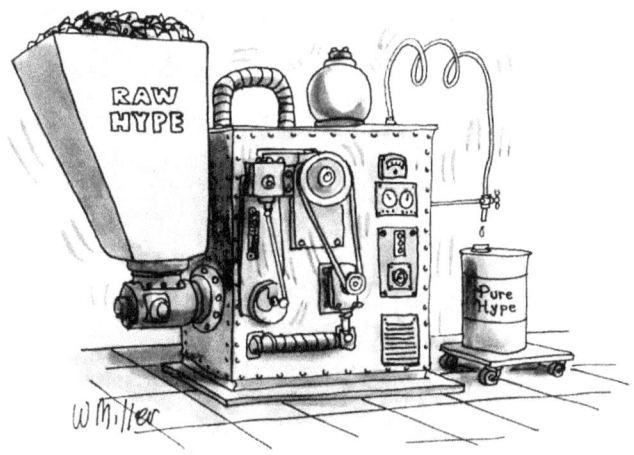

Think of ax murder and liposuction as means to extract the pure essence of your story.

Useful Advice from Someone Who Wrote Pretty Well

In the mind, as in the body, there is the necessity of getting rid of waste, and a man of active literary habits will write for the fire as well as for the press.

Cardan, Jérôme. *Aequanimitas.*

A (Possibly) True Picasso Ax Murder Story

Picasso was in his Paris studio with the owner of the gallery where his paintings were displayed and sold. The Spaniard was showing off his latest series of portraits, which he had labored for months to produce. The gallery owner was ecstatic. He couldn't wait to get these brilliant new works into the gallery and start selling them.

Suddenly Picasso seized a palette knife and strode to the first painting. To the gallery owner's horror, Picasso slashed the canvas from end to end. "Pablo! Arrete, Pablito!"

But Picasso didn't stop. Blade in hand, he marched down the line of paintings, reducing each one to ribbons.

The professional knows when he has fallen short of his own standards. He will murder his darlings without hesitation, if that's what it takes to stay true to the goddess and to his own expectations of excellence.

—Steven Pressfield. *Turning Pro.* New York: Black Irish Entertainment LLC, 2012.

Useful Advice from Someone Who Wrote Pretty Well

Remember the 1950s TV series Dragnet? Jack Webb, who created the show and starred as the no-nonsense Sergeant Joe Friday, became famous for the phrase: "Just the facts ma'am." (In fact Webb/Friday never used that memorable phrase, but actually said: "All we want are the facts, ma'am" and "All we know are the facts, ma'am.") Nevertheless, "just the facts," or in this case, "just the story," should be your mantra.

DON'T EVER DO THIS

AVOID CLICHÉS LIKE THE PLAGUE

When he saw her smile like an angel he decided he would hitch his wagon to a star by burning the midnight oil and giving all the tea in China to go out with her. She was truly a breath of fresh air, a sight for sore eyes.

His heart skipped a beat and he had a spring in his step even though it was raining cats and dogs.

The trouble was she had ants in her pants and didn't let any grass grow under her feet because the early bird gets the worm. She realized that at the end of the day, when the sun sets in the west, there are two sides to every question.

So he kept a stiff upper lip, tied up some loose ends, and gave heartfelt thanks as he prepared for her a mouth-watering feast fit for a queen that he hoped would tantalize her tastebuds and warm the cockles of her heart. He put his heart and soul into preparing a very unique gourmet gastronomic extravaganza. Later, her stomach growled and she was sick as a dog.

DON'T OVERCOOK THE DINNER

As in this drawing by Henri Matisse, sometimes simple is better than complicated. Sometimes a haiku works as well as an epic poem.

Useful Advice from Someone
Who Wrote Pretty Well

Substitute "damn" every time you're inclined to write "very" – your editor will delete it and the writing will be just as it should be.

—Mark Twain

Kids, Try This at Home

·········· FIND THE VIBRATION ·········

Get out your editing pen and slash and burn all the clichés and gee-whiz adjectives in this food travel article. (Extra points, note how Deanna Ramsay starts decently with a dialogue lead but then gets lazy – she ignores the opportunity to continue to use conversation, she doesn't seek other opinions, avoids writing in scenes, and refuses to involve herself in the story; there's too much passive voice and Tell, not Show.)

Answers are at the end in italics – hint: I count fourteen annoying clichés and gee-whiz phrases, roughly one every thirty words.

"Wednesday is market day. I was thinking of preparing a traditional Malukan meal for you guys that night. Will you still be here?"

The answer to Pak Asis's question was a resounding yes. Having already perused Saparua's twice-a-week market that Saturday and grazed on various sago-based sweets, sampling the savory food of this part of Maluku sounded perfect.

But, the spread Asis provided at Penginapan Putih Lessi Indah, which he runs, that night surpassed all expectations.

There was papeda – the ubiquitous gelatinous sago – and fish curry. There was fresh grilled fish and papaya flower. Assorted other green vegetables mixed with shaved coconut. A variety of local sweet potatoes and cassava. Citrusy sambal called colo colo. And more.

The meal, termed makan patita, had everyone groaning with delight and getting up for seconds and thirds. Usually prepared for special occasions, the flavors were unique and fresh, sour and spicy, and distinctly memorable.

Actually, most meals in Central Maluku were memorable. As were the desserts.

The area possesses a shocking amount of banana varieties, which are then crafted into a range of moist, addictive sweets. One woman's tiny stall just across from the Ambon Plaza Mall offered at least a dozen, if not more, desserts to choose from. Pie-like creations of coconut, banana or pandanus. Mounds of sticky rice with creamy coconut and gula merah. Banana halves dotted with sugar and peanuts. Cakes with layers of custard and subtle sweetness. The variety was endless and all of it was delicious.

Then along the central streets of the city of Ambon just around sunset, stalls would emerge with small tables laden with painted pots. They all sold the same thing, nasi kuning, each iteration better than the one before.

Offering more incredible Malukan flavors, Rumah Makan Paradise on Jl. Philip Latumahina in central Ambon is the place to gorge. Select the vegetables and starches (meaning cassava and potato varieties in these parts) from the already prepared food behind the counter, then order a grilled fish and papeda. Enjoy a meal that seems very much too good to be true.

When paying the bill, a jar full of clear liquid caught the eye. The woman said it was her own version of sopi, in which she had various herbs soaking at the bottom. The Malukan palm wine was crisp and extremely drinkable, and happily on offer in many parts of the region.

But aside from sopi, the other beverage of choice – in Ambon at least – seems to be coffee. Rumah kopi sit on practically every corner in Ambon's city center, filled with men chatting, smoking and playing chess.

The coffee at the constantly crowded Joas on Jl. Said Perintah is beyond fantastic. Hot and strong, dark and fresh, it is so good it is almost indescribable. Just go there.

—Deanna Ramsay. "Feasting in the East." Jakarta Post. August 31, 2012.

1. was a *resounding yes*; 2. sampling the savory food of this part of Maluku *sounded perfect*. 3. ... that night *surpassed all expectations*; 4. had everyone *groaning with delight*; 5. and *distinctly memorable*; 6. a dozen, *if not more*, desserts. The variety was *endless* and all of it was *delicious*; 7. nasi kuning, *each iteration better than the one before*; 8. more *incredible* Malukan flavors meal that seems *very much too good to be true*; 9. liquid c*aught the eye*; 10. on Jl. Said Perintah is *beyond fantastic*; 11. dark and fresh, *it is so good it is almost indescribable*.

Useful Advice from Someone Who Wrote Pretty Well

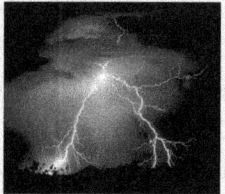

God only exhibits his thunder and lightning at intervals, and so they always command attention. These are God's adjectives. You thunder and lightning too much, the reader ceases to get under the bed, by and by.

—Mark Twain

In most cases, conciseness is a good thing.

DON'T EVER DO THIS

NEVER WRITE LIKE A BAD PRESS RELEASE

❧

The biggest abusers of fast-food adjectives are public relations people who think glowing adjectives enhance their message. The biggest enablers are editors at newspapers and magazines who publish this drivel. Here's one example:

> Three-time World Pizza Champion Danilo co will be entertaining guests at Ramada Resort Khao Lak all this month with fantastic displays of floury-fingered finesse and dough-handling dexterity.
>
> Sangrigoli will be demonstrating his pizza acrobatics and serving up expertly crafted specimens of Italy's unofficial national dish at Sassi's Beach Club at this hotel in Phangnga province.
>
> A certified master from the Scuola Italiana Pizzaioli, Sangrigoli is no stranger to impressing an audience with pizza-based performances, having won the title of European Champion at the 2006 Pizza World Cup in Barcelona as well as holding the Guinness World Record for baking 504 pizzas in 103 minutes.
>
> He is the first competitor to win both the Acrobatic and Baking categories in Italy's Pizza Championship, evidence – if any is needed – that this chef has both style and substance.
>
> When guests aren't diving, nature-gazing, rafting or trekking around Khao Lak to take in the stunning natural beauty of the area, Sangrigoli's pizza twirling can be admired and its results enjoyed from 7 pm every Wednesday evening.
>
> —Bangkok Post, December 10, 2012.

KEEP OUT OF THE JARGON JUNGLE

Jargon = empty calories.

In a 2012 press release the World Economic Forum predicted we face:

> A dystopian world, unsafe safeguards, and the dark side of connectivity are this year's major risk cases.

What does that mean?

∞

Or how about this call for papers for an academic publication?

> This anthology of essays explores the historical and contemporary dimensions of representations of knowledge in Borneo as they are associated with social spaces and places where power and contesting strategies are enacted. Taking representation as the central reference point, authors are invited to contribute essays that variously embrace or resist the assumptions particular representations generate, politicizing their implications or challenging discourse around such articulations.
>
> We seek essays that explore the interconnections and synergies between theory, method and politics in the field of representation, and in the light of complex and changing socio-political and cultural issues that affect countries, peoples, institutions and practices in Borneo. The editors are especially interested in scholarly essays on gendered agency, indigenous subjectivity or identity and, in general, on the representation and understanding of local traditional knowledges in Borneo as they relate to cultures of consumption and as cultures for planning and development.

∞

As Al Gore wrote:

> If we took the same approach to Christmas songs that we take to the language of federal rules and regulations, instead of "Silent Night," we'd be singing about "noise-mitigated post-daylight time intervals."

Watch out, intimidation can backfire.

DON'T EVER DO THIS

DON'T BE A POMPOUS ASS

You might have written this way in college (I certainly did), like the author of this letter wrote to his girlfriend. Don't do this as a grown-up.

> I will hazard these statements – [T.S.] Eliot contains the same ecstatic vision which runs from Münzer to Yeats. However, he retains a grounding in the social reality/order of his time. Facing what he perceives as a choice between ecstatic chaos and lifeless mechanistic order, he accedes to maintaining a separation of asexual purity and brutal sexual reality … Of course, the dichotomy he maintains is reactionary, but it's due to a deep fatalism, not ignorance … And this fatalism is born out of the relation between fertility and death, which I touched on in my last letter – life feeds on itself. A fatalism I share with the western tradition at times.
>
> —Barack Obama. while studying at Columbia.

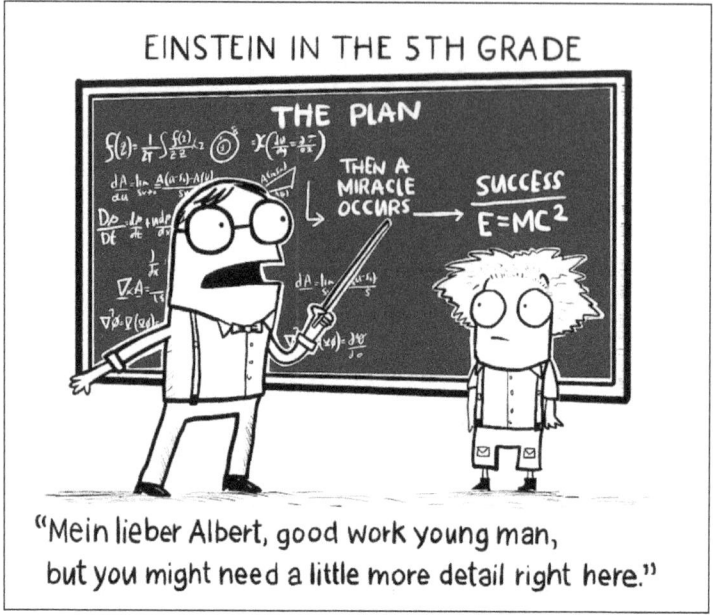

Illustration: Sarah Steenland

Think of your writing as a geometry proof – take us through your thought processes. Don't invoke miracles.

THE IMPORTANCE OF LOGIC

Don't leave out important signposts of logic.

Here's an example of a young writer with a distinctive voice telling her story.

Hanna Jones starts with a strong anecdote lead that introduces a quest with big questions. Will she save a life? Will she make a difference?

I am 4,000 miles from Tatsfield [England] and, with the windchill, it's minus 45 centigrade. I'm getting ready to leave my cozy house and go to work, I load up my pistol, strap on my duty belt, pull on my Kevlar gloves, zip up my jacket and – most important – check that the muskrat fur is pulled tight around my head. It looks funny, but I need its warmth. I stop outside and am careful not to slip as I tread the crunching snow and ice along the pathway to my truck. My throat stings as I take those first few numbing breaths. My eyelashes stick as I blink, and part of me would like to stay home. But I have a purpose. Maybe I'll save a life today. Maybe I'll make a difference.

And then she introduces her backstory.

I look up and gasp at the sight of the northern lights, bright and vivid, dancing across the star-filled sky. How did I end up here? It's a far cry from life as a teenager in Tatsfield. After studying at Oxted School I had no idea what I was going to do next. I had no strong ambitions, no "callings", career-wise. While my friends dedicated themselves to training toward becoming doctors or vets or teachers, I plugged away and simply hoped that one day my "calling" would be made known.

And then one day, after my studies were finished, I moved to Canada, still with no clear career plans.

And here's where she leaves the reader hanging, by not telling us the full story, like leaping from appetizer to dessert. Why Canada and why become a Mountie? Was she an ice hockey player? Were her parents in law enforcement? Was she inspired by a *Die Hard* movie? Did the Great Policeman in the Sky speak to her? Was she searching for romance? Or did she just like the cool red uniforms the Mounties wear? And, most important, does she answer the earlier questions she posed? Does she save a life or make a difference?

Instead, Jones leaves us hanging and tells us about her training.

Within just under three years I was a Canadian Mountie. I had completed a year of basic police training at a local college, followed by a gruelling six months at the RCMP "Depot" – a tough, military-style 'bootcamp' where only the toughest survive.

—Hannah Jones. "Tatsfield Teenager to Canadian Mountie."
Parish Magazine, Tatsfield, UK. December 2012.

Useful Advice from Someone Who Wrote Pretty Well

Leave out the parts readers tend to skip.

—Elmore Leonard

If you're not clear about the article's direction
then the reader won't know where to go.

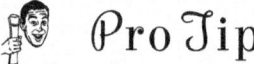 Pro Tip

Hire an Ax Murderer

Every writer needs one good editor. Get one you trust, who is not emotionally involved with you or your work. At the early stage of your career, do not ask a family member or close friend for serious editing advice.

CONSIDER A LIDGET

When you've got a wandering story, consider holding it together with a lidget. (Don't bother looking it up; I just invented the term.)

A lidget is a "literary widget" and is a technique for holding together disparate elements of a story, much like straw holds together bricks.

Think of it this way. A lidget is a recurring incident or series of asides that keep popping up regularly throughout the article.

In most cases, set the lidget in italics.

Lidgets work best in longer articles. In a 2,000-word story you might want four to five lidgets. Each lidget can be as short as a sentence, never longer than a paragraph. If your lidgets are taking up too much intellectual space in the article, then you need to rethink your focus.

LIDGETS IN ACTION

Here's an example of lidgets in my article about the copy painters of Vietnam. I decided to focus on one painting in particular, Leonardo da Vinci's Mona Lisa.

This is a short article, about 900 words, and I used three lidgets (which I set in italics on the original). In longer articles of around 4,000 words, I've used up to eleven lidgets, which might be pushing the limits of lidgetry.

She has many identities and genders.
She was kidnapped, maybe by Picasso.
She lived in the Palace of Versailles.
She spent time in Bonaparte's bedroom.
Nat King Cole, Cole Porter, Santana, Bob Dylan, and Britney Spears sang about her.
She appeared, twice, in The Simpsons.
She has no eyebrows or eyelashes.

She is the world's most famous painting. Created by Leonardo da Vinci in the early sixteenth century, the Mona Lisa (called *La Gioconda* in Italian and *La Joconde* in French) has been subject to the highest form of flattery – painters the world over have copied her likeness.

And Ground Zero for Mona Lisa copies is Vietnam. In the hothouse commercial atmosphere of Ho Chi Minh City and, to a lesser extent, Hanoi, Vietnam's artists churn out hundreds, perhaps thousands, of Mona Lisa paintings a year.

Kha Huen, a soft-faced 29-year-old artist in Ho Chi Minh City, takes about three days to paint a Mona Lisa. "I can do a Monet, Dalí, or Van Gogh in one day," he says over soft drinks at a café, "but the Mona Lisa has more details." Working as an in-house artist at a downtown art shop, Kha paints about thirty Mona Lisas a year, which sell for around $50. There are perhaps a hundred painters in Ho Chi Minh City creating Mona Lisas, he estimates.

Visitors to Ho Chi Minh City can hardly walk 50 meters without passing in front of an art shop. On the walls hang copy paintings of Botero's fat people with small heads, Warhol's Marilyn, Van Gogh's sunflowers, and Dali's melted watches. Like "copy-watches" and "copy-golf shirts," copy-paintings seem to be just another commodity to be sold in this overheated economy . But while the latest Hollywood movie or Swiss watch is protected by copyright and trademark regulations, a painting by da Vinci is free game.

Few pieces of art have been the subject of so much artsy analysis. For example, Professor Margaret Livingstone of Harvard University used the Mona Lisa smile to illustrate her theory that the human eye uses two types of vision, foveal (or direct vision, which is good for detail) and peripheral. "The elusive quality of the Mona Lisa's smile can be explained by the fact that her smile is almost entirely in low spatial frequencies," Livingstone said, "and so is seen best by your peripheral vision."

Like most copy artists in Ho Chi Minh City, Vy Vi spends his days in the middle of a small shop, sitting on a small stool in front of an easel, copying works of Klimt and Hooper. When he gets lucky a businessman will walk in, set down a photograph of his kids, and ask for a painted portrait that is as close to the original photograph as possible. There's not much request for creative license in this business. Vy Vi explains that his Mona Lisa usually requires six days, but he sometimes feels uneasy working on the famous face. "It's so well known that people will see if I make a mistake," he says. He paints some twenty Mona Lisas a year, which cost $43, about the standard price throughout the country.

Some of the Vietnamese Mona Lisas are excellent. Some are clearly "just off" in some way – either the color is wrong or the background is too sharp or too soft, or the details on her dress too ornate, or her smile is a bit, well, just not right.

The famous Mona Lisa smile is the trickiest thing to get right, Vu Dan Thang, a Hanoi-based artist says.

The question of what lies behind her half-smile has spurred debate for centuries. Who was she? What secrets does she keep?

Art historians have speculated that she is Leonardo's secret mistress. She is pregnant. She is an aristocratic lady with her own private secrets. She is following Leonardo's mischievous instruction to project an enigmatic image. Sigmund Freud thought she was a remembrance of Leonardo's mother. Italian art historian Angelo Paratico goes a step further, speculating that she is actually a Chinese slave who was Leonardo's mother – according to Paratico there are several proofs of da Vinci's Chinese ancestry, "For instance, the fact he was writing with his left hand from left to right ... and he was also a vegetarian, which was not common" [among Europeans]. Others speculate that she is Leonardo's male assistant and lover. That she is Leonardo himself, in drag.

The Vietnamese artists I met acknowledged that they are simply copying art, and trying to do so in an artistically valid way.

So where's the line between copy-art and fake?

Michelangelo was found guilty of forging a marble sculpture of Cupid for his patron, Lorenzo di Cosimo de Medici, rubbing his newly wrought work with soil before passing it off as an antiquity. Picasso was thought to have signed off on a painting that wasn't done by him.

Thomas Hoving, former director of New York City's Metropolitan Museum of Art, estimates that as much as forty percent of art in the market today is either a "half-forgery," meaning genuinely old works that have been altered to be attributed to a more valuable style or artist, or outright fakes.

Obviously, none of the Vietnam street paintings would ever be confused with the priceless masterpiece hanging in the Louvre. But an artist takes pride in his work, and I wondered how satisfying is it to copy Mona Lisa, day in, day out.

"It's challenging," Doan Le Quang, a Hanoi-based artist said. "But I'd rather do my own thing." I ask if I could see some of his paintings. He sifts among the Gauguins and Magrittes and Renoirs and pulls out a few idyllic landscapes of Vietnamese countryside scenes. They are attractive, although not to my taste. Does his shop sell a lot of these scenes of water buffalo and rice fields, thatched roof houses and temples? "A few," he says shyly. But not as many as these, he admits, pointing to a Klimt's golden woman and Monet's water lilies.

—Paul Spencer Sochaczewski. "Mona Lisa on My Mind."
Curious Encounters of the Human Kind – Southeast Asia. Geneva: Explorer's Eye Press, 2016.

It's easy. The great pieces of writing show creative genius,
but they also need clarity, logic, and structure.

Less Is More

Always.

Unless You're Mae West

Who said: "Too much of a good thing can be wonderful."

Clarity Is Key

Do not obfuscate the reader. She must know, at all times, where the action is taking place, who is speaking. You can have mysteries, but don't leave the reader confused about who the characters are and who's saying what.

*Make things clear for the reader. Generally, less is more,
except for those times when a bit more is better.*

 Pro Tip

Spider Web

In longer pieces beginners tend to introduce interesting events and characters that don't reappear. Such floating incidents leave the reader confused.

Each incident, each character needs to have a relationship with at least two other incidents or characters. The characters should be locked in the same spider web.

The stronger the relationships (preferably some kind of Nancy Reagan conflict relationship), the better.

DON'T EVER DO THIS

AVOID HOOPTEDOODLE

In Sweet Thursday, John Steinbeck created the term hooptedoodle to describe an often-narcissistic passage where the author breaks away from the main plot and shows off. It can be entertaining and a showcase for the writer's skill. It can also be irritating. Best to use sparingly.

Steinbeck's character Mack described it:

> "Sometimes I want a book to break loose with a bunch of hooptedoodle. The guy's writing it, give him a chance to do a little hooptedoodle. Spin up some pretty words maybe, or sing a little song with language. That's nice. But I wish it was set aside so I don't have to read it. I don't want hoopte-doodle to get mixed up in the story. So if the guy that's writing it wants hooptedoodle, he ought to put it right at first. Then I can skip if I want, or maybe go back to it after I know how the story came out."

IF YOU MUST SHOW OFF, DO IT WITH STYLE

Hooptedoodle can be likened to a basketball player who makes an ostentatious slam dunk.

In classical music the concept of hooptedoodle occurs in the composition of fiendishly difficult pieces and in the cadenzas of single-instrument concertos in which the performer is encouraged to improvise and show off.

Consider nineteenth-century composer and violinist Nicolò Paganini. His music was so difficult that he was one of the few musicians able to perform his works. To show off he would deliberately snap one or two strings on his violin and continue playing as if nothing had changed. Some observers thought his uncanny skill resulted from a pact with the devil. Not to diminish Paganini's genius, but he was aided by a lucky chronic illness. He had Ehlers-Danlos syndrome, marked by excessive flexibility of the joints. "This enabled Paganini to perform the astonishing double-stoppings and roulades for which he was famous," according to Philip Sandblom in his book *Creativity and Disease*. "His wrist was so loose that he could move and twist it in all directions. Although his hand was not disproportional, he could thus double its reach and play in the first three positions without shifting."

For a contemporary violinist with performing flair, see Ruggiero Ricci's album *Virtuoso Showpieces*.

CUT FLUFF LIKE MICHELANGELO

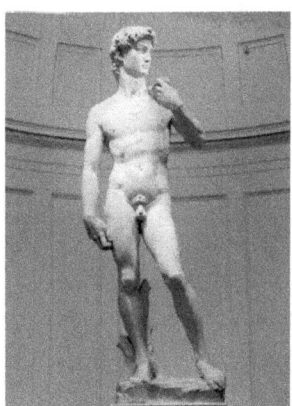

Mickey and his pal Gianni walk into a bar ...

They're getting mellow on grappa, and the conversation turns to art.

"Mickey, Mickey, tell me, how did you create David from that big piece of marble?" Gianni asks.

And Mickey answers: "Easy. I just chipped away everything that wasn't David."

Don't Forget English Comp 101

I've been relentless about the need for the writer to create her own voice, to be creative, to seek intimacy with the reader.

But it's all for naught if the writer uses sloppy grammar. You know the rules – avoid fast-food adverbs and adjectives by using active verbs and strong nouns, and all that.

Grammar (and its cousins spelling and fact-checking) gives your story credibility. Abuse it at your own peril.

Active Verbs and Strong Nouns

Make nouns and verbs do the heavy lifting.

∞

If I say the word *food*, what do you think of?

How about *Triple Cherry Garcia with hot fudge, whipped cream, and bits of crumbled brownie on top.*

∞

Same for *vehicle* vs. *fire-engine red Corvette.*

∞

Watch the progression of this sentence, which gains precision and power just by using active verbs and specific nouns:

A person enters a space.

A *man* enters a space.

A man enters a *church*.

A *priest* enters a church.

A priest *limps* into a church.

A *pope* limps into a church.

A pope *staggers* into a church.

A pope staggers into a *cathedral*.

A pope staggers into *St. Peter's*.

Pope Benedict XVI staggers into St. Peter's.

SHOW, DON'T TELL

This is one of the cornerstones of good writing, and every writing coach will advise you to follow this precept. Why does it work? By *showing* you put more drama into the scene. We believe what we see, we distrust what we are told.

∞

Telling: He stood six feet eight inches tall.

Showing: "Damn short architects," he muttered as he banged his head on the top of the door frame.

∞

Telling: She was upset with her husband's behavior.

Showing: "Get out of my house, you two-timing bastard," she shouted, throwing her husband's favorite Ming vase at his head.

∞

Telling: Jennifer was a very happy young woman when Freddie proposed.

Showing: "It's like Christmas and my birthday and the first snow of winter, all rolled into one," Jennifer said as she hugged her best friend and danced around the room.

Useful Advice from Someone
Who Wrote Pretty Well

Don't tell me the moon is shining; show me the glint of light on broken glass.

—Anton Chekhov

USING SHOW, DON'T TELL

When you *tell* you risk an info dump. When you *show* you put us in the action. An effective way to "show" is to put the information in the context of the scene.

Bemis D. R. Johnson restrains himself from describing the character as fat, obese, Oblomov-like, gross, rotund, tubby, disgusting, corpulent, or chubby. Nevertheless, even without these adjectives we get a pretty good idea of his girth.

> There was little passion; they investigated the oddities of each other's bodies like two interstellar sexologists compiling research to carry back to their respective planets ... She rolled over on her back to offer herself but the man's belly prevented any penetration. He tried again from the rear, with no success. The girl looked confused, but eager to please, so when he slid onto the mat and lifted her on top of him and then down onto his stub of an erection, she broke out into a smile of satisfaction that lasted only for the few short moments that he was able to contain himself.
>
> —Bemis D.R. Johnson. *Restitution*. In preparation.

Novelist and writing coach Nancy Kress shows how exposition (telling the story) can be transformed into dramatization (showing the story). Note that when she "shows" us the story, she writes a scene.

First the "telling" version:

> Prince Victor married the beautiful Lady Gianina in a huge celebration that lasted four days. Nobles attended from as far away as Balustrina. Immediately after the wedding, the royal couple left for a honeymoon at the castle of Tibinol in the remote, beautiful highlands. There, Gianina discovered that she didn't like her new husband at all.

Is this "showing" version better?

> The new royal couple settled themselves in the coach, and it began to move forward. Gianina smiled at her husband. "Tell me, my lord, what Tibinol is like."
>
> "Like any other highland castle, I suppose."
>
> "Is it beautiful?"
>
> "If you like wilds. I don't," Victor said, looking bored.
>
> "What kind of scenery do you like best, then?"
>
> "I don't like scenery at all. And I especially don't like women who keep asking pointless questions."
>
> Gianina felt as if she'd been punched in the stomach. What had she said wrong?
>
> —Nancy Kress. "Show and Tell." *Writer's Digest*, July 2000.

Show, Don't Tell Is Another Way of Moving from Cold to Hot

Theodore A. Rees Cheney created this exercise to illustrate what he called "informative and suggestive description." For me it could be dubbed "moving from cold to hot using Show, Don't Tell."

He starts cold:

> Cabin for sale. 20 x 20 log. 1 Bdrm.
> Sm. kitch. FP. 5 ac. Stream. Shed.

And then he heats it up:

Dear folks,

I'm thinking of buying a terrific log cabin up on the Deerkill River – you know, up near where you used to go back in the old days, Dad. It's got plenty of room downstairs with a bedroom loft up under the slanting log roof. I'll love lying there and looking up at those rough hewn timbers thinking about Abe Lincoln and all the other greats (like me) who lived in log cabins. I understand the logs have the highest insulation value of any materials – and they look so great, outside and in. And what a fireplace! I could fit a six-foot Yule log in there next Christmas. And it's got all the fire tools and hooks for hanging pots over the fire and everything. There's this great shed attached to the back, sort of a lean-to, that I can convert into a place for writing. Do you think you could lend me ...

—Theodore A. Rees Cheney. *Writing Creative Nonfiction*. Berkeley, California: Ten Speed Press, 2000.

DON'T EVER DO THIS

MAINTAIN LOGIC IN TIME AND PLACE

❖

Don't say this: She entered the room after opening the door.

CHEKHOV'S GUN - EVERYTHING HAS A PURPOSE; IF NOT, DON'T INTRODUCE IT

"If it's not going to be fired, it shouldn't be hanging there."

In Playwriting 101 you learn the role of Chekhov's gun:

If you show a rifle on the mantelpiece in the first act, you have to show someone shoot it in the third act.

And the corollary:

You cannot fire a gun in the third act that wasn't introduced in the first act.

How does this work in creative nonfiction?

Let's say your story's climax involves your slim and fashionable wife beating up a mugger while you're on vacation in Rio. For this to be believable, you have to indicate her feistiness, maybe even mention her brown belt in karate, early in the piece.

Here's a fictional example: the pet rabbit in *Fatal Attraction*. Early in the film we see the kids playing with their pet rabbit, showing us a happy suburban family. At the end of the film we see Thumper boiling in a pot of spaghetti water, indicating things are about to get rather messy.

FRAME AND FOCUS

Lee Gutkind, who *Vanity Fair* called "the Godfather of creative nonfiction," used the terms frame and focus to describe the binding agents that hold a nonfiction article together.

The frame, according to Gutkind, "represents a way of ordering [the] writer's narrative so that the elements ... are presented in an interesting and orderly fashion." Focus, he says, "is the overall theme, meaning, or intent of a nonfiction effort." Put another way, the frame is the story structure, the architecture – which I earlier suggested could be linear or circular – while focus is the recurring main idea – the red stripe in the barber's pole.

Frame and focus are techniques to structure your article or book by maintaining a single-mindedness to the main theme.

Gutkind is an old-school kind of journalist who sometimes spends years living with and observing the subjects of his books. His voice is strong but he seldom puts himself foremost in the scene.

In his book on writing creative nonfiction, Gutkind describes the background (the frame in his terms) for one of his most touching stories. For me this is a classical circular structure that starts with an anecdote and uses the Scheherazade Scenario.

Many Sleepless Nights, my book about the world of organ transplantation, begins when 15-year-old Richie Becker, a healthy and handsome teenager from Charlotte, N.C., discovers that his father is going to sell the sports car that he had hoped would one day be his. In a spontaneous and thoughtless gesture of defiance, Richie, who had never been behind the wheel, secretly takes his father's sports car on a joy ride. Three blocks from his home, he wraps the car around a tree and is subsequently declared brain dead at the local hospital. Devastated by the experience, but hoping for some positive outcome to such a senseless tragedy, Richie's father, Dick, donates his son's organs for transplantation.

Then the story flashes back a half century, detailing surgeons' first attempts at transplantation and all of the experimentation and controversy leading up to the development and acceptance of transplant techniques. I introduce Winkle Fulk, a mother of four, dying with an incurable heart disease, and Pvt. Rebecca Treat, a recent high school graduate with hepatitis, who is in a coma and near death.

Richie Becker's liver is transplanted into Rebecca, while his heart and lungs are sewn into Mrs. Fulk by Dr. Bartley Griffith. The last scene of the book 370 pages later finishes the frame three years later when Winkle Fulk travels to Charlotte, N.C., a reunion I arranged to allow the folks to personally thank Richie's father for his son's gift of life.

And then Gutkind offers the actual ending to the piece. I challenge you not to be touched.

At the end of the evening, just as we were about to say goodbye and return to the motel, Dick Becker stood up in the center of the living room of his house, paused, and then walked slowly and hesitantly over toward Winkle Fulk, who had once stood alone at the precipice of death. He eased himself down on his knees, took Winkle Fulk by the shoulder and simultaneously drew her closer, as he leaned forward and placed his ear gently but firmly between her breasts and then at her back.

Everyone in that room was suddenly and silently breathless, watching as Dick Becker listened for the last time to the absolutely astounding miracle of organ transplantation: the heart and the lungs of his dead son Richie, beating faithfully and unceasingly inside this stranger's warm and loving chest.

—Lee Gutkind. *The Art of Creative Nonfiction*. New York: John Wiley & Sons, Inc., 1997.

୭୬

Simon Winchester traveled to Cochin [now Kochi] in southern India in 1999, a year before the Millennium. He could certainly have written an interesting travel story about the region, one of the most complex and interesting corners of culture on the planet. But he took his *Condé Nast Traveler* story to a different dimension by focusing on a news hook – the hype then raging about the upcoming Millennium. He used that frame (a linear story arc following his quest in south India), and a focus (the upcoming Millennium) to ask Indian Christians, Jews, Hindus, Muslims, and Jains about what the Millennium meant to them, and in the process came away with a far more interesting story than he might have had.

Winchester starts off slowly and needs a few hundred words of scene setting before coming to his nut paragraph:

The New Millennium. It jars just a little, sounding a trifle unfamiliar, a bit too foreign. And yes, on reflection it has to be said that the word millennium is actually seldom heard in today's India. And with reason: In India, where they like to insist that they invented the clock, the calendar, most of algebra, and much of geometry; where their mathematicians originated the numeric symbols in use throughout the world today; and where there is a profound general interest in the concept of time, there most decidedly won't be a great fuss about the millennium's arrival.

One explanation is political, the other religious.

Winchester then contrasts the beliefs of Christians in Cochin, for whom January 1, 2000, has significance, with the views of Cochin's Hindus, Jains, Jews, Tamils, and Muslims for whom January 1, 2000, is just another day.

His writing incorporates the use of details, dialogue, and a mini-scene.

A Cochin calendar is a daunting icon of arithmetical complexity. It looks, at first blush, like any other. It has the number of the year at the top – 1174, since most Keralans, and most Cochin inhabitants, are Hindus. Closer examination, however, shows that it also has the year according to several other calendars (but not all of them) written in small type alongside. And in each of the thirty-odd boxes that represent one day in a particular Hindu month, there is, as on a Western calendar, the dominant Hindu number; and written in the four corners of each box are other numbers in a smaller typeface that represent the days for everyone else. Further, there are myriad footnotes, brackets, asterisks, and curious lunar devices, and lots of different numbers in different colors that turn out to represent feast days and holy days for the remembrance of saints and pilgrims, wars and battles and treaties, and the deaths and births of the long-forgotten divinities of all the competing and contrasting beliefs.

The solving of Fermat's Last Theorem, it seems, is nothing compared to working out the date in these parts. I once made the mistake of asking an elderly Saraswat Brahmin just what year it was. "I will have to find out," he replied, pulling out a vastly thick, dust-covered book and poring over it for fully ten minutes before looking up, blinking like a turtle, and replying simply, "It depends."

—Simon Winchester. "Whose Millennium Is It Anyway?"
Condé Nast Traveler, March 1999.

And then Winchester takes us on a journey through Cochin with a valid quest that results in encounters with verbose Hindu priests, lonely Jews, pious Muslims, earnest Christians, and courteous Jains.

∽

Here's a frame and focus technique in a personal essay. Note how Andrew Biggs regularly brings back his friend Six's anxiety about missing the plane; I've *italicized* the Six-anxiety passages (but Biggs doesn't). You could consider these italicized passages as lidgets. His story has the added benefit of incorporating a ticking clock – in fact the entire personal essay is predicated on a ticking clock – the scheduled departure of the plane. By the way, this piece is some 1,150 words, which is toward the outer limit word-count for an editor-friendly personal essay of this type.

With 15 minutes to go before our flight to Phuket leaves, Six is in a flap. "Come on Biggs," she says, slinging her Double Bay bag over her shoulder and straightening her bright pink maxi dress. We are sitting in the glorified food hall at Suvarnabhumi where a cup of coffee costs half my weekly salary.

Despite the airport's impractical expanse, there's not five minutes between here and A6, the farthest gate away where our flight to Phuket allegedly takes off at 11 AM.

Six is one of my nearest and dearest friends who visits Thailand annually to escape Sydney, where she is a TV celebrity known as much for her acute journalistic abilities as she is for her Queensland accent. Because of such roots, she has a mouth on her like a Lumpini Park public toilet that flushes incessantly in the company of those who are near and dear to her.

Anyway, she is starting to get toey *(anxious).* As she stands up I just shake my head. "No need to rush, Six," I say. "The plane won't leave for another half an hour, at least."

"You don't know that, Biggs! Come on. It's a quarter to 11."

"Six, sit down and relax," I say. She is the only person in the world who addresses me by my last name. I am the only person remaining who calls her by her nickname of 25 years ago. "The ticket says 11 AM, but the plane won't leave till at least 11.20."

Her eyes widen and more Queensland vernacular spews forth in and around the following words: "How do you know that, Biggs?"

How do I know that? Where does one begin to tell a highly strung Aussie used to Germanic precision that time in this country is fluid? And that fluidity need not be another source of stress, and that in fact, it could be the Thais have it right and we westerners are the ones barking up the wrong tree?

I was just like Six (minus the obscenities) when I first arrived here 20 years ago. I came from the world of Australian newspapers where missing a deadline meant your job. In Australia, a 5 PM deadline meant 5 pm on the dot. In Thailand, a 5 PM deadline also meant 5 PM on the dot ... but if you should send it at 5.30 or 6, or thereabouts, that's okay too.

I initially threw Six-like hissy fits, but soon realized nothing I could do would change the relaxed, carefree attitude Thais had towards time. It was a good 12 months before the next step – realising that attitude was generally the way to go.

Generally. Once I had a starring role in a Thai horror-comedy movie called Sars Wars, about a new strain of the SARS virus that turned you into zombies. I had 11 shooting days and on the first, they told me to be there at 8 AM for make-up for a shoot that started at 11 AM.

This was only five years ago, so despite a full 15 years in Thailand my western genes dominated and I foolishly woke at 6 that day, caught a cab at 7 and was in at the designated high-rise on Asoke by 7.45. Foolish, foolish Andrew. Not even on time. He arrives *before* time.

Of course, I could have switched on the lights and air-conditioning since I was the first to arrive. By 9 AM the first of the make-up staff trickled in. I was in the chair by 10 AM, as three people started to work reconstructing my face with latex as the first scene to be shot was the one where my head gets blown off (Dammit! I should have written "Spoilers" at the top of this paragraph! Now you know what happens!).

It took three hours. By 1.30 PM I was ready to go. "Just take a seat over there and we'll call you when we're ready," a staffer told me. Unable to read owing to painful red contact lenses, I just sat and sat until 6.30 PM. That's right. A full five hours sitting doing nothing but dabbing my eyes with Visine. And they told me get there at 8 AM!

"Biggs! Six is now giving birth to a litter of Siamese kittens. "It's five minutes before take-off. Get a move on!"

There is an even better story I could have told Six. Ten years ago I did an ad for yoghurt, and again the staff went to great pains to tell me the schedule was tight and expensive so please be there by 10 AM "on the dot." I was, and to my surprise the Thai staff ushered me through to the make-up room quickly and efficiently. By 11 AM I was in the studio, standing in place while sound and lighting crews meticulously went through their preparations. You try standing on one spot for an hour while slabs of technical people adjust lights and boom mikes. By 11.59 everything was ready to go. Because the scene was static and thus not difficult to film, I figured in my head: "This'll all be over by 12.30."

Ding dong. Midday. The director announced: *Kin khao.* Time for lunch.

Everybody dropped tools and made their ways to the buffet, leaving me standing like an idiot, primed up, made up, lines learned and ready to go. The one time everything went according to schedule – only to be foiled by the one thing that can disrupt even the best laid plans: *Kin khao.*

Like I said, I think the Thais have it right. While we stress ourselves out with a life of Rolex like schedules, the Thais are happy and relaxed with approximates that only a Rolex watch purchased for 400 baht off Patpong can offer.

On a recent TV shoot I happened to meet a gorgeous Thai-Swiss model who grew up in Switzerland and only recently came to Thailand. Over lunch she lamented: "You know, I had to get up at 6.30 every morning to catch a bus to school that left at exactly two minutes past seven. If I got to the bus stop at three minutes past seven, the bus would have gone!" She shook her head. I could literally see her dominant Thai genes shouldering themselves past their western counterparts in what only can be described as Punctuality Disgust.

"You're not always right, y'know," Six is saying as she hurtles down the Suvarnabhumi people mover towards A6, her Maxi dress flapping as it tries to keep up. "Surely 11 o'clock means 11 o'clock."

Nothing I can say can persuade Six that I'm right. We arrive at the gate with only one minute to spare. After which we sit down and I again try to explain the civility of life in a society where time is not of the essence.

I have more than enough time to do this. Our plane takes off at 11.30.

—Andrew Biggs. "The Time Bandits."
Bangkok Post. November 29, 2009. [italics added]

YOU DON'T HAVE TO WRITE WAR AND PEACE

Long isn't necessarily better. It's possible the reader doesn't need to know your nephew's favorite pizza topping.

Here are two short personal essays that are focused and blessedly to the point. Note how both stories use a circular structure – they finish not too far from where they begin.

This piece introduces memorable imagery and a touching portrait of a tough family that doesn't take itself too seriously. And I will always remember the iconic phrase, "Maybe it's time to drink the good stuff."

After 77 years of keeping her Nordic feet firmly rooted into the earth, my mom has been recruited against her will into the astronaut program. She has emphysema, and is tethered by a lifeline to a humming oxygen machine she has dubbed R2D2. It has taken her a while to get used to having just 50 feet of mobility, and she did pretty well until she created a Gordian knot by weaving her line with the gardening hose. Who would have thought that planting daisies could result in a near-death experience?

She always has been a good sport, tough and even-natured, but this limit of 50 feet of line has stretched her Norwegian stoicism. I can't decide if it is good or bad that she doesn't realize that this oxygen line will be part of her wardrobe for the duration. This accessory just doesn't go with her perfectly ironed Irish-linen dresses. As I am the constant bearer of reality and all grim news in my family, I am going to take this one duty off. I am not saying a word.

In wild contrast to my placid mother the rest of the clan are like screwing in a 200-watt light bulb in a lamp marked "don't exceed 60." We don't fit in her world, possess every bad habit that she spent a lifetime rejecting and don't much care what the world thinks. She was the maypole – the center to all our wild creative dancing round and round – stabilizing us into a form of social normality. Now I am the maypole. The moment has arrived, a moment I have secretly dreaded, the transfer of the baton – mother/daughter is now daughter/mother. I am the responsible one. I'm the one who tells her daughter, "don't run with scissors."

I have always felt distant from my mother's stoic physical and emotional evenness. She never acknowledged my pain or anyone else's, and especially never gave in to her own troubles. My siblings and I have suffered through anorexia, bulimia, psychological breaks and herniated disks without her acknowledgement.

She has strict mental discipline, never says anything even slightly unkind, never cusses. She is so strong that I never saw her eat an ice cream cone, even though she never denied us kids that pleasure – "sugar kills" she probably wanted to say but didn't out of fear of giving us Rocky Road nightmares. She had just one bad habit – smoking, which of course accounts for her reliance on a vacuum cleaner-sized pump. The root of her shame about being an astronaut on earth is that everyone will know she smoked. Her one little bad habit is out of the bag, and she thinks she will be blamed for it. She won't go out at all, even when I offered to hook myself up with my own matching oxygen pack so the supposed shame could be shared.

So my righteous, stubborn, aloof but never unkind mother finds herself to be the one thing she always feared we would become – different. I don't know if it's her helplessness, or the fact that she finally has achieved a form of strangeness, but I love her more than I ever did. Growing up I felt I could never touch her – she was too perfect and I was too raggedy, too edgy. Now I see her unsure of herself, needing love more than she ever let on and I react with a tenderness and desire to connect that surprises me.

I wonder constantly how long we will have her. I wonder if she knows. She must, we're not dumb in my family. I remember when my Uncle Knopf was diagnosed with kidney cancer. Over the years Uncle Knopf had been given hundreds of bottles of fine wine by grateful writers he had edited and published, but he kept the vintage Bordeaux stashed in the cellar and insisted on drinking *vin ordinaire*. The doctor, aware that the clock was ticking, finally told him, "Knopf, maybe it's time to start drinking the good stuff."

So now that I'm the grown-up in the family here's my plan. Follow the Uncle Knopf stratagem. Get my mom to eat the frosting, and when that's gone, lather on some more and let her lick the spoon. I'm going to keep laughing, to love bigger and to make it feel as normal as possible for both of us that she is sucking air on a line. This is a family plan I can push with enthusiasm. Warmth, embraces, forgiveness will be poured out every day on demand into our largest crystal goblets and drunk with abandonment and gratitude. We will toast my mom, the tethered explorer.

"My Astronaut Mommy." Participant in my writing workshop.

This short personal essay was written for radio, and that format forces the writer to write musically and concisely. Like the earlier piece, it uses a generational theme to good effect.

My sister once produced what I now realize was an important philosophical insight while standing in front of a mirror applying yet another magic potion to her blemished adolescent complexion. "It's all an illusion," she said with sudden passion. "You *think* you're getting rid of a pimple, but actually, all that's happening is that you're endlessly chasing it round and round your face." And with that, she snapped the lid back on the potion and left the room. At the time, I must admit, I wasn't particularly struck. Being four years younger, I was smugly content with *my* complexion. But nowadays I often think of her remark. Here I am, constantly striving toward some mythical perfect day when I'll finish my play, have a tidy house, cheerful children, money in the bank, supper on the table, and – if possible – thin legs. It never happens, of course. But the funny thing is that anytime I get even close to this idyllic state – let's say when I've dealt with everything except the play, the money and the legs – some new worry always materializes out of thin air. Like the air conditioner breaks. Or the mailman destroys our storm door. And suddenly, I'm spending all day on the phone discussing doors and compressors. "Oh well … as soon as *this* is dealt with," I think, ever the optimist, "I'll get back to working on the Grand Plan." But somehow it never works out that way.

Parenting is pretty much like chasing a pimple round your face too, I've decided. I used to think that it was something you could learn, get good at, and then just keep on doing – like riding a bike, maybe. But as soon as my husband and I get vaguely on top of one issue – how to get our four-year-old to eat a green vegetable for example, then our baby daughter produces some new behavior – continuous raucous screaming springs to mind – that has us scratching our heads again and heading back to the drawing board. And so it goes on, and on – an endless circular dance of parental authority versus child's ingenuity, the acne lotion versus the pimple … Meanwhile, of course, the house is a mess, my play is frozen in time, supper exists only in the back of our minds, money is non-existent and my legs don't bear thinking about.

Still, there is at least one way that I'm ahead of the game. In twelve years or so, when my son hits adolescence, I shall be ready with a piece of advice that should save him countless hours of anguish. "Don't even try to get rid of them," I shall say as he peers disconsolately into the mirror. "They're nothing but a philosophical concept."

> —Jennifer Davidson. Participant in my writing workshop. "Chasing Pimples,"
> aired on NPR's "All Things Considered" in 1991, published in her book
> *Stop Smelling My Rose!* Redgrove Press, 1997.

WRITING TIP #7

Cinema - Write like Steven Spielberg Directs

THINK OF ANY MOVIE

The commercial feature film recounts a hero's journey. The film is comprised of scenes, characters, dialogue, settings, details. Music and sound effects tell you whether the scene is tense or flippant. The film is shot from specific points of view that direct your attention to a particular character. Sometimes there are close-ups, sometimes long shots. There is pace – slow and languorous or sharp and edgy. There are countless visual cues to complement the action – an arch of an actor's eyebrow, an embarrassed tear. The film uses music and sound effects. The viewer is manipulated by the director's choices.

Which is what you do as a writer. *The reader has no clues about what's going on except those you give him.* The skill lies in knowing how much to give, and how to do it.

MAKE US SEE THE ACTION

Listen to the action in this passage. Better yet, read it aloud – I'm certain you will read it at a quick pace because George Howe Colt intended it to have vibrancy and pace.

Ted Kennedy is on the run. He's running for reelection, he's constantly running against his past, and right now he's running through the Capitol Rotunda. If he paused for a second, he'd have no more chance of progressing unimpeded than a tourist in Marrakech has of making it through a bazaar without being collared by panhandlers. Whenever his speed is less than warp, Kennedy becomes a magnet for gawkers, askers of favors, critics, groupies. He can't afford that today. He's late for a crucial meeting on a bill he's sponsoring that will make it a federal crime to block the access to abortion clinics. He zooms through the halls, scattering tourists in his wake, leaving them with dazed expressions and the word *Kennedy* on their lips. At six feet, with big belly straining inside his double-breasted suit, he doesn't look built for speed. He lumbers with a faintly bearish gait but goes at such a clip that his two young aides have to skip to keep up. The elevator takes 20 seconds to arrive, 20 seconds that cannot be wasted. "Let me see the book," Kennedy says, reaching for a thick briefing book. His concentration is fierce.

—George Howe Colt. "Is Ted Kennedy's Midlife Crisis Finally Over?" *Life*, August 1994.

Or the fictional inspiration for the above passage, from the White Rabbit:

> I'm late
> I'm late
> For a very important date
> No time to say "Hello, Goodbye"
> I'm late, I'm late, I'm late.

> > —Lewis Carroll. *Alice's Adventures in Wonderland & Through the Looking-Glass.*
> > Reissue edition. New York: Bantam, 1984.

STAND TALL

Tom Wolfe is a master of writing visually.

Magdalena was standing up belligerently – her fists on her hips and her elbows winged out – as Mother and Daughter traded hisses and growls and eyetooth glowers. Mother was sitting forward on the couch with *her* elbows winged out – and the heels of her hands pressed down on the front edge of the frame, a veritable feline, ready to spring, claws, rip guts out, eat livers whole, and bite heads off by sinking both sets of incisors into the soft centers of the temples. Her father, if Magdalena knew anything about it, was possessed by a fervent desire to evaporate. Too bad he had sunk so far down into the easy chair. He'd have to be an acrobat to slip away unnoticed. Their fights mortified him ... but he had long since given up trying to control his two cats.

—Tom Wolfe. *Back to Blood.* New York: Vintage, 2013.

PUT IN THE SOUND EFFECTS

Remember the old radio shows where some guy created the sound of horse's hooves by clopping half-coconut shells on a wooden board? Create your own sound effects.

On January 10, between 4.45 and 5.00 a.m., the inhabitants of the Karluk awoke to a sound like gunfire ... it grew louder. Then it sounded like drums, and then thunder. Suddenly, there was a harsh, grating noise, and the Karluk shuddered violently ... The ice continued its deafening symphony, until McKinlay covered his ears and thought he would go crazy from the noise alone ... The ice was grinding, churning, like an explosion of thunderclouds overhead, and then it engulfed them.

—Jennifer Niven. "Stranded at the Top of the World." *Talk*, November 2000.

And more aural and visual images (and a terrific quote) in an article about the 60th annual Oxford and Cambridge Varsity Blind Wine-Tasting Competition.

The competitors twirled and sniffed and inspected, some holding their noses while sipping, others warming their glasses between their thighs, all of them scratching notes on their tasting sheets.

There were plenty of curious sounds, a dissonant chorus of slurping and sluicing and spitting, marked by the occasional chime of crystal on crystal and the creaking of wooden floorboards beneath a plush carpet. One Cambridge competitor, aerating her wines in her mouth, produced a sound akin to the pressurized rush of an airplane vacuum toilet.

"I've been mocked a couple of times," said the woman, Vaiva Imbrasaite, 23, a Lithuanian doctoral student in computer science. "It can, however, be a useful party trick," Ms. Imbrasaite said.

—Scott Sayare. "A Long Rivalry Resumes, Over Sips and Crackers."
The New York Times, February 27, 2013.

Useful Advice from Someone Who Wrote Pretty Well

While I am carrying on a conversation with someone, I find that I am drawing with my eyes. I find myself observing how his shirt collar comes around from behind his neck and perhaps casts a slight shadow on one side. I observe how the wrinkles in his sleeve form and how his arm may be resting on the edge of the chair. I observe how the features on his face move back and forth in perspective as he rotates his head. It actually is a form of sketching and I believe that it is the next best thing to drawing itself. I sometimes feel it is obsessive, but at least it accomplishes something for me.

—Charles Schulz, creator of Peanuts

MUSIC AND ELEGANCE

We all can dance and sing and play a sport. But not everybody can dance like Fred Astaire and Ginger Rogers, or sing like Placido Domingo, or swing a golf club like Freddie Couples.

Here's where good becomes elegant.

It's when adequate writing takes flight.

Sometimes writing soars, but it must never draw attention to itself.

Not everybody can write elegantly. It cannot be forced. It cannot be faked. But you can recognize it, and maybe take a few steps in the direction of elegance. Some turns of phrase I particularly like from two of America's most elegant writers are the following:

Both parties deprecated war; but one of them would make war rather than let the nation survive; and the other would accept war rather than let it perish. And the war came ..."

—Abraham Lincoln. Second Inaugural Address.

With malice toward none; with charity for all; with firmness in the right, as God gives us to see the right.

—Abraham Lincoln. Second Inaugural Address.

People who like this sort of thing will find this the sort of thing they like.

—Abraham Lincoln. Quoted in *Collections and Recollections* by G.W. E. Russell. 1898.

And, in a different context (fiction, but you get the point):

From 30 feet away she looked like a lot of class. From 10 feet away she looked like something made up to be seen from 30 feet away.

—Raymond Chandler. *The High Window*. New York: Alfred A. Knopf, 1942.

I was as hollow and empty as the spaces between stars.

—Raymond Chandler. *The Long Goodbye*. New York: Hamish Hamilton, 1953.

The girl gave him a look which ought to have stuck at least four inches out of his back.

—Raymond Chandler. *The Long Goodbye*. New York: Hamish Hamilton, 1953.

It seemed like a nice neighborhood to have bad habits in.

—Raymond Chandler. *The Big Sleep*. New York: Alfred A. Knopf, 1939.

"You're broke, eh?"

"I been shaking two nickels together for a month, trying to get them to mate."

—Raymond Chandler. *The Big Sleep*. New York: Alfred A. Knopf, 1939.

I'm an occasional drinker, the kind of guy who goes out for a beer and wakes up in Singapore with a full beard.

—Raymond Chandler. "The King in Yellow." *Dime Detective*, March 1938.

∽

Here's P.J. O'Rourke writing elegantly about elegance.

I did, however, want to hear Jesse Jackson speak. He is the only living American politician with a mastery of classical rhetoric. Assonance, alliteration, litotes, pleonasm, parallelism, exclamation, climax and epigrams – to listen to Jesse Jackson is to hear everything mankind has learned about public speaking since Demosthenes. Thus Jackson, the advocate for people who believe themselves to be excluded from Western culture, was the only 1988 presidential candidate to exhibit any of it.

—P.J. O'Rourke. *Parliament of Whores*. New York: Vintage, 1991.

∽

And Maureen Dowd waxing eloquent in an Op-Ed.

Will it mean that Mr. Obama ends up being the one-term Democratic tunnel between the first black president, as Bill Clinton has been dubbed, and the first female president – the organic arugula in a messy, meaty Clinton sandwich?

Much was made of the alpha tone of the second presidential debate. But it was more like a parody of alpha, a couple of pampered, manicured Harvard princes kicking up "gorilla dust," as Ross Perot calls it. In a truly commanding performance, you don't jab fingers, invade space, bark interruptions ...

Mr. Obama's contempt for Mr. Romney gleamed through as Mitt got all OCD with Candy Crowley about the rules, and rambled on about his weird retro worldview, where women in binders have to bound home to make dinner, where the problem of too-easy access to assault weapons could be helped if, gosh, we just tell "our kids that before they have babies, they ought to think about getting married to someone."

As Massachusetts governor, Mr. Romney signed a ban on certain assault weapons. But now he has "Romnesia," as Mr. Obama bitingly calls it, so Mitt is always distancing himself from himself.

In some ways, the two rivals are alike: cold, deliberative fish, self-regarding elitists with upbringings out of the norm and trouble connecting at times, as when Mr. Obama echoed Jon Stewart's word "optimal" on "The Daily Show" and sounded aloof about the tragedy in Libya: "If four Americans get killed, it's not optimal." The mother of one of those Americans, Sean Smith, told *The Daily Mail* of London, "It's insensitive to say my son is not very optimal; he is also very dead."

These candidates are, in some respects, natural antagonists. Their rancor seems especially intense, fueled by jagged ads and a long period of mud-wrestling on the head of a pin.

> —Maureen Dowd. "Pampered Princes Fling Gorilla Dust: Obama and Romney Are Natural Antagonists, but They Have Some Similarities." *The New York Times*, October 22, 2012.

Read your work aloud and it will be evident whether it's elegant, like this passage, or jarring.

The English are humorous but melancholy, law-abiding but loathe being bossed about, and say "Still, mustn't grumble" after a lengthy grumble, which cheers them up enormously. We eschew flowery language but use endless evasions and circumlocutions that sound polite to us, but maddeningly vague to others ... We say "presumably," "possibly," "arguably" and "perhaps," qualifiers meant to be considerately unassertive ...

We love understatement ... In general we avoid plain-speaking, unless we're the Duke of Edinburgh, who said to the President of Nigeria in his finest nightie-type national fig, "You look like you're ready for bed." Others might think it, but presumably you have to be in the line of succession to 16 different thrones to blurt it out loud.

—Christopher Hart. Review of *SORRY! The English and Their Manners* by Henry Hitchings. *The Sunday Times*, January 6, 2013.

Useful Advice from Someone Who Wrote Pretty Well

Style is knowing who you are, what you want to say, and not giving a damn.

—Gore Vidal

MUSICAL LISTS

Boring lists can be transformed into interesting passages:

Wikipedia (who compiles this stuff, bless them) has a page devoted to creatures named after celebrities. Some highlights: *Agra schwarzeneggeri,* a species of carabid beetle from Costa Rica with a biceps-like middle femora. Frank Zappa has at least three creatures bearing his name, including a jellyfish. George W. Bush, Dick Cheney, Donald Rumsfeld, and Darth Vader have beetles named after them. Adolph Hitler has a blind cave beetle from Slovenia, while SpongeBob SquarePants has a musky-smelling fungus from Malaysia. Mozart, Beethoven, John Lennon, Mick Jagger, Keith Richards, Sid Vicious and Freddy Mercury all have their creatures, as do Buddha and Confucius (feathered dinosaur). A spider has been named after the baseball pitcher Dizzy Dean; it uses a sticky ball on the end of a thread to catch its prey. Marilyn Monroe is honored by *Norasaphus monroeae*, a fossil trilobite with an hourglass-shaped glabella, while Greta Garbo has a wasp described as "a solitary female."

—Paul Spencer Sochaczewski. *An Inordinate Fondness for Beetles*.
Singapore: Editions Didier Millet, 2012.

∾

Here's the elegance of Bill Bryson describing, in list form, the tenacity of Shakespeare scholars.

Faced with a wealth of text but a poverty of context, scholars have focused obsessively on what they *can* know. They have counted every word he wrote, logged every dib and jot. They can tell us (and have done so) that Shakespeare's works contain 138,198 commas, 26,794 colons, and 15,785 question marks; that ears are spoken of 401 times in his plays; that *dunghill* is used 10 times and *dullard* twice; that his characters refer to love 2,259 times but to hate just 183 times; that he used *damned* 105 times and *bloody* 226 times, but *bloody-minded* only twice; that he wrote *hath* 2,069 times but *has* just 409 times; that all together he left us 884,647 words, made up of 31,959 speeches, spread over 118,406 lines.

—Bill Bryson. *Shakespeare*. New York: Harper Perennial. 2007.

AND SIMPLE NARRATIVE CAN BE ELEGANT

They definitely need some new astrologers at the royal court in Kathmandu. It was the seers of the spheres, casting their ancient divinations and decoding the celestial motions, who laid the trap. They calculated that the heavens were not in alignment for a royal wedding. The crown prince had picked the wrong bride. The auspicious date and the harmonious mate were still years in the future. The queen listened to them too closely – or, some say, they listened to her too closely – and rejected her son's plan to marry his girlfriend.

—Patrick Symmes. "The Last Days of the Mountain Kingdom." *Outside*, September 2001.

∞

[The Himalayan yak is] a lovely long-haired animal, like a cow on its way to the opera.

—Paul Theroux. *Riding the Iron Rooster: By Train Through China*.
New York: Houghton Mifflin, 1988.

∞

The old deposed dictator, Mubarak, held physically captive in the penumbra by his former minions, continues to inhabit the national imagination like an undead pharaoh thought still to be wielding dark powers.

—Jon Lee Anderson. "The Demons in Egypt." *New Yorker*, July 5, 2013.

ELEGANCE TAKES MANY FORMS

I've put this excerpt in the "elegance" section but I could have used it to illustrate many themes in this book – voice, details, conflict. Tom Wolfe doesn't use the word "I" at all in this article, one of his most famous, but we know he was there by the details he provides. (He actually crashed the party, using David Halberstam's invitation, but that's another story).

Mmmmmmmmmmmmmmmm. These are nice. Little Roquefort cheese morsels rolled in crushed nuts. Very tasty. Very subtle. It's the way the dry sackiness of the nuts tiptoes up against the dour savor of the cheese that is so nice, so subtle. Wonder what the Black Panthers eat here on the hors d'oeuvre trail? Do the Panthers like little Roquefort cheese morsels rolled in crushed nuts this way, and asparagus tips in mayonnaise dabs, and *meatballs petites au Coq Hardi*, all of which are at this very moment being offered to them on gadrooned silver platters by maids in black uniforms with hand-ironed white aprons ... The butler will bring them their drinks ... Deny it if you wish to, but such are the *pensées métaphysiques* that rush through one's head on these Radical Chic evenings just now in New York. For example, does that huge Black Panther there in the hallway, the one shaking

236

hands with Felicia Bernstein herself, the one with the black leather coat and the dark glasses and the absolutely unbelievable Afro, Fuzzy-Wuzzy-scale, in fact, is he, a Black Panther, going on to pick up a Roquefort cheese morsel rolled in crushed nuts from off the tray, from a maid in uniform, and just pop it down the gullet without so much as missing a beat of Felicia's perfect Mary Astor voice …

—Tom Wolfe. "Radical Chic." *New York Magazine*, June 8, 1970.

∞

And another, very different elegant voice.

I was in a difficult relationship. His name was Nick Di Stefano, he was a sportswriter I had known for years, and I had been seeing him, on and off, for eight months. He was Italian, which in my family is considered practically Jewish, except that (1) as children, Italians don't talk back to their parents, and (2) as adults, the men Run Around. Naturally, being so troublesome, we find them very appealing, and anyway, I had always liked Nick. He was smart; he knew all the lyrics to *The Pajama Game*; he dressed like a forties sharpie; he had the requisite newspaper Up-Yours Attitude toward authority. Also, there is something very nice about a relationship in which you have known each other a long time and are in the same business. We watched old movies from his collection, and he cooked and told me how much he loved his mother and took me dancing. Then he waltzed off to Miami for a weekend with an old girlfriend, and that was the end of Nick, Chapter One. She, it turned out, wanted to just be friends. Now when Nick is with me he is often petulant, seeing himself as the tragic hero of a doomed love affair, a role I have traditionally tried to reserve for myself.

—Joyce Wadler. "My Breast: One Woman's Cancer Story."
New York Magazine, April 13 and April 20, 1992.

∞

And another:

Ni Sabuk, the mother of Siladri and Madé Kerti, had no time for nonsense. She thought it nonsense to make pets of animals, for instance, or to dye one's hair, or to get in out of the rain. She disliked frenzy. If the ritual trance became too violent during mystery plays – with half-naked men sobbing and bending knives against their bellies – Ni Sabuk was unimpressed.

"Show-offs," she'd say, getting up in the middle of it all to go home. "Where are my sandals?"

Ni Sabuk had been a widow as long as her sons could remember. Her husband fell dead of a stroke while helping her give birth to Madé Kerti. If anyone politely inquired how she'd lost her husband, she'd say, "He died in childbirth."

—Diana Darling. *The Painted Alphabet*. Singapore: Editions Didier Millet, 2012.

ELEGANCE CAN BE PRAGMATIC

Elegant writing can be created by something as subtle as changing the emphasis, as in these examples created by Nancy Kress.

OK

1. The Chicago cops knocked on Jeremy's door and arrested him for murder, although he'd thought that everything was forgotten and that he was certainly safe after forty-two years had passed.

Better

2. Forty-two years later, when Jeremy thought everything was forgotten and he was certainly safe, the Chicago cops knocked on his door and arrested him for murder.

–Nancy Kress. "Bringing Up the Rear." *Writer's Digest*, November 2001.

GO ON, HAVE FUN

And how could you not write elegantly about Napoleon's penis, allegedly snipped off by a snitty Italian doctor performing the autopsy on the French hero.

Officially, the little general's privates are where they've always been: with the remainder of the body, in its crypt beneath the gold dome at the Hotel des Invalides. Unofficially though, there is now growing concern among the French that their Napoleonic unmentionables may be elsewhere; that a bone of contention may exist between France and the United States; and that, perhaps, their noble heritage may derive in part from a legacy that is not so much gilded, but gelded.

And then Mikelbank follows with a catchy transition paragraph:

History teaches that by the time he defeated Napoleon's fleet at Trafalgar, Lord Horatio Nelson had already suffered the loss of an eye and an arm. But that was nothing compared to his adversary's alleged later loss.

—Peter Mikelbank. "A Small Piece of History: Napoleon and the Case of the Missing Member." *Washington Post*, October 4, 1992.

And consider this jitterbug passage from Harry Rolnick, describing balut, a duck embryo eaten fresh from the shell:

After eighteen days, one has more than elementary egg yolk and egg white with which to deal. The embryo is so well established that a biology student could make out the duck's budding bill, thorax, and spiked little claws. Consequently, to most foreigners and a few queasy Western-educated Filipinos, eating balut is odious.

Yet, to speak of a Filipino duck right-to-life movement would be a canard. The balut, after all, is a national treasure. And unlike most national treasures (which are mainly quack icons), the balut is actually delicious.

—Harry Rolnick. *Spice Chronicles: Exotic Tales of a Hungry Traveler.* Santa Ana: Seven Locks Press, 2006.

🎭 Pro Tip

Be Open to Iconic Phrases

Remember the key scene in Gone with the Wind? The one where Scarlett begs Rhett to stay? Rhett doesn't say "You know Scarlett, your wishes really don't matter much to me." Instead he utters one of the most iconic lines in the movies: "Frankly my dear, I don't give a damn."

Same for Terminator ("Hasta la vista, baby"), Dirty Harry ("Go ahead, make my day"), Dorothy ("Toto, I've got a feeling we're not in Kansas anymore."), Han Solo ("May the Force be with you."), and you know who ("Shaken, not stirred.").

Obviously, if you're writing nonfiction, you can't invent lines like these, but you can be open to them and recognize them when they pop up.

ELEGANCE REQUIRES CONTENT, A SENSE OF MUSIC, AND A GOOD DELIVERY IN THE RIGHT CONTEXT

Consider the music and elegance in the epic phrase attributed to John F. Kennedy (and perhaps written by Theodore Sorensen) in his 1961 inaugural address:

And so, my fellow Americans: ask not what your country can do for you – ask what you can do for your country. My fellow citizens of the world: ask not what America will do for you, but what together we can do for the freedom of man.

This is an example of creative borrowing from other authors and honing the phrase from clunkiness into memorable music. (These sentiments, if not these words, were in the oratorical lexicon of Ancient Roman politicians, and a similar quote is sometimes attributed to Roman statesman and orator Marcus Tullius Cicero in a 64 BCE speech, but he might have borrowed it from Decimus Junius Juvenal.) Here's the genealogy:

As soon as any man says of the affairs of the state, what does it matter to me? the state may be given up as lost.

> —J.J. Rousseau (in translation). According to Arthur M. Schlesinger, Jr., Kennedy had noted this quote in a loose-leaf notebook in 1945.

Recall what our country has done for each of us, and to ask ourselves what we can do for our country in return.

> —Oliver Wendell Holmes, in an 1884 Memorial Day speech.

As has often been said, the youth who loves his Alma Mater will always ask, not "What can she do for me?" but "What can I do for her?"

> —Le Baron Russell Briggs. "Routine and Ideals." *College Life*. 1904.

In the great fulfillment we must have a citizenship less concerned about what the government can do for it and more anxious about what it can do for the nation.

> —Warren Harding, at the 1916 Republican convention.

Are you a politician asking what your country can do for you or a zealous one asking what you can do for your country? If you are the first, then you are a parasite; if the second, then you are an oasis in a desert.

> —Khalil Gibran, in his 1925 article "The New Frontier" (curious coincidence with JFK) urging his fellow Lebanese to revolt against Turkish occupation.

Is this the time for us to be asking, What have you [Spain] done for us? We should be asking what can we do for you?

> —Spoken by Captain Felipe Arrellanos in the 1958–1959 series of the Walt Disney TV show *Zorro*, episode "Invitation to Death."

(Or the more refreshing, if less musical, statement by Edward Abbey: "A patriot must always be ready to defend his country against his government.")

Useful Advice from Someone Who Wrote Pretty Well

This sentence has five words. Here are five more words. Five-word sentences are fine. But several together become monotonous. Listen to what is happening. The writing is getting boring. The sound of it drones. It's like a stuck record. The ear demands some variety. Now listen. I vary the sentence length, and I create music. Music. The writing sings. It has a pleasant rhythm, a lilt, a harmony. I use short sentences. And I use sentences of medium length. And sometimes when I am certain the reader is rested, I will engage him with a sentence of considerable length, a sentence that burns with energy and builds with all the impetus of a crescendo, the roll of the drums, the crash of the cymbals – sounds that say listen to this, it is important.

So write with a combination of short, medium, and long sentences. Create a sound that pleases the reader's ear. Don't just write words. Write music.

—Gary Provost. *100 Ways to Improve Your Writing.*
New York: New American Library, 1985.

THE RHYTHM METHOD

Gary Provost, again, (the best writing teacher I ever had) pointed out the music in parallel structure:

NOT PARALLEL	PARALLEL
Fish gotta swim, and flying is something that birds must do.	Fish gotta swim, birds gotta fly.
First I came. Then I saw. Conquering came next.	I came. I saw. I conquered.
When one has been seen by you, you've seen them all.	When you've seen one, you've seen them all.

—Gary Provost. *100 Ways to Improve Your Writing.*
New York: New American Library, 1985.

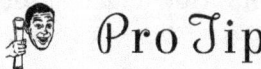

Pro Tip

Create Memorable Descriptors

You need chutzpah and talent to pull this off. It means inventing clever phrases to describe Big Ideas. Tom Wolfe is a useful role model – in Bonfire of the Vanities, he created Social X-Rays and Masters of the Universe, and elsewhere, the Right Stuff, the Me Decade and Radical Chic. In Soul of the Tiger, Jeff McNeely and I created the concept of Eco-Cultural Revolutions to describe the five revolutionary changes that define how we relate to nature.

Do you capitalize descriptors like these? I think if you use the phrase regularly and consistently in an article, you can claim it's a name and get away with upper case. But opinions differ: the Financial Times reports every week on the choices made by a noted fashionista and starts the column by asking the individual to describe her "personal style signifier," a catchy descriptor which, for some reason, they don't capitalize (but I would).

AVOID THE "INFO DUMP"
ELEGANCE IN DESCRIPTION

Ah, the dreaded info dump, sometimes known as the expository lump. Where the writer breaks out of her charming writer personality that makes readers say: "I'd sure like to meet that gal" and dumps a bunch of information on the reader, like a deep-fried East European dumpling plopping onto a plate filled with steamed vegetables.

How can you get the reader to digest information? Nancy Kress suggests four options:

* Action: Somebody *does* Something
* Description: Somebody *sees* Something
* Dialogue: Two Somebodies *discuss* Something
* Thoughts: Somebody *thinks* about Something

–Nancy Kress. "Turning Exposition into Action." *Writer's Digest*, March 1998. [italics added]

She also addresses the question: "How much is too much?" The answer: It depends. The amount of information you need to provide is contingent on how exotic the location is, your own writing style, and the voice of the piece and expectations of the reader.

∞

Let's say you are writing about Grandma Chen, who left China penniless, then through hard work and a deft touch at the mahjong table, became one of Singapore's leading real estate tycoons.

How much information does the reader need?

Well, first of all, is the reader familiar with China, with Singapore, with mahjong, with the real estate business?

And how long is your story?

And where does most of the story take place – in a village in Canton, in a gambling den, in the board room of a Singapore skyscraper?

∞

Redmond O'Hanlon makes information fascinating. Here he is preparing for an Amazon adventure:

> But it was the candiru, the toothpick-fish, a tiny catfish adapted for a parasitic life in the gills and cloaca of bigger fish, which swam most persistently into my dreams on troubled nights ... In the Amazons, should you have too much to drink, say, and inadvertently urinate as you swim, any homeless candiru, attracted by the smell, will take you for a big fish and swim excitedly up your stream of uric acid, enter your urethra like a worm into its burrow and, raising its gill-covers, stick out a set of retrorse spines. Nothing can be done. The pain, apparently, is spectacular. You must get to a hospital before your bladder bursts; you must ask a surgeon to cut off your penis.
>
> —Redmond O'Hanlon. *In Trouble Again*. London: Hamish Hamilton, 1988.

∞

Bill Bryson writes similarly engagingly about dangerous critters:

It was the height of the season for box jellyfish ... not to be trifled with ...

"So you're telling me," said Allan, for whom all this was new, "that if I waded into the water now I would die?"

"In the most wretched and abject agony known to man," I replied.

"Jesus," he muttered.

"And don't pick up any of the seashells," I added, stopping him from leaning over to pick up a seashell. I explained to him about coneshells – the venomous creatures that lurk inside some of the handsomest shells, waiting for a human hand to sink their vile pincers into.

"... They've got lethal seashells here?"

"There are more things that will kill you up here than anywhere else in Australia, and that's saying a lot, believe me."

I told him about ... The loathsome, sluggish stonefish, so called because it is indistinguishable from a rock, but with the difference that it has twelve spikes on its back that are sharp enough to pierce the sole of a sneaker, injecting the hapless sufferer with a myotoxin bearing a molecular weight of 150,000.

"And what does that mean exactly?"

"Pain beyond description followed shortly by muscular paralysis, respiratory depression, cardiac palpitations and a severe disinclination to boogie. You might similarly be discommoded by a firefish, which are easier to spot but no less hurtful. There's even a jellyfish called the snottie."

"You're making all this up," he said, but without conviction.

"Oh, but I'm not."

—Bill Bryson. *Down Under*. New York: Doubleday, 2000.

 ## Kids, Try This at Home

.... READ YOUR BOOK OUT LOUD TO DETECT AN INFO DUMP ....

Amazing how helpful this is to get a sense of music and pace.

INFO ENHANCEMENT IN THE MIDDLE

There's another way to introduce facts, anecdotes, jokes that are not essential to the story, but that enhances its flavor, like salt, pepper, and sugar do in cooking. I do this in personal essays in the range of 1,000–3,000 words and stick the info enhancement in the middle. The key rule is that the info must support and be relevant to the main story and that there should be a natural flow. If you can't make it flow then perhaps it belongs in a sidebar. Or maybe you don't need it at all – ax murder.

∽

Here's mid-article info-enhancement in an article about why I turned down a knight-hood.

It starts with a Provocative Statement lead.

> I turned down a knighthood recently. It was a tough decision – I liked the sound of "Sir Paul."
>
> I had replied to a classified ad in the *International Herald Tribune* that had offered "an economically available, State Sanctioned Hereditary Knighthood."
>
> Turns out that some wannabe nobles have resurrected the Knights Templar, a prominent and powerful group of medieval Christian noblemen who protected pilgrims on the crusader routes to Jerusalem.
>
> The Knights Templar were created by the Catholic church in 1127, and were wiped out by the same hand, when Pope Clement V's bull *Vox in excelso* of March 22, 1312, abolished the group, despite its being vigorously championed by celebrities such as Dante Alighieri. Two years later the Church ordered Knights Templar Grand Master Jacques de Molay burned at the stake.
>
> The literature surrounding the Knights Templar weaves historical fact, fantastical tales, conspiracy theories, metaphysics and religious geopolitics. Some writers claim that the image of what is now called the Shroud of Turin is actually Jacques de Molay's. An abundant shadow literature claims that the Knights Templar were the origin of Freemasonry, that they had links to the fabled continent of Atlantis,

that they possessed the Ark of the Covenant and the Holy Grail. They featured in Dan Brown's bestseller *The Da Vinci Code*.

Several years ago a group of mostly British visionaries incorporated the Ancient and Noble Order of Knights Templar as a nonprofit organization in Israel. For just a single $5,000 fee, and fees of $500 year (less than my golf club fees), I could be honored in an investiture involving apanages and escutcheons. I'd get to wear a special ring and have use of two castles and the opportunity to buy privately bottled Knights Templar Bordeaux.

And even better, the title comes with citizenship of a new country they're creating, code-named Savantis.

"Only five people know where it is," said Knights Templar Chancellor Savant Graham Renshaw-Heron. But from reading between the lines I figure they're buying an island in the Philippines or the Caribbean. According to Sir Graham, the thousand or so locals are enthusiastic about becoming Savantists and living under five dukes who will control the country. The nation will become a beacon of hearty, mostly British-bred, capitalistic enthusiasm, with economic benefits accruing from the planned casinos, resorts, golf courses, offshore banking, and flags of convenience shipping.

I asked my friend Dan about whether he too wanted to sign up – I figured we could get a two-for-one deal, maybe even a free toaster.

"Those guys don't need their own country," he said. "They're already on their own planet."

The Knights Templar certainly have a history of geographical expansion. The medieval group had a fleet larger than that of most countries – Columbus flew the Templar's red cross on his sails. William Mann, author of *The Labyrinth of the Grail*, claims that the Knights Templar "possessed the 'secret' of being able to fix longitudinal positions long before it became common practice," and that this "sacred geometry," allowed Neolithic to Roman era "societies who were in on the secret" to circumnavigate the world and settle corners of the world that are far removed from Europe.

So, the idea that the new Knights Templar might start their own country has a certain fuzzy logic – after all, the original Knights Templar bought the island of Cyprus. And I love the idea of starting your own country. In fact I propose something similar in my novel *Earthlove*, in which a nature conservation organization thinks about buying a tropical archipelago and establishing a Republic of Rich

Misunderstood Heads of State to provide secure luxury housing for deposed dictators who otherwise might face pesky legal efforts to divest them of their fortunes. Instead of wandering around the world seeking asylum, Baby Doc could have leased an island of his own, as might have Ferdinand Marcos, Idi Amin, Mobuto Sese Seko and other rich despots.

Here is the info enhancement.

But can you start a new country just like that?

Well, countries are being created and destroyed all the time. The United States, of course, didn't exist before 1776. Italy didn't exist before 1866, and even then it was missing Rome, which joined in 1870. A vast swath of African and Asian countries were big pink blotches on the colonial maps before the post-WWII period, and the 1990s breakup of the Soviet Union and Yugoslavia created nation-building opportunities for many territories that previously were only known to geographers and stamp collectors. The United Nations had just 157 country members in 1981, but this number expanded quickly – Switzerland just became the 190th member of the United Nations, leaving the Vatican as the only generally recognized country out of the international body. Palestine and Tibet? Watch this space.

Most of these new countries of course were created by standard causes – wars, revolutions, political uprisings, collapse of empires.

But don't discount human ingenuity in the nation-building process.

For $145 you can become a citizen of the Principality of Castellania in Austria, where Prince Ralph I, formerly a burgher named Otto Hubner, has sold more than 2,000 citizenships in 25 years of independence. Or why not become a Sealander? In 1967 Englishman Roy Bates reinvented himself as Prince Roy of Sealand and took over an abandoned World War II anti-aircraft tower off Britain's east coast. "I have always liked the idea of liberty," he told the British newspaper *The Mirror*, "and this was the ultimate way of achieving it."

In November 1998, Philippine police raided a hotel in Olongapo, near Subic Bay, and arrested a Briton, an Australian and a Malaysian. They had been running an Internet scam that offered passports for a fictitious nation called the Dominion of Melchizedck, named after Jerusalem's high priest to whom Abraham gave a tenth of his fortune in reward for rescuing Lot and his family from Sodom.

The Dominion of Melchizedek's bubble burst when a man who identified himself as "His Serene Highness Gerald-Dennis Sayn-Wittgenstein-Hohenstein" tried to open bank accounts in Hong Kong with checks issued by phony Melchizedek banks. The 22-year-old unemployed Austrian, who had been living in the passenger terminal at Kai Tak airport in Hong Kong, turned out to be a baker, not a prince. During his trial (he was convicted for bank fraud and jailed for six months), it was learned that he had visited a number of Asian countries with his Melchizedek "diplomatic passport."

And back to the main story.

Savantis, which Sir Graham assured me is "just an inch away from receiving United Nations recognition," would be a kind, gentle, and I hope, legitimate place. I could see myself as social director at the Savantis Golf Club perhaps, or professor of creative writing at Savantis University.

One thing is sure though, and that is there will never be a Gay Pride Day in Savantis. The Knights Templar constitution, which preaches that "there are no, nor shall there ever be, any political, religious or racial affiliations, obligations or favours of any nature," draws the line on the issue of homosexuality. They are very clear: "While it may be recognized that certain governments, and for their own reasons, have de-criminalized acts of homosexuality, it is the avowed policy of this Noble Order to unreservedly condemn and decry all such activities."

Jacques de Molay was accused of being a homosexual. He was arrested on the morning of October 13, 1307, and spent the next seven years in prison undergoing extreme tortures to force him to issue a confession that would damn the order in the eyes of the people and the Catholic Church.

Although de Molay confessed under duress to denying Christ and trampling on the Holy Cross, he steadfastly denounced the accusations that the initiation ritual consisted of homosexual practices.

Now while I have gay friends I'm not in favor of them receiving special treatment, good or bad, in society. Let them do what they want as consenting adults.

But I don't much like the idea of Savantis telling anyone, in particular me, how to run his life. Nevertheless, I grudgingly admire the Knights Templar's fighting spirit, encouraging the "abandoning of all wimpish thoughts whether this or that cannot or should be attempted."

The Knights Templar documentation is wholeheartedly libertarian and appeals to anyone who thinks there is entirely too much government in our lives. Savantis will be a place where: "Further and more self-evident human rights such as the absence of oppressive alimony laws, childish seat belt laws, alcoholic consumption laws, the punishment of success by the successful being forced to support the unsuccessful, or the energetic being obliged to support the slothful, shall also be Constitutionally and conspicuously absent, while the inherent rights of self-defence, privacy, protection of property, etc. shall be immutably enshrined in The Constitution of Savantis, which shall become blended with the Constitution of this Noble Order ..."

It's their right, of course, to decide who can become a Savantis citizen and what the codes of ethics are. Northern Australia, among many places, prohibits homosexuality. Vibrators and sex toys are outlawed in Kansas. And adultery will, theoretically at least, get you arrested in New York.

When I questioned the civil liberty issue Sir Graham argued: "Your golf club wouldn't allow me to play in just a bathing suit. They're allowed to set their own standards of behavior. So are we."

I didn't like the possibility that these guys, and they're all guys since women can't hold Savantis office, could conceivably change the constitution in a few years and tell me, say, that the Missionary Position is the only approved posture.

But I really I like the sound of Sir Paul. The truth is, I was tempted. I left myself a phone message ("Sir Paul, this is Steven Spielberg. I'd like to make a film of your novel.") to see how it sounded. It sounded just fine. (I'm rather used to honorifics, actually. My mom called me Angel. My wife calls me Hunk. Other acquaintances have called me more colorful titles.)

But I've always rejected honors. I refused to join the high school honor society. I refused to join a fraternity. With the exception of my golf club, I'm sympathetic to Groucho Marx's dictum "I wouldn't belong to any club that would have me as a member."

But still, "Sir Paul" has a certain ring (and a reasonable price tag). Maybe I was too hasty. Maybe I could work my way up the Templar totem pole. Since I'm a writer, I could be eventually be known as "The Prince Formerly Known as Artist."

—Paul Spencer Sochaczewski. "Almost a Knight to Remember."
The Sultan and the Mermaid Queen. Singapore: Editions Didier Millet, 2008.

TRIPLE WHAMMY - THE RULE OF THREE

For some reason we like examples to come in sets of threes. This is as common a phenomenon, and equally impossible to figure out, as the reason why aerobics instructors worldwide use a count of eight.

David A. Fryxell, writing in *Writer's Digest*, noted some of the iconic uses of the Rule of Three: Snap, crackle, and pop. Three gifts of the magi: gold, frankincense, and myrrh. Thomas Jefferson's three inalienable rights: life, liberty, and the pursuit of happiness. The use of "so" three times by Winston Churchill: "Never in the field of human conflict was so much owed by so many to so few."[3] Martin Luther King's triple freedom: "Free at last! Free at last! Thank God Almighty, we are free at last!"

This paragraph by John Keay uses one group of four and three groups of threes, which I've *italicized* and [numbered] for easy reference. Note that the Triple Whammy works for verbs, for parallel phrases, and for nouns. And I like the elegance of his final sentence.

> In fact, during the late 1960s and early seventies over half a million combatants passed up and down the [Ho Chi Minh] Trail – on foot [1], on bikes [2], in lorries [3], on stretchers [4]. So did several million tons of armaments [1], munitions [2] and provisions [3]. The Trail was extended [1] down to the Bolovens plateau for access to the Delta and Cambodia; elsewhere it was frequently realigned [2]; and increasingly it was fortified [3] with bunkers [1], artillery [2] and anti-aircraft

---

[3] And another, lesser-known Churchill Triple Whammy – he was commenting on the early nineteenth-century practice of "impressment," in which British ships patrolling the Atlantic would seize sailors and drag them into the miseries of the British Navy, which Churchill described as "rum, buggery, and the lash."

batteries [3]. For over this route that did not exist [1], through a country that was not involved [2], there soon raged a war that was not acknowledged [3].

—John Keay. *Mad About the Mekong*. London: HarperCollins, 2005.

∞

Here's a triple Triple Whammy:

When he had finished reading and rereading the book, he would place it with all the other books about his brethren. Books about Bianchi [1] and Speck [2] and Bundy [3], about earlier ones – Mors [1] and Lucas [2] and Pommeroy [3] – and others; books about killers and their minds [1], about killers and their victims [2], about killers and those who hunted them [3].

—Jan Burke. *Bones*. New York: Simon & Schuster, 2000.

∞

Diana Darling uses a multitude of threes:

Bali then was a richly growing swarm in the world, humming with the afterclash of cymbals [1] and gongs [2] and slow soprano hand bells [3]. It was a scented place. There was the perfume of mangoes [1] and dung [2] and frangipani [3], and the subtler scents of molds [1], hot wax on cloth [2], and woodsmoke on the skin of lovers [3]. Bali was a shimmering world suspended between heaven and hell, and its people were operatic in their art [1], ferocious in war [2], and tender to their superiors [3].

—Diana Darling. *The Painted Alphabet*. Singapore: Editions Didier Millet, 2012.

∞

And a different type of cultural scene:

Except Atlanta. There was not a recumbent bum [1], importunate panhandler [2], or cardboard pied-à-terre [3] visible within parking distance of downtown.

—P.J. O'Rourke. *Parliament of Whores*. New York: Vintage, 1991.

A tasteful description:

Flom was fat (a hundred pounds overweight, one lawyer said ...) [1], physically unattractive (to a partner, he resembled a frog) [2], and indifferent to social niceties (he would fart in public or jab a cigar close to the face of someone he was talking to, without apology) [3].

—Lincoln Caplan. *Skadden: Power, Money, and the Rise of a Legal Empire.* New York: Farrar, Straus, and Giroux, 1993.

And this joyful Triple Whammy:

It was there [British Museum] in 1872 that George Smith, a self-taught Assyriologist ... made a sensational discovery: a version of the flood story written in cuneiform. So overwhelmed was he by the implications of his find that he immediately leapt to his feet [1], ran around the room [2], and started taking off his clothes [3].

—Tom Holland. "So Much Older Than the Bible." Book review of *The Ark Before Noah: Decoding the Story of the Flood*, by Irving Finkel. *The Guardian*, February 15, 2014.

🎙 Pro Tip

Characters Have Their Own Musical Signatures

The tendency is that the dialogue for all your characters sounds the same (usually, they all sound like you). In long pieces give each character a distinctive rhythm, a unique voice, a characteristic tempo. Think of a famous opera, like La Bohème, in which Mimi has her musical signature, as does Rodolfo.

Another example: Listen to the confrontation scene in the musical Les Misérables in which Javert and Valjean confront each other. Their distinct individual musical themes reverberate throughout the musical whenever these two characters appear.

LITERARY DIALOGUE IS NOT NORMAL CONVERSATION

Normal conversation is to literary dialogue what grape juice is to aged cognac.

Literary dialogue is not retyped day-to-day talk.

Literary dialogue should sound like casual conversation, but it is quite different. Dialogue has to serve the story. In nonfiction, dialogue should not only be truthful, it should have the *appearance of truth*, it should have verisimilitude. Put another way, it should *sound* like conversation, but conversation distilled down to its essence.

LINEAR DIALOGUE / OBLIQUE DIALOGUE

Linear dialogue is a direct question/direct answer type of exchange. It tends to be dull.

Oblique dialogue veers off into unexpected directions. Learn to use it.

Oblique dialogue hits you at an angle. It surprises, opens a door the reader hadn't anticipated.

The constant caveat, if you're writing nonfiction, which is the focus of this book, is that you can't invent dialogue. But you can be alert for it and make the most of it when you come across it. (This is a contentious point – in many scenes, particularly when the quote isn't important for the public record, all writers filter, mold, and manipulate dialogue to suit the demands of the story. I guess the guiding principle is to remain true to the original content and intent.)

Linear Dialogue (at a bar):

"You come here often?"

"Sometimes. How about you?"

"When I'm not working."

"Oh yeah, what do you do?"

"I'm a lawyer. How about you?"

"Me too. What firm?"

"Hookem, Fleecem, and Billem. Downtown, big brown building."

"Can I get you a drink?"

"Why not? A martini if you don't mind."

"Sounds good. I'll have one myself."

and so on until the reader is asleep.

Oblique Dialogue (same bar):

"You come here often?"

"You're pretty pushy. You must be a Wall Street guy."

"My fifth wife said the same. Actually I'm a lawyer."

"Corporate or defense?"

"I get serial killers off."

"My boyfriend might be interested in talking to you. He's out on bail."

"Embezzling or fraud?"

"He dismembers irritating jerks for a living."

"Oh."

"Here he comes now."

THE NONFICTION DIALOGUE CONUNDRUM

The energy in this scene by P.J. O'Rourke comes from oblique dialogue. It is imaginary dialogue but sounds authentic when presented in O'Rourke's voice. (It also presents a conundrum for the writer and reader because the book is positioned as nonfiction/ personal travel. The dialogue is clearly surgically enhanced; if the article was a woman entered in the Miss America Pageant, would it be allowed to compete? I think people expect a bit – okay, a lot – of hyperbole from O'Rourke because the essence of what he says is true. Do you agree?)

> To travel to the rest of Lebanon you just hail a taxi. The country is only one hundred and twenty miles long and forty miles wide, and no Lebanese cab driver has to call home to ask his wife if he can take off for a couple of days. Settle the price first. This won't be easy. It's not the way of the Levant to come to the point. I asked Akbar, one of the Commodore's taximen, how much he'd charge to take me through the Israeli lines and into South Lebanon.

"I have been in this business twenty-seven years," he said.

"Yes," I said, "but how much is it going to cost me?"

"I will tell you later."

"Give me a rough idea."

"Would you like a coffee?"

"What's your hourly rate?"

"Across the street – fine rugs at the best price. I will get you a discount."

"What do you charge by the mile?"

"I have a cousin in Detroit."

"Akbar," I shouted, "what's it going to cost?!"

"If you do not like my price, I tell you what," Akbar gestured grandly, "you do not hire me any more again."

Make sure your driver knows English well enough to translate. Lebanese English is often a triumph of memorization over understanding. "I come from the village of Baabdat," the driver will say in quite an acceptable accent, "it is very beautiful there in the mountains."

"Right," you'll say, "but you better pull over, that guy behind the sandbags is levelling an anti-tank gun at us."

"You do?" the driver will say. "Is that in Texas? I have a nephew in Houston."

—P.J. O'Rourke. *Holidays in Hell*. New York: Grove Press, 1989.

There is little absolute truth in most memoirs. Before you embellish reality, look in the mirror.

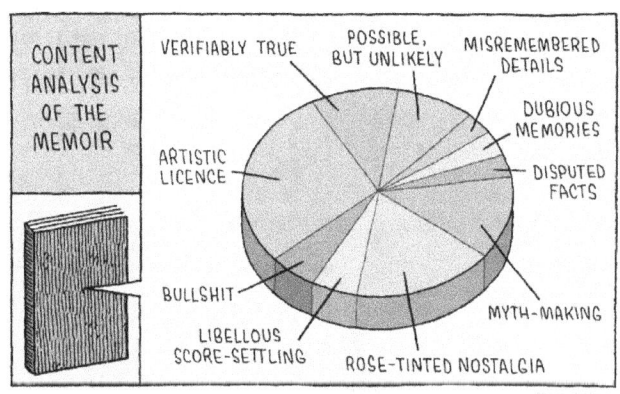

Illustration: Tom Gauld. The Guardian. *February 2, 2014*

DON'T EVER DO THIS

DON'T INVENT IMPORTANT DIALOGUE

❧

Houghton Mifflin Harcourt withdrew Jonah Lehrer's New York Times bestseller Imagine: How Creativity Works because the author fabricated quotes he attributed in the book to Bob Dylan. This is certainly not the first scandal of this type to ruin an author's credibility. The invention of quotes, or its first cousin plagiarism, is not uncommon but it's wrong. What might happen if you did it in your article or book? Perhaps nothing, except a niggling guilty conscience. But lying can damage your career and make you liable to lawsuits. Admittedly, there is a gray area when you retell a story and write remembered dialogue to fit a narrative structure. The basic guideline: if you position the piece as nonfiction, it means the reader expects it to be true. Put yourself in the reader's shoes and your actions should be clear.

CAPTURED CONVERSATION

Most dialogue involves the writer as a participant. But sometimes the writer is there simply as a fly-on-the-wall reporter, resulting in what Theodore A. Rees Cheney refers to as "captured conversation." In Joe McGinniss's profile of Richard M. Nixon, the captured conversation conveys Nixon's famed "shiftiness" without putting it so bluntly. (And his use of Nixon's full name is a subtle way to describe the guy's rigidity.)

He took his position on the front of the heavy brown desk. He liked to lean against a desk, or sit on the edge of one, while he taped commercials, because he felt this made him seem informal. There were about twenty people, technicians and advisors, gathered in a semi-circle around the cameras. Richard Nixon looked at them and frowned.

"Now when we start," he said, "don't have anybody who is not directly involved in this in my range of vision. So I don't go shifting my eyes."

"Yes, sir. All right, clear the stage. Everybody who's not actually doing something get off the stage, please. Get off the stage ..."

"Now, when you give me the fifteen-second cue, give it to me right under the camera so I don't shift my eyes."

—Joe McGinniss. *The Selling of the President*. New York: Simon & Schuster, 1968.

DON'T EVER DO THIS

"AS YOU KNOW, JOHN ..."

❦

Dialogue can be a clumsy way to convey information.

Dialogue should illustrate character and move the story. Be cautious in using dialogue to provide information or tell the back story.

Here's an example of "As you know, John," something you should never do.

Two men are seated at a bar.

Harry: "Good to see you again, John."

John: "And you too, Harry."

Harry: "As you know, John, we were born Siamese twins, connected at birth at our foreheads, which means that we share certain yet-to-be-investigated but undoubtedly profound similarities in our thinking patterns and behaviors. But we had a good surgeon – the famous Ethiopian refugee named Amondilla who later in life died while trying to perform a sex change operation on himself – and after we were separated you were adopted by a Romanian circus family and became a famous East European acrobat until you were convicted of smuggling heroin into Italy, after which you became a Transcendental Meditation guru, while I was left abandoned at an orphanage in Seattle where I was adopted by Meyer Lansky's great-nephew who raised me to be the brains behind his plans to start a gambling casino in Ulan Bator."

> John: "Yes, I remember that well, Harry. Whatever became of your fourth wife, the girl who had red hair, big boobs, and a crush on Sean Connery and who broke into MI6 in London looking for him?"

Surely no successful writer would use such a heavy-handed device. Actually, you see it all the time:

> "I did some research on you. I hope you don't mind. You have an impressive background – a B.S. in criminal psychology and premed, with a master's in behavioral psychology, a forensic fellowship at Quantico. Eight short years with the FBI and already you're one of their top profilers of serial killers. If I calculated right, you're only thirty-two. That's got to feel good – to have accomplished so much."

> —Alex Kava. *A Perfect Evil*. Richmond, UK., Mira Books, 2000.

GOD IS IN THE DETAILS[4]

Without details I don't believe you.

Details are the mortar that holds together the bricks. The chili in the curry. The wag in the tail.

Details prove to the reader that you were there, that you are a good journalist, that what you are saying is true and we can believe you.

Details are what readers remember ("How did she dare wear a purple wedding dress?")

Details illustrate bigger truths.

In this passage Chris Jones provides an abundance of details to set the scene and help us appreciate the meticulous preparation Apolo Ohno undertakes. Would the article

---

[4] Or maybe it's the Devil. You can spend an intriguing couple of hours researching the various origins of this popular expression.

have been as effective if Jones had simply stated, "Apolo Ohno takes great care in fine-tuning his racing skates."?

> [Speed skater Apolo Ohno leads a life] that's one part machinist, one part monk.
>
> First he finds his tool kit, a Tupperware bin filled with wrenches and stones, and next he takes out his skates, which are locked into a jig, blades up. The boots are hard plastic, burgundy and gray; the blades are seventeen inches long – as long as home plate is wide – and silver and gold, like his four-year-old medals ... Everything in Apolo Ohno's life hangs on the sharpness and balance of these blades. They are his foundation.
>
> They are also curved slightly to the left to help him grab the corners, but after this morning's practice session and another hundred laps, he felt as if they weren't quite right. By using a radius gauge that can detect flaws to the thousandth of an inch, he finds the wobble – a whisper, really, but plenty enough to keep him up at night. He works the kink with a tool called a bender, crimping the blade and measuring it again and again until the radius gauge tells him that all is right with his world. Then he locks his skates back in their jig and scrapes a square, flat, diamond-laced stone over the blades. He stops occasionally to pluck the metal with his fingertips, like a harpist working his strings ... Finally, he runs another, small stone along the sides of the blades to shave off whatever microscopic burrs his earlier work produced. At last, they are perfect.
>
> —Chris Jones. "One Thing Perfectly." *Esquire*, February 2006.

☙

And this chilling passage. How did the writer get this information – particularly the detail of the recorded cell phone message – about the death of golfer Payne Stewart, when the cabin of the private plane in which he was traveling lost pressure, leaving the plane still flying but all the passengers dead? In particular feel the impact of one Story of One detail – the recorded cell phone message.

> Unfortunately, Tracey Stewart, Payne's Australian-born wife, was watching events unfold on television just like the rest of the world. It had been only four hours since she had kissed her husband goodbye. Now she was hearing people on television tell her the man she loved was dead in the seat of an airplane, and that the plane

might have to be blown out of the sky! After prefacing everything with such disclaimers as "we are guessing at this stage," and "this is one of several possibilities," the experts speculated on the various ways in which Payne Stewart might have perished, while Tracey sat transfixed in their Orlando home frantically dialing Payne's cell phone number.

"You've reached Payne Stewart's phone," Payne's recorded voice said in his distinct and ever-jovial Ozark twang. "He's not with it right now, so leave him a message and I'll tell him you called and he'll get back to you. Thank you."

As time dragged on, Tracey realized the reports must be true ... All she had at the moment was his voice on the end of the cell phone. "He's not with it right now, so leave him a message ..."

—Steve Eubanks. *At the Turn*. New York: Crown, 2001.

❧

Here's another. This article is thick with informative details; indeed that's one reason everyone seems to love reading Malcolm Gladwell. He does his tasting at Zabar's, where his ketchup visionary is squashed between the sushi and the gefilte fish. I dare you to forget that detail.

And it is because of Grey Poupon that a man named Jim Wigon decided, four years ago, to enter the ketchup business. Isn't the ketchup business today exactly where mustard was thirty years ago? There is Heinz and, far behind, Hunt's and Del Monte and a handful of private-label brands. Jim Wigon wanted to create the Grey Poupon of ketchup.

Wigon is from Boston. He's a thickset man in his early fifties, with a full salt-and-pepper beard. He runs his ketchup business – under the brand World's Best Ketchup – out of the catering business of his partner, Nick Schiarizzi, in Norwood, Massachusetts, just off Route 1, in a low-slung building behind an industrial equipment rental shop. He starts with red peppers, Spanish onions, garlic, and a high-end tomato paste. Basil is chopped by hand, because the buffalo chopper bruises the leaves. He uses maple syrup, not corn syrup, which gives him a quarter of the sugar of Heinz. He pours his ketchup into a clear glass ten-ounce jar, and sells it for three times the price of Heinz, and for the past few years he has crisscrossed the country, peddling World's Best in six flavors – regular, sweet, dill, garlic, caramelized onion, and basil – to specialty grocery stores and supermarkets. If you were in Zabar's on Manhattan's Upper West Side a few months ago, you would have seen him at the front of the store, in a spot between the sushi and the gefilte fish. He was wearing a World's Best baseball cap, a white shirt, and a red-stained apron. In front of him, on a small table, was a silver tureen filled with miniature chicken and beef meatballs, a box of toothpicks, and a dozen or so open jars of his ketchup. "Try my ketchup!" Wigon said, over and over, to anyone who passed. "If you don't try it, you're doomed to eat Heinz the rest of your life."

—Malcolm Gladwell. "The Ketchup Conundrum." *New Yorker*, September 6, 2004.

∽

Here's another clever use of details (bet you'll remember the "cracked G"). And note the second Nancy Reagan word, "but," which in the last line signals a new and important plot twist.

At the beginning of her career as a professional musician, Abbie Conant was in Italy, playing trombone for the Royal Opera of Turin. This was in 1980. That summer, she applied for eleven openings for various orchestra jobs throughout Europe. She got one response: The Munich Philharmonic Orchestra. "Dear Herr Abbie Conant," the letter began. In retrospect, that mistake should have tripped every alarm bell in Conant's mind.

The audition was held in the Deutsches Museum in Munich ... There were thirty-three candidates, and each played behind a screen, making them invisible to the selection committee. Screened auditions were rare in Europe at that time. But one of the applicants was the son of someone in one of the Munich orchestras, so, for the sake of fairness, the Philharmonic decided to make the first round of auditions blind. Conant was number sixteen. She played Ferdinand David's Konzertino for Trombone, which is the warhorse audition piece in Germany, and missed one note (she cracked a G). She said to herself, "That's it," and went backstage and started packing up her belongings to go home. But the committee thought otherwise.

—Malcolm Gladwell. *Blink*. New York: Little, Brown, 2005.

∽

And a telling observation expressed in a single detail – the missing chicken.

The real argument against the Sandinistas isn't made by the civil opposition or the human-rights do-gooders, much less by the *contras* or Ollie North or the Great Communicator his own dumb self. The real argument is made by invisible chickens. There are no chickens, no chickens at all in the Eastern market, the largest market in Managua.

It doesn't matter what kind of awfulness happens in Latin America – and practically every kind of awfulness does – there are always chickens. No Peruvian mountain village is so poor that you can drive through it without running over a chicken. No Mexico City slum is so urban but dawn comes in with rooster crows as loud as Los Lobos live in your breakfast nook. No oppression is so thoroughgoing that there's not a cockfight on Sunday with the loser fried up, *¡muy gusto!,* with the feet still on. But there were no chickens in Managua.

—P.J. O'Rourke. Holidays in Hell. New York: Grove Press, 1989.

I love the detail of the Latin instructions for the ATM machine (it's also a Triple Whammy).

John Paul II has been the great conservative pope. But he has also been, as pontiffs go, relatively funky. He is the first to wear a wristwatch. He watches football on satellite TV. He has installed a papal lift and built a hotel inside the Vatican.

The 21st century has crept into the Papal City by stealth. Cash points now dispense euros – though the instructions are in Latin: *Inserto, Scidulam, Factundum.*

—Tessa Boase. "Everything but the Pope." Financial Times, March 30, 2002.

Here writers report about a senseless murder. They did their homework, interviewing (no doubt distraught) staff at the restaurant to get the order and value, and checking with police (or the police report) to obtain details of how Liu was murdered.

Prosecutors said they [five youths accused of killing the owner/delivery guy from a Chinese restaurant] wanted to eat without paying, so they used a cell phone to call in their $60 order – for General Tso's chicken, shrimp egg foo young, chicken with broccoli and shrimp lo mein – to be delivered to a vacant house. When the owner,

Jin-Sheng Liu, 44, arrived with the delivery shortly before midnight, he was jumped from behind, covered with a sheet and pummeled to death with repeated head blows from fists and at least one brick.

—David Barstow and Sarah Kershaw. "5 Youths Accused of Killing Man for Takeout Dinner." *International Herald Tribune*, September 8, 2000.

∞

Sometimes a writer will give you an overdose of details, as in this fictional excerpt, to convince you he was there and that he knows about what he writes.

First, they cut the fence. Then they dug out the rock ballast from beneath the crosstie nearest the bridge, on the side of the train's scheduled approach. When a hole was cleared the size of an apple box, Hayduke consulted his demolition card (GTA 5-10-9), handy little item, pocket-size, sealed in plastic, which he had liberated from Special Forces during his previous career. He reviewed the formula: one kilogram equals 2.20 pounds; we want three charges 1.25 kilograms each, let's say three pounds each charge, to be on the safe side.

"Okay, Seldom," he says, "that excavation's big enough; you dig another five ties down. I'll place the charge."

Hayduke steps off the railway, back to the sealed boxes waiting on the dune. He rips open the first case – DuPont Straight, 60 percent nitroglycerin, velocity 18,200 feet per pound, quick-shattering action. He removes six cartridges, tube-shaped sticks eight inches long, eight ounces heavy, wrapped in paraffined paper.

—Edward Abbey. *The Monkey Wrench Gang*. Lippincott Williams & Wilkins, 1975.

∞

I had to dig to get these details for an article about how Vietnamese street kids learn the restaurant business. It was tough to get this information. None of the people working at Koto when I visited had been present when Clinton dined there. I had to find the waiter who had served Clinton, shake his memory about the order, and get an update on his career progression.

The cooks were busy, but without interrupting their work managed to smile for a quick photo. I tried to imagine the scene in 2001 when the restaurant was given three hours notice that former U.S. President Bill Clinton, and his 130-strong entourage, was going to have lunch at Koto. As an added challenge, the VIP group had to be fed during the 25 minutes allotted in their tight schedule. Clinton asked his trainee waiter, 18-year-old Phung Van Hai, what was good. The president, known for his love affair with food, ordered grilled vegetables and hummus in a baguette, washed down with a banana milkshake, a café latte and a Diet Coke. Clinton left satisfied; Phung Van Hai now has a steady job at the Hanoi Sheraton.

—Paul Spencer Sochaczewski. "Into the Frying Pan." *International Herald Tribune.* March 10, 2005. Reprinted in *The Sultan and the Mermaid Queen.* Singapore: Editions Didier Millet, 2008.

 Kids, Try This at Home

. . . . USE DETAILS (AND ACTIVE VERBS) . . . .
TO SPICE UP YOUR CV

Which is more convincing?

I was creative director of Flim-Flam Advertising for six years, handling numerous leading companies.

Or this one?

As creative director for Flim-Flam Advertising, I developed a campaign to launch strawberry-flavored fish nuggets, which within one year became Almost-Real Foods' bestselling product; developed an ad campaign during which Orange Orangutan's blood-flavored energy drink rose from sixth position to second within three months; and my TV campaign for my client United-Trust-Us-We're-Bankers Bank generated one hundred thousand new sub-prime mortgages. During my six years with Flim-Flam, the agency's revenues increased by 400% and I won, four times, the Golden Cistern award presented annually by the Global Shucksters Association for the most innovative use of social media in promoting German hip-hop artists.

STRUCTURE YOUR DETAILS CAREFULLY

Here are two passages created by Nancy Kress. The second passage uses more details, and incorporates the Nancy Reagan Principle by showing the contrast between expensive construction and fittings with the neglect one might expect in a shanty town. Which passage works better?

1. Elsie's bathroom was ten feet square, an unusual size and shape for a bathroom. All the fittings and decorations were expensive, but they hadn't been taken care of very well. Elsie had always been a sloppy housekeeper, and she hadn't improved with age. Both floor and walls had been ruined.

2. Elsie's bathroom, so large that it echoed, had clearly been a battlefield between money and neglect. Neglect had won. Thick blue towels, sopping wet, had warped the teak parquet floor. Mildew flourished on hand-painted tiles. The toilet reeked, overpowering the oils and perfumes in their delicate French glass bottles.

–Nancy Kress. "Perfection in Details." *Writer's Digest*, December 2001.

WHAT ABOUT DETAILS WHEN YOU CAN'T REPORT FROM THE SCENE?

WWF once asked me to write a feature article about a conservation project in the Pechoro-Ilych forest in the Ural Mountains. I had never been to this Netherlands-sized spread of pine and spruce and had little frame of reference. Getting the facts was easy. But I needed a sense of place, quotes from local people. I spent an hour with Hartmut, a WWF colleague who had been to the project area many times. He provided key details about the project, but I wanted the blood and guts of the story. I gave him a list of points I wanted him to ask the Russians next time he saw them. Later, with details he provided, I wrote the article. Here's part of what I wrote:

The Chagin family, which lives in Ust-Unja in the buffer zone of the reserve, requires a pile of firewood as big as their log cabin house to get them through the winter, and they rely on horse-drawn sleds to drag the wood along the muddy trails. Fedor Chagin fishes for grayling and pike, and hunts moose and capercaillie, a large wood-grouse. His wife Nadja, an accountant at the local post office, works feverishly during the May-September growing season to cultivate potatoes, cabbages, cucumbers, tomatoes, and beets. They sometimes produce a restorative health tonic from birch juice, and collect, for conditions ranging from bronchitis to baldness, a few of the 2,500 types of medicinal plants used in Komi. This variety indicates both a staggering biodiversity for such a northern region as well as an impressive heritage of living with the land.

Men from Ust-Unja travel as far as 260 kilometers upriver to gather sufficient hay to feed the cows and horses during the long winter. They build simple rafts for the long float down, which might take several days, hollowing out living quarters in the floating haystacks. Hartmut Jungius, WWF's director of the Eastern European program, notes that timing for the return trip is critical, since if the men delay their voyage until too late in the season the water level will drop and they might become stranded.

—Paul Spencer Sochaczewski. "Distant Pressures Threaten Isolated Russian Forest." Commission for WWF.

When it was published I got a nice note from a Russian colleague, saying, "It was as if you'd been here."

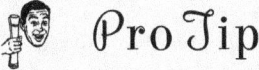

Pro Tip

Name Important People

You've met someone who occupies more than one sentence in your story. She might have taught you how to grind corn to make tortillas; she might have taken you by the hand when she saw you were lost. She might have been your guide or porter. If she appears in the story and has something important to say, identify her. Don't refer to her as a "villager" or a "guide." This person has a name.

USE VISUALS, OR WRITE VISUALLY: PART I

Discovered in Madagascar. World's smallest lizard. 29 mm (1.15 inches). You have a choice of how cold or how hot to present this new creature.

How big is 29 mm? That's a cold, left brain statistic, forcing the reader to do strenuous mental calculations.

If you have control over the visuals in your article, use pictures to heat it up. Here's that tiny lizard in visual form.

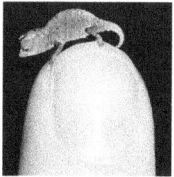

No control over visuals? Then create a hot written picture. Something like: "The new lizard is so small that it can sleep happily on my thumb; I could easily hold an entire breeding population in my palm."

USE VISUALS, OR WRITE VISUALLY: PART II

If you're writing nonfiction and you are in control of the graphic design, think about how graphics can support your message

The two covers on the following page are from reports I produced when I was with International Osteoporosis Foundation.

In the first example, the report is about the poor communication between doctors and patients. Patients said "doctors don't explain things properly," while doctors said "patients don't listen properly." (My sympathy in this case goes to patients.) These are cold, left-brain statements – the reader is asked to decipher what they mean in her own context. To make the messages hotter (more accessible), we chose a photo of a woman in the osteoporosis target age group (roughly 50+) looking skeptically at a smug, good-looking doctor. Note their body language.

In the second example, the report tried to suggest a strategy to help patients stay on treatment. The main photo was a patient and a doctor talking, but not yet in synch because they are separated by a broken jigsaw puzzle.

And if you can't control the graphics? Then write graphically. Each of these reports contained anecdotes and comments from both patients and doctors. Stats alone don't provide enough of an emotional hook to grab the reader.

Visuals enhance most nonfiction stories.

WRITING LONG STUFF

Many of the examples in this book relate to relatively short personal essays and personal travel stories. The ideas apply as well to longer pieces, of course, but with book-length personal stories, say a family history, another factor comes into play: it's sometimes called the story arc or the three-act structure.

The story arc is the structure in storytelling that keeps the reader turning the page. It might be based on an Aristotelian "fall from grace" (or the reverse, a rise to the heights), or a Joseph Campbell-like quest exemplified by a hero's journey. Readers and cinema-goers subconsciously expect that popular books and movies follow a traditional story arc.

The three-act structure is a classic story structure for books, plays, and movies, generally comprised of the Setup, the Confrontation, and the Resolution.

Writer Tim Lott puts it another way, using Jack and the Beanstalk as "an example of essential story structure." Writing in the *Guardian* he says:

> There is stasis – Jack and his mother living an ordinary life. There is the inciting incident – they run out of money. There is the quest – Jack sets out to sell the cow. There is the hero's journey – Jack visits the giant's lair where he faces tests and perils. There is climax – the giant chases Jack down the beanstalk. There is resolution, when Jack cuts down the beanstalk and kills the giant, and the reversal, when Jack and his mother, once poor, become rich.

This can get highly technical. There are hundreds of workshops and books about plotting longer stories; they generally make me nervous   too much like high school English comp class – but the following Pro Tip offer a useful template.

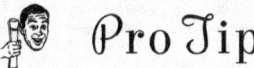 *Pro Tip*

Figure Out Your Story Arc

Here's one simple guide to determine a story arc that's both helpful and not overly irritating, the eponymous Gary Provost Sentence.

Once upon a time _____

(something happened to a person/inciting incident)

and he/she _____

(decided to pursue a prize)

so he/she _____

(devised a plan of action/strategy)

and even though _____

(there were forces trying to stop him/her/conflict)

he/she moved forward because _____

(there was a lot at stake)

and just as _____

(things seemed as bad as they could get/bleakest moment)

he/she learned _____

(an important lesson)

and when _____

(offered the prize)

he/she had to _____

(decide whether or not to take it)

and in making that decision, he/she _____

(satisfied a need/hole)

that _____

(had been created by something in his/her past/backstory.)

—Gary Provost. Used in the Gary Provost-created Writers Retreat Workshops

WRITING TIP #8

The Story of One - Tragedy or Disaster?

This young woman from rural China changed my life.

I was working with WWF – at that time called World Wildlife Fund. I had just returned to Switzerland from Xishuangbanna, a corner of southern China on the Mekong River that borders Laos and Burma. I was asked to make a presentation to the staff about my trip; I wasn't too confident speaking before an audience, even an audience of non-threatening colleagues.

So I gathered a few 35mm slides and memorized the facts of our forest conservation program – how much money we spent, how many Land Rovers we purchased, how many people we employed, and how many hectares of forest we (claimed) we protected.

I knew all the facts, but I didn't know the story behind the facts. My presentation was going to be cold, intellectual, boring.

Then, while rehearsing, I kept thinking about this one slide, this one young woman. I dug into my notes and found her name: Bo Wan Kan. A member of the Dai ethnic group. Fourteen years old. Three brothers and one sister. She had completed primary school, then went to work in the fields alongside her parents.

I looked at the photo of Bo Wan Kan by the riverside. The water was clean and plentiful. Dragonflies, a sign of a healthy environment, flitted around her. It was a beautiful scene, rather idyllic.

It struck me what the whole WWF project was about: one person and her dependence on water. No one had framed it in that simple a concept, but that was it. By protecting the forest, we were ensuring that Bo Wan Kan and her fellow villagers had water for cooking and drinking and bathing. Water for the crops. Water for life.

I also realized that there were big stakes involved – if Bo Wan Kan *didn't* have water, her health, culture, and opportunities might be in jeopardy.

So I made a much shorter presentation than I had first planned, focusing on the human story with hardly any statistics.

WHAT'S THE DIFFERENCE BETWEEN DISASTER AND TRAGEDY?

A disaster affects many nameless people. A tragedy affects one person, who has a name, a favorite cocktail, and a pet cat named Rasputin. The tragedy is the Story of One that introduces a disaster – The Story of Many.

THE STORY OF ONE AND THE STORY OF MANY

Use the Story of One (one incident, one example, one detail) to hook the reader with a hot connection, and then you can pull back and talk about the cooler Story of Many (usually a big statistic that is hard to visualize).

USE THE STORY OF ONE TO PUT A FACE ON STATISTICS

The 2004 Indian Ocean tsunami killed more than 230,000 people.

That's a lot of pain and suffering.

But I can't visualize 230,000 people; it's too big a number.

But I *can* visualize the Story of One, as in this scene:

Ali, a 37-year-old fisherman living in a small village in Aceh province, Sumatra, went to sea on the night of December 25, 2004. He returned around four in the morning with a basketful of fish.

Shortly before dawn Ali's wife Siti, a 35-year-old mother of two, strapped the basket containing eight still-wriggling fish to her bicycle and got ready to pedal two kilometers to the coastal fish market to sell the catch. It was the day after Christmas, a holiday she knew about but didn't celebrate.

Siti's seven-year-old daughter Aminah wanted to go to the market with her mother, as did her ten-year-old son Ahmad. "No way," Siti told them. "Today's a school day. You can come with me to the market on Saturday."

And so Siti went to the market while her husband Ali loaded the two kids on his motorcycle and took them to school on top of the hill in town, a few kilometers away.

As they reached the school, Ali and the children heard a rumble like a freight train. In one moment the birds took wing and people turned toward the ocean.

They watched the tsunami hit.

From his elevated vantage point Ali, Ahmad, and Aminah could see it happening, as if in slow motion. It looked to him as if the world was coming to an end. *What sins have we done to deserve this?* He watched, helpless and confused. What happened to Siti? What happened to his house, his boat, his community? What happened to his future?

Siti was never seen again; Ali, Ahmad, and Aminah were safe, but without a wife and mother.

After catching us with the Story of One, you can then go into the nut paragraph with a statement that tells the Story of Many:

The tsunami that ravaged the Indian Ocean on Boxing Day, 2004, killed more than 230,000 people (no one is quite sure of the exact number) and left millions injured, homeless, and without much of a future. The challenge now is to help the survivors regain their livelihoods and confidence.

The Story of One can represent the Story of Many.

THE STORY OF ONE – A HANDY TOOL

Here's how Pulitzer Prize-winning columnist George Will uses a powerful Story of One to introduce a general discussion about the breakdown of the American welfare system. After his hot lead Will then goes on to discuss political and financial reasons why such incidents happen regularly.

When police, responding to her call, arrived at her East Harlem tenement, she was hysterical: "The dog ate my baby."

The baby girl had been four days old, twelve hours "home" from the hospital. Home was two rooms and a kitchen on the sixth floor, furnished with a rug, a folding chair, and nothing else, no bed, no crib.

"Is the baby dead?" asked an officer.

"Yes," the mother said, "I saw the baby's insides."

Her dog, a German shepherd, had not been fed for five days. She explained: "I left the baby on the floor with the dog to protect it." She had bought the dog in July for protection from human menaces.

> —George Will. "On Her Own in the City." *Washington Post*. Excerpted in Theodore A. Rees Cheney. *Writing Creative Nonfiction*. Berkeley: Ten Speed Press, 2000.

I went to the 1999 Geneva Salon des Inventions and was impressed by the range of inventions on display and the enthusiasm of their creators.

I could have written a story in "list" form – the hundreds of inventions featured in the Salon included many innovations that had insignificant redeeming social value (but plenty of reader appeal): a Korean concoction that minimizes hangovers, a fly swatter with built-in tweezers so that you don't have to actually touch the squashed insect, a toilet seat with a built-in scale, and a device to attach a windsurfing sail to a wheelchair.

But I chose the Story of One to introduce the Story of Many.

What was this unusual creation? It's a disposable funnel-like device called the Lae-Ine, which, according to Ineke Dantuma, the device's Dutch inventor, "enables women to water like gentlemen."

Dantuma noted that "most ladies envy men because of their possibility to urinate standing, without the need to touch anything in their vicinity." And the product's promotional material noted that it ensured "No more wind under the bumbs [sic] of ladies."

> —Paul Spencer Sochaczewski. "A Matter of Convenience for the Ladies."
> *Mensa Magazine*, May 1998.

Conor McKeever uses the Story of One – an incorrect polygraph test to illustrate the bigger point he made later that "a 1997 survey of psychologists estimate the polygraph's accuracy to be around 61% – not much better than chance."

> When Bill Wegerly came home to find his wife murdered in their bed, his world fell apart. To make it worse, he became the prime suspect in her murder and, without an alibi, no one would believe his innocence. In a bid to clear his name, he agreed to a police polygraph test, but failed. Twice. By the time he was finally exonerated, in light of new evidence, it was too late – Bill and his children had spent twenty years living as social outcasts, damned by the very machine that should have saved them.
>
> —Conon McKeever. "Polygraphs: Are They Telling the Truth?"
> I, *Science*, Winter 2012/2013.

WRITING TIP #9

NEWS

RELATE TO THE NEWS, LEARN NEWS TECHNIQUES

There are two major points in this chapter.

The first: Consider relating your story to a news story. A discovery. A trial. An uprising. A volcanic eruption, a sporting event, a new public opinion poll. It could be as mundane as a big increase in gasoline prices, or as important as a salmonella outbreak. You might find resonance in a business statistic noting that the adventure travel market is up twenty-five percent, or that the exchange rate of the dong to the dollar is down by half, making this a good time to visit Vietnam. If no news story comes to mind, you can try to link your story to an anniversary - your article on a resurgence in log cabin architecture might coincide with an anniversary of Abraham Lincoln's birth.

The second. Learn how leading newspapers and magazines structure their stories, and follow a similar style.

I sold a bunch of articles about Alfred Russel Wallace in 2009, which was the 150th anniversary of the publication of Charles Darwin's landmark book *Origin of Species*, an anniversary that generated considerable media attention. What's the connection? Wallace, while in Southeast Asia, independently developed a theory of natural selection and sent it to Darwin in England. Darwin deliberately sidelined, and perhaps plagiarized Wallace, who was a younger, lesser-known naturalist. Once I got that link across, I could go anywhere I liked with the Wallace story.

Here's how I started one of those pieces:

> This year marks the 150th anniversary of the publication of Charles Darwin's *Origin of Species*, a landmark book which dramatically changed how we think about ourselves and the world in which we live.
>
> Charles Darwin has been lionized as one of the giants of western thought for his theory of evolution.
>
> But what about Alfred Russel Wallace, a contemporary of Darwin's who independently developed the theory of natural selection during his eight-year sojourn in Southeast Asia? Why did Darwin become a household name while Wallace became a historical footnote?
>
> —Paul Spencer Sochaczewski. "An Inordinate Fondness for Beetles."
> *Bangkok Post*, March 10, 2011.

And another news-oriented lead, linking China's current global power surge with a cultural/historic anniversary from the Ming Dynasty:

> The United States and the countries of Southeast Asia are struggling to know how to respond to the rapid growth of China's military power. Is it the natural outcome of China's economic growth, or does it presage a desire on China's part to throw its weight around in world affairs?
>
> Southeast Asia, on the other hand, does present an historical precedent – one that should be attracting particular attention in 2005. This year is the 600th anniversary of the first of seven great voyages to south and west by China's most famous admiral, Zheng He.
>
> —Philip Bowring. "China's Growing Might and the Spirit of Zheng He."
> *International Herald Tribune*, August 2, 2005.

Think of the Beatles's song: "Do you want to know a secret?" Can you write your article so that you investigate a secret? "What's the secret of longevity of folks in Hunza?" Or "Hidden courtyards you can visit in Paris." Or "My husband doesn't know I was secretly married to O.J. Simpson."

THE STORY ANGLE MIGHT EVOLVE ONCE YOU GET A NEWS HOOK

I've been interested in white elephants for some time. Because the animals are incarnations of Buddha, the Buddhist kings of Burma, Thailand, Laos, and Cambodia collected white elephants as symbols of their royal power and righteousness. I had heard that Burma had three white elephants, which were on public display. A friend in Rangoon managed to get me a meeting with Lt. Col (retired) U Shu Maung, a senior official at the Ministry of Forests who had responsibility for capturing and displaying the white elephants (this was in 2000, well before Aung San Suu Kyi's release from house arrest, when the country was firmly in the grip of the military leaders and journalists were not welcome). During the course of the interview, U Shu Maung made a comment, perhaps tongue-in-cheek, about how the white elephants justified the rule of the country's generals. And then the obvious hit me – of course that's what they were doing – the leaders of the military junta were using white elephants to position themselves as powerful modern Buddhist kings. My story took on a new, timely, newsy edge. Here's an excerpt:

> The official *New Light of Myanmar* newspaper does not hesitate to predict that the discovery of the country's three white elephants heralded a new era of prosperity. "Throughout history, white elephants emerged during the time of Myanmar kings and governments who ruled the nation discharging the ten kingly duties," the government newspaper reported. "It is said that the white elephant brings peace, stability and prosperity ... a good omen when the State is endeavoring to build a peaceful, modern and developed nation."
>
> To some skeptics white elephants are just animals with recessive genes that give them albino-like characteristics and other curious attributes like fan-shaped tails and ears, or a white palate or genitals. But to true believers, and to people like Burma's military leaders who use the white elephants to legitimize their positions on the top of the hierarchal totem pole, white elephants are true incarnations of Lord Buddha and are as sacred to many Buddhists as a savior born to a virgin is to Catholics.
>
> —Paul Spencer Sochaczewski. "Burma's Generals Hope White Elephants Provide Jumbo Support." *Geographical.* September, 2005. Reprinted in *The Sultan and the Mermaid Queen.* Singapore: Editions Didier Millet, 2008.

LEARN TO WRITE A STRAIGHTFORWARD NEWS FEATURE

Sarah Lyall's story about how Britain's health care system is failing to provide adequate service for its patients is an example of a cleanly structured news feature. I've cut it down and annotated it to show how she's using a number of techniques described earlier: anecdote lead, quotes from experts, the use of the Story of One to support the Story of Many, use of statistics to add verisimilitude (this woman has done her homework!), introduction of a news hook (what's Tony Blair going to do?), and plenty of Nancy Reagan conflicts that are enhanced by Nancy Reagan words: "but," "however," "nevertheless," "in spite of."

Lyall starts with an anecdote lead that sets up the basic Nancy Reagan problem. Jackie O'Donnell's story becomes the Story of One that Lyall uses to represent the Story of Many. Note the use (twice in one paragraph) of the Nancy Reagan word "but" to enhance the seriousness of the problem and accentuate the conflict.

> Jackie O'Donnell's oncologist couldn't have been more clear about her prospects.
>
> Suffering from advanced ovarian cancer, with five inoperable tumors after surgery, Mrs. O'Donnell urgently needed aggressive chemotherapy. But, the doctor explained, her local health authority would not pay for the treatment he was recommending, a drug that can prolong life for a year or more and is routinely used in the United States, Europe and some parts of Britain. If Mrs. O'Donnell wanted it, it would not be free, as most treatments are in the government-financed National Health Service, but would cost her $16,000.
>
> "I just didn't believe it, because in this country we were brought up to believe that we would get the best treatment available," said Mrs. O'Donnell, now 55. She chose her life over her budget, put the bills in a drawer when she could not pay them, and has been in remission since last spring. "It's hard, when it stares you in the face that what you thought was really all nonsense."

Lyall then uses a nut graph that highlights the Story of Many.

> In a country where cancer care horror stories are as common as the winter flu, Mrs. O'Donnell's is striking only because it is so familiar. Doctors, health-care advocates and even the government say that Britain's record on cancer, the country's second biggest killer after cardiovascular disease, is nothing short of disgraceful, a stark example of the limitations of Britain's fraying system of socialized medicine.
>
> Problems in the health service, advocates and doctors say, are so pervasive that literally billions of dollars directed specifically at cancer are needed. But cancer is

not the only disease making demands on a system struggling to cope with rising patient expectations and increasingly stretched resources.

She uses a news hook.

Health care has already become one of the major political headaches confronting Prime Minister Tony Blair, who is debating whether to increase the government's health spending and, if so, by how much.

And a second nut graph:

In cancer, the problems include a chronic lack of money, specialists and cancer treatment centers; a lack of national standards that means that treatment is available in some parts of the country but not others; and a tendency at times to postpone aggressive treatment until it becomes too late.

Now she gives us a statistic – 25,000 people – that represents the Story of Many.

Cancer programs are so underfinanced and chaotically managed, the World Health Organization says, that 25,000 people die unnecessarily of cancer in Britain each year – people who would most likely have survived if they lived in countries with better standards of treatment, like France, Germany or the United States.

And here's the first expert quote (note the Nancy Reagan conflict generated when he compares Britain to a Third World country):

"The phrase 'third world cancer care' has hung heavy over the National Health Service for years," Gordon McVie, director general of the Cancer Research Campaign, one of Britain's largest cancer charities, wrote recently in *The Daily Mail*. "Today it is no longer a sound bite; it describes a reality."

Lyall does two interesting things here. First, she introduces a Story of An Anonymous One (a critically ill patient), which introduces a Story of Many (the statistic "500 patients die a year"). And she wakes us up by shifting to present tense.

The problems in the overstretched National Health Service are not limited to cancer. It is hard to pick up a newspaper these days without seeing signs of a system in trouble. A critically ill patient is shunted from place to place in a desperate 100-mile search for an intensive-care bed, and finally dies in the ambulance. A new study shows that 500 patients die a year while on the national waiting list for heart operations.

Another anecdotal Story of One (this time naming the person), with a quote from Mavis Skeet's daughter, Jane. Note how she shifts from present tense in the first paragraph below to standard simple past tense, then back to present. This type of tense-shifting can get tricky – you can try it, but be careful.

In a particularly grim instance, a 73-year-old woman with advanced esophageal cancer has the misfortune of being scheduled for surgery in mid-December, when operations are routinely canceled to make way for emergency patients suffering from pneumonia and the like.

The operation on the woman, Mavis Skeet, was scheduled, and canceled, four times over the next five weeks: first because the anesthesiologist had the flu, and the next three times because no intensive care beds were available. After the fourth cancellation, an ultrasound scan showed that the tumor had spread and was now inoperable.

Mrs. Skeet is now in a hospital, being fed through a stomach tube and receiving chemotherapy, waiting for the inevitable, her daughter, Jane, said in an interview. "They haven't given us a timetable, but it's spread so quickly in five weeks that anybody can work it out," she said.

Lyall then uses another Nancy Reagan – "some successes" and an implied "but." Then another expert quote, with a narrative intro, then statistics – a cold interlude in the midst of hot anecdotes. In my opinion this is a left-brain overload – the excessive use of statistics slows down the piece.

Experts say that in a system with some successes – the infant mortality rates in Britain are lower than those in the United States, for instance – there are few areas where the situation is so demonstrably bad as it is in cancer. "The health service has been chronically underfunded in the last 10 or 15 years and is desperately short of money, and I'm not aware of where things are any worse than in cancer," said Dr. Tim Maughan, a clinical oncologist specializing in gastrointestinal cancer and lymphoma at Velindre Hospital in Cardiff, Wales.

According to the most recent studies, a British man with lung cancer has a 6 percent chance of surviving for five years after treatment, compared with a 12 percent chance in France and a 13 percent chance in the United States. For colon cancer in men, the five-year survival rates are 41 percent in Britain, 59 percent in the Netherlands, and 64 percent in the United States.

And for breast cancer in women, the figures are 67 percent in Britain, 72 percent in Germany, and 84 percent in the United States.

Even the relentlessly optimistic government of Mr. Blair has begun, however reluctantly, to acknowledge that its cancer care is, in fact, bad. Last summer, Mr. Blair pledged to try to reduce the death rate from cancer for people under 75 by 20 percent in the next 10 years, saving 100,000 lives.

Back to a news hook in which Lyall introduces a new Nancy Reagan – how will the politicians fix the mess? I think she overwhelms us with numbers, but perhaps that was intentional. (I would have put many of the statistics into a sidebar.)

It is unclear exactly how he plans to do this, short of injecting billions more dollars into the system or changing the way it is financed. Britain currently spends £55.7 billion – about $89 billion – a year on health care, or 6.8 percent of its gross domestic product – nearly all of it public money. There is little political will in Britain to move to a more cash-rich European or American-based model. Germany spends about 10.7 percent of its gross domestic product on health care, and the United States, about 14 percent.

In a recent television interview, Mr. Blair appeared to promise that Britain would bring its health spending up the European levels by 2006, but when Treasury officials calculated that that would cost perhaps an extra $12 billion a year, money that would have to come out of roads and schools, the promise was hastily downgraded to an "aspiration." Mr. Blair has already made an extra $21 billion available to the health service over three years, but much of that is being taken up by steep salary increases for workers …

—Sarah Lyall, "In Britain's Health Service, Sick Itself, Cancer Care Is Dismal."
The New York Times, February 10, 2000.

Use News to Save an "Information" Article

I wrote an article about an interesting subject – hyperthermophiles – unusual and rarely studied critters that live in the deepest parts of the ocean.

The story was enlightening and full of fun facts: they live near volcanic vents at the bottom of the deep ocean in totally dark, highly pressured environments. Some deep-ocean bacteria are able to get their energy from chemicals; they might form a third superfamily of life, distinct from that of plants and animals. Some life forms live in water so hot – up to 112 degrees centigrade (235 degrees Fahrenheit) – that they are kept from boiling only by the enormous pressures deep in the ocean. They thrive on hydrogen sulfide, which is poisonous to most other forms of life. A large tube worm grows to more than one meter in length without the benefit of either a mouth or a digestive system.

Interesting stuff, but it had no edge.

I got hold of two then-current news hooks and these points gave the article a new vibrancy.

> Scientists and dreamers alike have been enthralled by recent discoveries of planets outside our solar system which might harbor life, and speculation that minute specks of life possibly live on Mars.
>
> Later this year, researchers will begin to hunt in earnest for the microscopic Martians, which may be similar to the first forms of terrestrial life on Earth. The scientists might have more success, however, if they stayed on Earth and explored the deep oceans.
>
> —Paul Spencer Sochaczewski. "Down Deep." *E-Magazine*, July 1996.

Before I found the news hook, my article was floating. Now it had anchors.

Quote Other Experts – It Makes You Look Smarter

Here's something that seems odd, but it's true. You may be an expert in your field, but you will be perceived as even *more* of an expert if you quote others.

∾

In his 5,400-word *New Yorker* story "The Ketchup Conundrum," Malcolm Gladwell quotes twelve experts (thirteen including Plato), and has detailed conversations with seven of them. That tells me that a) he does his homework, b) he isn't afraid to put in the hours to seek out and meet people, c) he has a good filtering system since he must have interviewed at least twice that number of people resulting in thousands of words of notes to sift through, and d) he probably had a terrific time meeting these unusual characters.

∾

See how a carefully selected quote enhances this short passage:

> Jesse [Jackson] and Mike [Dukakis] emerged from the strange-bedfellow room on Monday morning of convention week claiming to still respect each other. They then engaged in a kind of lukewarm political necking that *New Republic* editor Fred Barnes called "kiss on the lips but no tongue."
>
> —P.J. O'Rourke. *Parliament of Whores*. New York: Vintage, 1991.

∾

I used details, anecdotes, a historical expert quote, and a contemporary expert quote to convey the isolation of the Pechoro-Ilych forest in Russia:

> The village of Jaksha used to be an important trading center where skins, dried meat and fish and whale parts from the Arctic were transported to the markets in distant western Russia. In 1917, historian F.P. Dobrokhotov wrote that "the lack of communications [here] is a real tragedy," and that in order to cross the watershed to transport goods coming in from the northern flowing rivers to those flowing south, "one has to launch an expedition, similar to those of Central Africa In the days of

Livingstone." Even today, a visit to the Pechoro-Ilych Reserve requires two flights from Moscow, a long journey on bad roads, an even longer river trip, and probably substantial delays.

Following the collapse of the Soviet system, state support to the nature reserve dropped drastically, meeting only ten percent of operating costs with no money for fuel, boats, telephones, or even for mail.

"Something as simple as communications, which other protected areas take for granted, are missing," notes Przemyslaw Majewski, the leader of the Swiss government-funded WWF project in Komi.

During a visit to the remote post of Ust Liaga on the Ilych River, Majewski says, half the research group was transported by helicopter to another location some one hundred kilometers away. Due to poor weather conditions the helicopter did not return for the rest of the group, and for several days radio contact was limited to frustrating "Boo-boo-baa-baa-zzzz-iiiii-boo-zzz" static. The helicopter returned three days later. Less lucky were students completing field work in the nearby national park, one week's walk from the nearest human settlement. They were stranded for three weeks while waiting for a helicopter, and survived by foraging for berries and mushrooms until rescued by another chopper.

—Paul Spencer Sochaczewski. "Distant Pressures Threaten Isolated Russian Forest."
Commission for WWF.

Useful Advice from Someone Who Wrote Pretty Well

Nora Ephron, who wrote the films Sleepless in Seattle and When Harry Met Sally, started as a newspaper reporter; she said she became a journalist because of her high school journalism teacher.

In the first day of journalism class, Ephron's teacher told the students they would write the lead of a newspaper story. The teacher reeled off the facts: "Kenneth L. Peters, the principal of Beverly Hills High School, announced today that the entire high school faculty will travel to Sacramento next Thursday for a colloquium in new teaching methods. Among the speakers will be anthropologist Margaret Mead, college president Dr. Robert Maynard Hutchins, and California governor Edmund 'Pat' Brown."

Ephron said she and the other budding journalists churned out leads that condensed the facts, along the lines of "Governor Pat Brown, Margaret Mead, and Robert Maynard Hutchins will address the Beverly Hills High School faculty Thursday in Sacramento."

The teacher read the leads out loud and tore them up, one by one. He then wrote the lead on the blackboard: "There will be no school next Thursday."

Ephron said, "It was a breathtaking moment. In that instant I realized that journalism was not just about regurgitating the facts but about figuring out the point. It wasn't enough to know the who, what, when, and where; you had to understand what it meant and why it mattered."

—Recounted by Chip Heath and Dan Heath. *Made to Stick: Why Some Ideas Survive and Others Die.* New York: Random House, 2007.

Think of the headline your story will generate.

GET THE NAME OF THE DOG

It's old advice given to rookie newspapermen. Get the name of the dog. Ask your interviewee to turn on the car radio so you can hear what she listens to. See if the dishes are piled in the sink or carefully washed and put away. Snoop like a cop in CSI.

Such details are important; they not only give a sense of character and place, but they show that the writer has done her homework, that she is a serious reporter.

Note the use of "dog names" in the following passage. No one expects the reader to remember the names of the computers, but the fact that the writer provided them gives the article gravitas. And the dumped human corpse – I love the way Preston throws that in. But before he could use it he had to dig to get that tidbit of information.

Gregory Volfovich Chudnovsky recently built a supercomputer in his apartment from mail-order parts. Gregory Chudnovsky is a number theorist. His apartment is situated near the top floor of a run-down building on the West Side of Manhattan, in a neighborhood near Columbia University. Not long ago, a human corpse was found dumped at the end of the block. The world's most powerful supercomputers include the Cray Y-MP C90, the Thinking Machines CM-5, the Hitachi S-820/80, the nCube, the Fujitsu parallel machine, the Kendall Square Research parallel machine, the nec SX-3, the Touchstone Delta, and Gregory Chudnovsky's apartment. The apartment seems to be a kind of container for the supercomputer at least as much as it is a container for people.

—Richard Preston. "The Mountains of Pi." *New Yorker*, March 2, 1992.

 Kids, Try This at Home

· · · · · · · · · TAKE A BREAK ONCE IN A WHILE · · · · · · · ·
AND ENJOY THE ENGLISH LANGUAGE AS SHE IS WRITTEN

Some of my favorite newspaper headlines:

Statistics show teen pregnancy drops off significantly after age 25.

Get 50% off or half price, whichever is lower.

One-armed man applauds the kindness of strangers.

An Australian Army vehicle worth $74,000 has gone missing
after being painted with camouflage.

Fish need water, Feds say.

Caskets found as workers demolish mausoleum.

Utah Poison Control Center reminds everyone not to take poisons.

Federal agents raid gun shop, find weapons.

∞

And I relish clever phrasings that pop up everywhere, like these "worst analogies ever written in a high school essay contest" winners:

John and Mary had never met.
They were like two hummingbirds who had also never met.

His thoughts tumbled in his head, making and breaking alliances like underpants in a dryer without Cling Free.

McBride fell 12 stories, hitting the pavement like a Hefty Bag filled with vegetable soup.

BUT BE CAREFUL

Don't assume you know everything. In 2012 I was upset by this phrase from *The Telegraph*: "A famous seventies advertisement for hairspray features a man watching admiringly as a woman with swinging hair and an enigmatic smile walks past. It bore the tag line: 'Is she or isn't she?'" I was certain that the writer was incorrectly referring to an iconic 1950s ad for Clairol hair coloring, written by Shirley Polykoff of ad agency Foote, Cone & Belding, which asked: "Does she ... or doesn't she?" But the Internet is a brilliant resource for checking things like this, and I searched for "is she or isn't she?" and found that yes indeed, the tagline was used in a 1970s UK campaign for Harmony hairspray.

Check everything.

Kids, Try This at Home

········ HOW DO YOU SPELL? ········

1. Famous Australian airline (begins with Q).

2. The double-numbered ubiquitous convenience store chain whose numbers add up to 18.

3. The global fast food chain with Golden Arches.

4. The popular Red- or Black-labeled Scotch whisky in the square bottle showing a perambulating gentleman.

5. The full name of the household product conglomerate P&G.

6. The South American country known for kidnappings, emeralds, and cocaine, named after famous explorer Christopher C.

If you don't know how to spell it, look it up.

I once misspelled the Scotch whisky (number 4 above) in an article in the International Herald Tribune (shame on me – but my self-abuse was mollified a bit when I read that Graham Greene made the same mistake in his novel A Burnt-Out Case). The editors didn't notice (shame on them). Perhaps no one else noticed except the manufacturers. But I was annoyed with myself for making such a rookie mistake.

Answers: 1. Qantas; 2. 7-Eleven; 3. McDonald's; 4. Johnnie Walker; 5. Procter & Gamble; 6. Colombia

Fake it at your own risk.

FIVE WS AND AN H – THE FIRST THING
YOU LEARN AS A CUB REPORTER

Illustration: Sarah Steenland

Journalism 101: The basic newspaper story should answer these questions:

Who? What? Where? When? Why? How?

Your nonfiction personal memoir should as well.

WRITE IN LAYERS

Imagine a chocolate layer cake with just one layer.
Imagine a curry with just one spice.
Imagine a radio station that played just one song.

A good article or book has two layers – the superficial story and the deeper subtext. Consider Michael Crichton's *Jurassic Park*. The story is about an eccentric billionaire who clones dinosaurs. The subtext, call it the theme if you want, which is more evident in the book than the movie, is about how scientific arrogance upsets our balance of civilization.

I like articles that make me think, that give me new insights. I like richness. I like the juxtaposition of silliness next to deep thoughts.

Achieving richness can be tricky, since it's easy to stick in too much tangential stuff and neglect your main obligation – to tell the story.

Then look at your own writing. Any possibilities of adding another layer to the cake?

HOW TO MAKE A BIOGRAPHY OR AUTOBIOGRAPHY JUMP

I've always argued for simplicity, but sometimes, particularly in book-length pieces, I break the guideline and create a deliberately complex structure.

Here's one tip. Don't structure a biography or family history chronologically. Write it thematically.

Here's what I mean. Most biographies/autobiographies begin "I was born in a circus dressing room to a mother who trained camels and a father who was a clown, then I grew up in Orlando with my cross-dressing Aunt Tilly who taught me to read tarot cards, then I got married to Zsa Zsa, then I became a police officer who infiltrated a drug gang, then ..."

Instead, write thematically. For example, a friend who is a world expert on nature conservation is working on his memoirs and is structuring his autobiography thematically:

* His first (and formative) job was working at the San Diego Zoo. He uses that experience to write about the role of zoos in nature conservation and regeneration of endangered species.

* He traveled to Nepal and for two years looked for the *yeti*. This experience opens several themes – the role of crypto-animals like the *yeti* in our life, the future of delicate mountain ecosystems, the pleasure (or not) of camping in blizzards while suffering altitude sickness.

* He somehow stays awake during mega-meetings at which the big conservation conventions are discussed. This soporific experience leads to a discussion of how and where the real work of conservation is done.

And so on.

I've been following Victorian-era naturalist Alfred Russel Wallace for some forty years and wrote *An Inordinate Fondness for Beetles*, which is based on "campfire conversations with Alfred." I played with various structures and found that a thematic structure worked best – one reviewer said I had "created a new genre of personal travel writing."

* A thematic structure is different to the way most "in the footsteps of" writers structure their books – the default structure is chronological and geographical. Instead I chose about twenty themes in which Wallace was interested and that he wrote about. They also happened to be subjects I explored during my decades of wandering around the territories that are now Malaysia, Singapore, and Indonesia. Wallace killed seventeen orangutans for their skins and

skeletons, but nursed a baby orangutan he had orphaned as if it was a human baby. This trigger incident led to a chapter about our relationship and fraternity with the other great apes – chimps, gorillas, and orangutans. Wallace wrote about the benefits of good colonialism and the evils of bad colonialism. With this trigger I devoted three chapters to colonialism-related themes, including positing the idea that brown-brown colonialism has replaced white-brown colonialism, and exploring the idea that racial arrogance supports environmental arrogance and why this dynamic is the key catalyst for tropical forest destruction. Wallace spent months alone, frustrated, and nearly broke. What kept him going? This idea encouraged me to write several chapters about why boys leave home, and how each person deals with loneliness in his own way.

* I also created imaginary conversations with Wallace, set on a real turtle-nesting beach in eastern Indonesia.

* And at the beginning of each chapter I set the historical context that related to the theme of that section.

* The book is filled with curious bits of information that I find relevant and intriguing, and hope that the reader will find equally seductive. For example, in the chapter on why there are so many beetles, I digress into a discussion of how having a new species named after you is one of the only certain ways to ensure immortality. I related how the early Dutch and Portuguese explorers came to give birds of paradise that designation. In the chapter on women's role in society (Wallace thought women should, and would, control society), I wandered into a discussion of Indonesian herbal medicine used by men to make them manlier (one concoction boasts it offers "a decided advantage over a number of similar preparations of quack reputation"). In the section on why boys collect stuff, I sidelined into the importance of Swedish botanist Carl Linnaeus, who famously thought of himself as the second Adam. "*Deus creavit, Linnaeus disposuit,*" he liked to say – God created, Linnaeus organized. The frontispiece of Linneaus's *Systema Naturae* depicts its author in the Garden of Eden, evidently applying binomial nomenclature to all the creatures of Creation.

Don't Ever Do This

DON'T CONFUSE A PLACE WITH A STORY

❧

You write to an editor: "I'm going to Rome. Rome is a terrific place. Would you like a story?"

Well, if the editor bothers to respond, she will certainly say: "Rome is indeed a terrific place. But you haven't told me a story."

So how about: "I'd like to do a story about how the movie industry has portrayed Rome, using my personal quest to visit locations used in the classic 1953 film Roman Holiday starring Audrey Hepburn and Gregory Peck as triggers. In doing so I will provide an unusual itinerary and helpful travel tips for visitors."

That's what Taras Grescoe did for his article "Roman Holiday."

After an overly languorous start describing the beauty of Rome, Grescoe admits:

> I'm ready to fall in love. You see, before coming to Rome, I made the pleasant mistake of watching Roman Holiday, that classic story of abandoning day-to-day responsibilities and unexpected infatuation …

He takes a couple of paragraphs to tell us a bit about the film and then:

> As a carefree jaunt through an enchanting place, Roman Holiday sets out a classic itinerary: From the Forum, where Peck first stumbles upon the groggy princess – still reeling from a sedative administered by her doctor, who wanted to make sure she'd have a good night's sleep before her day of appearances – to a café outside the Pantheon, where she has her first cigarette, to the banks of the Tiber, where they dance arm-in-arm, it's a whirlwind city tour by taxi, foot and scooter.

And then Grescoe invites us on that tour.

And, as an added bonus, he provides several service sidebars:

- The basics: Getting around, festivals, restaurants, hotels.

- Photowise: How the article's photographer approached his assignment.

- Shopwise: Shopping (a bit heavy on the fluffy fast-food adjectives, like "Rome's big flea market is an unforgettable extravaganza.").

- Media file: Links to some useful guidebooks and maps.

- Filmwise: Locations for key shots in the film Roman Holiday.

—Taras Grescoe. "Roman Holiday." National Geographic Traveler, July/August 2000.

THE PERSONAL TRAVEL ARTICLE

There are four types of travel articles, and you can put yourself in the middle of any of them.

1. **Quest**
2. **Profile**
3. **Event**
4. **Service**

These categories are not clear cut and there can be considerable overlap.

1. Quest

The best quests combine a pragmatic and measurable goal (let's say bicycling across Africa) with a spiritual search (proving your manhood after your wife left you for her yoga teacher.)

This is the kind of article that most people in my workshops want to write.

A few examples follow.

∞

Edward A. McCabe quit a high-flying advertising career to participate in the Paris/Dakar Rally with his girlfriend Carolyn. The big Nancy Reagan problems are that he was forty-eight, out of shape, spoke no French, had no factory support team like the other drivers, and had little experience with racing cars, rally driving, the Sahara Desert, or enduring the level of pain and frustration he was going to face. His story is a long personal quest that is both literate and exciting – the questions he poses reappear throughout: Will he finish the race? Will his relationship survive? What will he learn?

Some excerpts from his personal travel article:

> I spoke to an American who had run it twice and failed both times to finish. I asked him what I could do to train for it. He told me that running a marathon a week wouldn't be enough.

*

> I developed a list of objectives. They were pasted on the dash so we couldn't lose sight of their relative importance: (1) SURVIVE. (2) FINISH. (3) FINISH WELL. (4) BREAK EVEN.

*

> On these straight parts we go along in silence, too tired to talk. I'm closing on big trucks going 90 to 100. I get into their dust trails and can't see or breathe. I have to back off. Passing blind here is begging for early retirement. The track is lined with jagged rocks. Washboard is a word that can describe the road, but it can't begin to describe what the road is doing to us ... So intense are the bumps that the speedometer snaps loose from its mooring in the dashboard and adds to the surrounding racket. We can see screws from the car unscrewing themselves around us. The spare windshield breaks away from its mounting overhead and begins to bang against the roof, resounding like gunfire. The spare wheels have worked themselves loose and are bashing up and down on the wheel wells with such force that the metal begins to fracture.

*

> "Right a little. No, too much. Left! Okay. Hold it now. Hold it."

Hold it? My shoulders are numb from the shoulder harness cutting into them, my arms like lead from the vibrations. So far today I've been driving thirteen hours ...

And McCabe finishes his personal quest near where he starts, a circular structure:

I think it's about doing, about living. Even though I felt miserable much of the time, I felt more alive than I ever have before. With no time to ponder the meaning of anything, with only time to survive, you live.

—Edward A. McCabe. "Eight Thousand Miles of Bad Road." *Esquire*, July 1987.

The quest for food – sometimes exotic, sometimes pungent, always evocative – can be the trigger for a powerful quest story.

A personal travel quest doesn't have to be life-threatening or earth-shattering. Monique Filsnoël used a cooking lesson in Bali to reflect on the lessons relating food and life taught to her by her French grandmother. And she used a sidebar – you can guess what it was: Ibu Rai's curry recipe – to give her personal essay another layer and increase its salability.

"Did you enjoy riding on my husband's chariot?" Ibu Rai asked me as I slowly extricated myself from her husband Jika's 125 cc Honda.

The ride had been stiff, but mind-expanding. Ibu Rai and Jika lived in an isolated family compound set amidst emerald green paddy fields. We had dodged traffic leaving my guesthouse, but then the countryside became impossibly beautiful, and we passed surging rivers and disciplined groups of ducks marching along the roadside in the hills above Ubud. It was still early in the morning, and although my back was aching I felt the life reemerge in my cramped legs just as Bali's damp earth seemed to revive after the previous night's rain.

"Ready to learn how to make *real* curry?" Ibu Rai joked as she led me through the gates of the rambling house.

Filsnoël then explains how she came to meet her curry-mentor.

I was on vacation in Bali and had met Ibu Rai (Ibu, meaning "mother", is a common honorific used in Indonesia when speaking to an adult woman) and her husband Jika several days earlier at a friend's dinner party. I had been invited to sit beside a slender middle-aged woman wearing a pink-laced Balinese blouse. Speaking excellent English, she explained that she managed a restaurant in the tourist village of Ubud.

"You're French," she said calmly. "I can cook Italian and French cuisine, but I'm rusty. Maybe you can give me some new recipes."

"I'd rather you taught me to cook Balinese food."

"You like our food?"

"I love it, but curry remains a mystery."

"Why don't you come on Sunday, to my house? We'll cook together."

Filsnoël then introduces her grandmother and the impact *Indochine* (and curry) had on her French family.

I was six or seven when I had my first close encounter with curry. On a snowy, gray Sunday my parents and I drove across Chambéry, the small French city where I grew up, for dinner at my grandmother's.

My father carried me on his shoulders, and before we reached her front door we could smell that she was serving something strange, something outside my young frame of reference. This wasn't going to be the usual Sunday roast beef with chocolate cake.

"What do you suppose your grandma is cooking?" my father teased me as he rang the bell of her apartment.

I sneaked into the kitchen. I could just peer over the edge of the old wooden table. I watched Mémée put the finishing touches on her strange magic. The warm and peculiar combination of perfumes tickled my nose while my grandmother gave a last touch before serving her mysterious creation. She saw how curious I was and soberly explained the event with words that added even more mystery: *"C'est une vieille recette de mes amis qui vivent en Indochine."*

Filsnoël then ping-pongs between the wise coaching of Ibu Rai and curry-inspired memories of her childhood. Note the Nancy Reagan-inspired tension when she contrasts the unusual Balinese household with the French household with which she was more familiar, accented with liberal use of questions. First, back to Bali.

Unlike Mémée's light yellow kitchen, Ibu Rai's workplace was dark, the walls blackened by the wood fire that for years served as her only stove. The wood fire had been replaced by a gas cooker, but she hadn't bothered to wash and paint the walls. Maybe she felt the soot-look added to her culinary magic. Like Mémée's kitchen, Ibu Rai had a large window, but instead of looking out on the urban street, Ibu Rai's window gave her a view of the other pavilions in the compound, with the family temple far on the left side.

"All from my mother-in-law", Ibu Rai explained as I examined her utensils. Her cooking equipment was simple: a wooden board, a sharp and sturdy knife, a black stone mortar, a pestle, a frying pan and a red plastic bucket. Aside from a tall, white refrigerator all her tools were basic, all appeared worn out. How can she cook with these? I wondered.

Early that morning, well before I arrived, Ibu Rai had peeled and washed a variety of spices that were now drying on a bamboo tray. Inscrutable shapes and colors, displayed by an artist painting an exotic still life that was far removed from the French *nature morte* of apples, pears and grapes. My nose and eyes betrayed me. This looks like garlic, but it smells different. I finger roots and twigs. They all smell wonderful, but none smells like anything in my memory.

Not for the last time, Ibu Rai came to my rescue. "These sprigs are lemongrass, these leaves are basil, and these are the candlenuts and the peppercorns."

With her finger she fumbled into the tangled herbs and spices and extracted a beige-colored rhizome."This one is ginger, and the orange one is turmeric. Essential for the curry."

I picked up the turmeric and smelled its earthy tang, incredulous about how something that smelled like mildewed soil could make a curry palatable.

And then back to France.

"*Indochine, Indochine,*" I kept repeating. Indochina was a faraway land for a small girl. Indochina was also René, a tall and solidly built friend of my father's who intrigued and frightened me. René had two fingers missing from his left hand: "*Il a fait l'Indochine*" the grownups would whisper behind his back. This expression said everything. It conveyed respect and admiration for the Frenchmen who lived and fought there; it conveyed nostalgia of a colonial period that had run its course; it conveyed curiosity and fear and confusion about a distant and exotic land where people weren't the same as us.

And back to Bali. She introduces a modest ticking clock. And a very subtle element – throughout the story food is seen as comforting. In this section Ibu Rai "comforts" Filsnoël that it's okay to use an electric blender. A few paragraphs later Filsnoël's grandmother "comforts" her about a more serious matter - the death of the writer's father.

We had so much to do, but no time. Jika was returning in an hour, with Paul, my boyfriend. It would take a miracle to get everything ready for the lunch we promised them.

Ibu Rai placed several cloves of garlic on the mortar, along with small red and green chilies and slices of turmeric. She took the pestle, and twisting her wrist, crushed the spices. After four strong circular movements she reduced the multi-colored spices into a pungent yellow paste.

"Do you want to try?" she asked, handling me the pestle. It wasn't a request, but an order. Somehow I sensed that the alchemy of curry involved this physical work, this ability to help a few spices, innocuous and uninteresting by themselves, become part of something greater.

Can't be that hard. Just hold the pestle tight and twist your wrist, I murmured to myself. This was a serious matter. A Sunday morning to learn all the secrets; mixing and grinding the spices was one of them. I felt like an alchemist over the cauldron, impatient to witness the bubbling brew turn into gold.

After two circular movements my wrist was burning and the spices were barely dented.

"You can use an electric blender at home," Ibu Rai comforted me.

And back to France.

I was the only child at the dining room table and was treated like a queen. Mémée perched me on a soft feathered pillow placed on my chair. My sister was just a baby and my two brothers were still in the dreams of my parents. "Something special, *pour ma grande,*" Mémée said as she served me my first *poule au cari.*

And it's raining in Bali, with ancient truths.

Outside, the sky darkened. Long threads of rain thundered on the corrugated iron roof. In a corner, next to the refrigerator, a scruffy black dog ignored the thunder and slept curled on several layers of old newspapers. Bent over the kitchen counter, cutting, chopping, tasting, blending, Ibu Rai was like a *dalang*, the puppet master of the *wayang kulit*, the Indonesian shadow play. Just as a *dalang* takes inanimate leather puppets and gives them voices and personalities, Ibu Rai, her face lit by the gas fire and the occasional burst of lightning, was creating her own world, a world of perfumes and flavors and hospitality. The *dalang* creates a world designed to keep people amused, to teach them the ancient truths, to help them understand that they are part of something bigger than their daily existence. Ibu Rai's world was far less ambitious, but equally fascinating, and maybe just as important. She was creating a world for the senses and the heart. The rain was so loud that conversation was impossible. Absorbed in her art, Ibu Rai had forgotten my presence.

The tears flow in the now-outdated French kitchen, with some more words to remember.

Many years later my sister and I sought comfort around Mémée's wide round table. It seems that little had changed. Her kitchen appliances, once so modern, appeared dated and old fashioned. But of course everything had changed. We were adults, and my grandmother had lost height, and we two girls now stood a head taller than her. It was the day my father died, and we gathered here in our place of refuge, lost in time, lost in space. Mémée made us tea in her old black teapot. A tiny piece of the pot's nozzle was broken and the tea dripped in round brown spots on the tablecloth as she poured it. I sat with my elbows on the table, holding the cup with two hands. I stared at the amber swaying liquid. The steam was warm to my nose and my cheeks. Lost in the circling movement I heard Mémée's voice, as if coming from far, far away. "Girls, as long as you don't forget your father, he is not dead."

More tears blend in my tea. Now I can see she was probably right, death is when you forget. But at that time this thought did not bring me much comfort.

Filsnoël ends with a circular structure, finishing near where she started. Like the best circular structures, the physical setting at the end might be the same as at the beginning, but the dynamics have shifted – you can't swim in the same river twice.

The rain didn't last long, and a beam of sun enlightened Ibu Rai's kitchen. A bird, perched on the branch of the frangipani, sang, the backyard reappeared from the mist. The scruffy black dog stretched his paws and yawned before running off to the garden to terrorize the chickens. A large pot of chicken curry was simmering on the fire.

"A spoon of curry for you." Ibu Rai offered me a wooden spoon holding a yellow elixir and put it to my mouth, her hand curved underneath as if she was feeding her grandchild. I closed my eyes and surrendered to the biting flavor that was pacified by the balm of the coconut milk.

"This is delicious," I said. "But it doesn't taste like Grandma's curry from Indochina."

"Well, you are in Indonesia," Ibu Rai said, laughing. She began to display the food on celadon plates and trays: delicate satays, Balinese roasted pork, chicken curry, fish steamed in banana leaves, a bowl of fragrant rice grown in the family fields. My father would have enjoyed this moment; a meal of colors and perfumes, a meal to discover new tastes and to enrich the vocabulary of the senses.

Ibu Rai drew a bunch of hairy red fruits out of the refrigerator. "The rambutans will look nice on your pictures," she said arranging the fruits around the colorful dishes.

We carried the food to the terrace. Ibu Rai disappeared. A few minutes later she returned wearing a black and dark green sarong and a freshly ironed white shirt. She picked up a yellow frangipani flower and placed it in her black chignon.

We heard Jika's bike stop at the gate. The sun was now high and shining. Ibu Rai was silent, her gaze far away, above the walls of the compound.

—Monique Filsnoël. "Unraveling the Alchemy of Curry." Participant in my writing workshop.

❧

I went in search of the Burmese backwater town where Eric Blair (writing as George Orwell) wrote his novel *Burmese Days*. Here's the questing lead:

There are worse travel strategies than to visit places with evocative names.

There's Timbuktu, Congo and Okavango in Africa; and Salvador de Bahia, Darien and Patagonia in Latin America, names which purr with history and allure.

But Asia's resonant place names beckon to me above all others. There's Sumatra, Java and Borneo; Malacca, Vientiane, and Makassar; Kelantan, Kathmandu and Ayudhya. Not to mention the rivers: Ganges and Yangtze, Mahakam and Mekong. And the one I was headed towards: Ayeyarwaddy.

My destination was Katha, a small town on the Ayeyarwaddy (Irrawaddy). It was here, between 1926 and 1927, that a British policeman named Eric Blair spent six months as one of 90 British police officers in Burma. Eric Blair, who subsequently took the pen name George Orwell, based his 1934 novel *Burmese Days* on a fictionalized version of Katha.

—Paul Spencer Sochaczewski. "Orwell's Days." *Wall Street Journal.* August 3, 2007.
Reprinted in *Curious Encounters of the Human Kind – Myanmar.* Geneva:
Explorer's Eye Press, 2015.

❧

Jane Perlez used the writing of George Orwell to conduct a culinary quest.

George Orwell, who memorably sketched the stark existence of living on bread and thin soup in Paris in the 1930s, hardly seems like an obvious guide to exotic food in the tropics. Yet, in his classic novel *Burmese Days*, Orwell creates a vibrant scene of his hero and heroine wandering through market stalls filled with ripe pomelos the size of green moons, red bananas, dried fish, crimson chilies, ducks cured like hams, larvae of the rhinoceros beetle, heart-shaped betel leaves, and "baskets of heliotrope-colored prawns the size of lobsters."

The reality is that Perlez is forcing the issue – Orwell didn't write much about Burmese food and when he did he denigrated it, writing: "Almost the worst thing in Burma, the filthy, monstrous food." But nevertheless it's a useful device for what Perlez wants to achieve and we are hooked; she writes authoritatively and we will digest her experiences as if they had been stewed in an Orwellian broth.

As soon as we arrived, tired and dusty, for a late 4.30 lunch, Ma Aye Shwe asked one of her nieces – three of them work as her helpers – to catch a foot-long catfish from the pond just outside the kitchen window This was done rapidly by grabbing one of the fish by hand, giving it a wallop to kill it and then gutting it and chopping it up into about one-inch pieces. The niece sprinkled some salt on top of the pieces, some pieces of ginger as well, and threw the pieces into a pan of super hot fat ... In a second wok, the chef stir-fried some garlic, ginger and sliced tomatoes, added some water, added pieces of the fish, a huge bunch of basil leaves, and then covered it all for some 15 minutes, fanning the flames with rapid flicks of a reed fan ...

—Jane Perlez. "A Culinary Odyssey, on a Path Blazed by Orwell."
The New York Times, March 11, 2007.

A writer goes on a quest to Bangladesh in search of Big Weather.

It was not suntan weather when I arrived in Cox's Bazar, a town in the southeastern corner of Bangladesh, with a sodden strip of slum-lined beach pounded by the rust-colored surf of the Bay of Bengal. A driving rain fell hour after hour, day after day. The skin on the hands of the marketplace vendor who sold me his last coconut was shriveled from the moisture. Cox's Bazar had a defeated, used-up air. The people milling through the streets didn't bother with rain gear. There was no use.

—Mark Levine. "A Storm at the Bone." *Outside*, November 1998.

Patrick Kuh's quest is to understand the new Russia by visiting its leading restaurants. We get a glimpse into how peculiarities of late twentieth-century Russia through questions like: "How much do you tip the man with the machine gun?"

He drops me off in front of the Ukraina [Hotel]. As I go into the lobby, three men in ill-fitting suits eye me but let me pass. I take a right and go into the restaurant. The tall windows let in the weak light. The place is empty. Walking down the runner between the tables toward two watchful waiters and a cashier is like going to an interrogation. I make the symbol for food. "Nyet," they say. Anywhere in the hotel? They shrug. There must be something to eat in a hotel this size at two in the afternoon ...

The sixth floor proves even more deserted than the lobby ... I'm back at the window by the elevators. The Russian Parliament is directly across the river from here. The tanks that shelled it during the last nationalist coup attempt were positioned on the bridge below me. The river is gray, and Moscow never looked bleaker.

Suddenly, I hear music coming from some corridor, and I follow its trail. Finally, I see the Cyrillic sign РЕСТОРАН outside a door. This is the word that has brought me to this country. Now I know something about it. There are restaurants where people feed live mice to crocodiles. Restaurants where the waiters all had KGB military ranks. Places where nine tables make $17,000 a night. Places that use the Soviet flag to advertise. Mexican, Cuban, Chinese, Italian, and French. Fast food where you hear the soundtrack to *Pulp Fiction*. Slow food where you hear balalaikas. And restaurants like this sixth-floor apparition, where there are a few bottles of orange soda on the counter, a maid sitting down to a bowl of soup, and a couple of swarthy men sitting against the wall. There are restaurants where, even if you're hungry, you say it's not worth it.

—Patrick Kuh. "Comrade, Your Table Is Ready." *Esquire*, March 1997.

Tim Cahill starts with a classic quest device – a friend showed him a newspaper clipping that jump-starts his wanderlust.

The lead sentence in the London *Sunday Express* said that high in the mountains of Turkey "could lie a secret which will stun scientists, the return from the dead of a lost species." The article quoted Dr. Guven Eken of the Society for the Protection of Nature: "The Caspian tiger is considered to be extinct, but in southeast Turkey local hunters claim to have seen tigers in the mountains."

—Tim Cahil. "Anybody Seen a Tiger Around Here?" *Men's Journal*, June 2001.

2. Profile

Throughout the book I've been encouraging you to write about you. But sometimes the best way to write about yourself is to focus on another person.

Most profiles take place in the home territory of the subject, and a good profile is usually also a travel story.

 Pro Tip

Learn from Historical Films

Were you bored during history class in school? Too many battles and treaties to learn? But when the same events are put in dramatic form, focusing on one or two individuals, as they are in films, we have a human face to visualize, and the characters' stories make the history come alive.

It's the same with a personal travel story written as profile – you might have had a good safari in Botswana (all those photogenic animals, the lovely sunsets, the delicious food), but the more memorable focus might be a profile on your guide's ten-year-old daughter Josephine, who befriended your nine-year-old daughter Gail.

Here's my story about meeting Elmer, the emperor of China. Is this a personal essay or a profile? Perhaps a bit of both. Regardless, the story fell into my lap when I happened to meet Elmer, an accidental gift from the writing gods.

The lead is a provocative statement. Or is it dialogue? Or an anecdote?

> I had naively thought that China's 2,000-year-old imperial system ended when 12-year-old Aisin-Gioro Pu Yi, the last emperor, was overthrown in 1912.
>
> "Not so," declares Elmer. "*I'm* the last emperor."
>
> I meet the man I'll call Elmer, for reasons that will become clear, by chance. He stands next to me in front of the visitors' board at the East-West Center in Honolulu. "There are some Chinese visiting," he observes *sotto vocce*, as if he is speaking in Spy vs Spy code.
>
> We begin to talk. Elmer is suspicious at first. He is Chinese and royal. I am Anglo and common.
>
> Elmer is obviously an emperor of the people. Plain grey T-shirt. Dirty jeans. Flip-flops. Black hair, speckled grey, pulled into a ponytail. His briefcase is a folded piece of cardboard, from which he extracts a complicated genealogy, which links him directly and definitively, he explains, to the 17th-century Chou dynasty as well as to Chou En-lai, Sun Yat-sen and Chiang Kai-shek.

The narrative continues, posing the basic question – what if he's right?

> But what about Pu Yi I ask, the last emperor whose life was featured in Bertolucci's film.
>
> "Pu Yi was Ching dynasty. Manchurians. Invaders. My family are *real* Chinese," Emperor Elmer says.
>
> His genealogy, printed on the back of his CV, tells a contorted tale of usurped emperors and invaders, and of exiled royalty who emigrated to Hawaii. Shaky about Chinese family trees, I ask around and find that Elmer has been a bit, er, creative, with his historical narrative. One scholar thought that the emperor "learned his history from a fortune cookie."
>
> But hey, call me a dreamer. What if ... I invite Elmer for lunch, figuring that, just in case he is who he says he is, it couldn't hurt to be pals with the Big Guy.

Back to dialogue. And yes, I realize the food choices are ridiculously stereotypical, but they're true. Honest.

Elmer orders chop suey from the University of Hawaii's cafeteria. I have a hamburger.

Elmer isn't too clear about his strategy for gaining the throne. He wants to visit China, for the first time, to see his people. "Can you find funding for me?" he asks. He wants to bring western ideas to the Middle Kingdom, particularly the religion of the Jehovah's Witnesses. "Chinese are Semites," he explains obliquely. "Direct descendants of Noah."

I suggest it might be useful for American-born Elmer to learn a few phrases of Mandarin. "Uh?", the emperor-to-be grunts, which is the way he acknowledges new, seemingly apparent ideas, as in "This is how you network." "Uh?"

He bridles at the suggestion that he might also brush up a bit on Chinese politics and customs. He gets edgy. I've overstepped his royal space.

I ask him, respectfully, I hope, what qualifications he has to lead 1.2 billion people.

Elmer waves the genealogy. He went to college for four years but left before getting a degree, muttering "It was a fake sexual harassment case." He adds: "I'm stable, level headed. Have good common sense. I hope it's tough for someone to take advantage of me."

He doesn't think that China is ready for a democratic movement. What about the current generation of Chinese leaders? "They're doing the best they can."

"President [George H.W.] Bush had about the right kind of China policy," Elmer adds. But he's down on Henry Kissinger. Elmer points out that he once handed a letter to Kissinger, who was visiting Honolulu, asking for support. To Elmer's surprise, Kissinger spent all his time in Hawaii without seeking the emperor's counsel about how Sino-American relations would improve once Elmer took over the throne. So much for Kissinger's renowned geopolitical acumen.

An info enhancement:

Obviously chutzpah is a useful quality in a wannabe emperor. While speaking with Elmer I was reminded of Joshua Abraham Norton, a 19th-century English Jew who sold supplies to San Francisco gold rushers and then declared himself Emperor of America.

In 1859 Norton walked into the offices of the San Francisco *Bulletin* and presented them with this single sentence, which they ran on the next edition's front page:

"At the preemptory request of a large majority of the citizens of these United States, I, Joshua Norton ... declare and proclaim myself Emperor of these U.S., and in virtue of the authority thereby in me vested to hereby order and direct the representatives of the different States of the Union to assemble in Musical Hall of this city, on the 1st day of February next, then and there to make such alterations in the existing laws of the Union as may ameliorate the evils under which the country is laboring, and thereby cause confidence to exist, both at home and abroad, in our stability and integrity."

It was signed "Norton I. Emperor of the United States."

Like Elmer, Norton I had a common touch: he abjured seclusion and luxury, attending every public function by foot or bicycle. If he noticed someone performing some kind act he might spontaneously ennoble them, from which practice the expression "Queen for a day" was obtained.

In return for his noble generosity restaurants offered the emperor free dinners, he was given three seats at every theatrical performance (one for himself and one each for his famously well-behaved dogs, Bummer and Lazarus). The city itself paid for his uniforms, Bay Area newspapers published his proclamations and he had his own currency printed, which was accepted widely. He had a habit of levying taxes by walking into the offices of an old business friend and announcing an imperial assessment of ten million dollars or so, but could quickly be talked down to a cigar and small change. When he was arrested by an overzealous policeman "to be confined for treatment of a mental disorder" virtually every newspaper published editorials denouncing the action and Norton was released with a lengthy public apology from the chief of police.

Norton sent frequent cables to fellow rulers offering surprisingly well-informed advice. King Kamehameha of Hawaii (then the Sandwich Islands) was so taken with the Emperor's insight and understanding that towards the end of his life Kamehameha refused to recognize the U.S. State Department, saying he would deal only with representatives of Norton's empire.

When Norton I died in 1890 ten thousand people lined up to view his mortal remains; his funeral cortege was three kilometers long. At 2.39 pm, during his funeral, San Francisco experienced a total eclipse of the sun.

The article ends by closing the circle, resonating with the lead:

Elmer could use some heavenly miracles since his claim to the throne is in danger of disintegrating unless he gets some support.

Elmer explains that he has high-placed relatives in the Hawaiian political and social world. "But they won't help me," he says. "They're jealous. Afraid of my power. And the CIA wants to assassinate me." I agree not to use his real name.

We meet a couple of other times but since Elmer has no phone and no fixed domicile it is difficult to set up appointments.

Although we lose contact, I read about China's political travails with renewed interest. Could it happen? I can't recall a communist state deciding to re-establish a monarchy. But in Geneva, King Michael of Romania is talking comeback. It works in sports, and it works in politics. Emperor Elmer. He's tanned, rested and ready. Emperor Elmer. I like the sound.

—Paul Spencer Sochaczewski. "China's Emperor is Tanned, Rested and Ready." *Wall Street Journal*. December 13–15, 2002. Reprinted in *The Sultan and the Mermaid Queen*. Singapore: Editions Didier Millet, 2008.

Here's a personal essay with a provocative statement lead, in which the main profile character is a tree, with a circular structure and a touch of Gallic elegance at the end.

Yesterday, on my way to the office, I stopped to kiss a tree.

It was midafternoon, in the heart of the city, but if any of the passersby with whom I shared that singular moment took note of my act, not a one made the fact known to me.

Perhaps, to them, the tree and I were not separate from the ordinary gray texture of the day. Or perhaps, like me when late one night some months earlier I had come upon a man kissing that tree, they were not surprised because they knew that Paris does that to people: They take the city to heart and lose their heads.

My own stupor was nonetheless grand when several weeks after the first sighting I again witnessed such a scene. This time, as I passed in a cab on a rain-soaked and chilly night, a man and a woman reached around opposite sides of the trunk, their arms stretching to embrace not one another, but the tree rising elegantly between.

Quickly, I turned from the window to the rearview mirror, hoping to see reflected there a look of complicity on the cabbie's face. If he had seen what I had seen, he gave no sign of it. His eyes, reliably, were on the road; mine, predictably, shot back to the lovers. Although neither they nor the tree had moved, the instant had, leaving me with a sense of wonder.

Note the power of the question Amy Hollowell asks. In fact, the entire personal essay is full of questions that drive her quest to understand why the tree is special and why it made such an impact on her.

My interest had been irreversibly piqued: What was it with this tree?

Someone had told me once that it was the city's only remaining elm, the others having been ravaged by the disease that had devastated the species. Maybe elms once covered Paris; now, however, the wide boulevards sweep grandly under the arching limbs of chestnut and plane trees.

Yet here was this elm. I took to watching it, and my questions pressed: Why was it there, encircled gracefully by a thin chain and stout pillars, on a little island of its own on the place St. Gervais, in the Marais, near the Seine? Why did people kiss it? Why did I care?

My first consultants, as usual, were books – travel and guide books, history and botany books, encyclopedia and almanacs. What I found was knowledge thick and exhaustive, but no answers.

So I asked around. Anyone who would listen got an earful, but no one could offer as much in return. The rest of the story remained a mystery.

I took my quest to city hall. Surely within the grandiose Hôtel de Ville, that behemoth of French democracy, there was someone who knew the story of the lone elm.

Armed with nothing but a desire to know, I picked up the phone. After the customary holding pattern, I was informed that an answer could be provided a week from Thursday. My sense of urgency apparently was not shared.

Next, I tried the municipal park authority, where I was routed to a woman named Noëlle. I'm not sure what was more astounding: that she knew of the tree or that, after checking some details, she called me back within the hour, as promised.

What she had to say, however, was not astounding: This was not the last remaining elm in Paris, nor was it the oldest. That honor belonged to a tree in the Parc Montsouris. But my elm, as she called it, was the oldest of the elms planted by landscape designers in the late 19th century.

Noëlle could not explain the chain around the tree, nor was she aware of the kissing phenomenon. She knew only the facts, which, of course, were not at all what I wanted.

What, then, did I want? It was only months later, after the elm's flush of summer green had turned gold and then fallen, after winter had settled in, that I knew. But the answer was not in my head.

She creates music – "It was just a tree."

I found it yesterday on my way to work. As I rounded the corner of the church on the square, the elm came into view. It was just a tree. I stepped over the chain and touched the ridged bark. It was just a tree.

Then as I leaned forward and kissed the elm, I knew that the answer was in the act. It was just a tree, and, as with the city, I took it to heart and lost my head.

—Amy Hollowell. "A Kiss for an Old Elm and Its Durable City."
International Herald Tribune, January 19, 1995.

∾

Linda Spalding wrote a profile about orangutan researcher Birutė Galdikas. It's a classic quest, in this case Spalding's quest to meet and understand Galdikas and in the process learn a bit about our own place in the ape-human continuum. (Annoyingly, Spalding refers to the Indonesian capital as Djakarta; the city's name was changed to Jakarta in

1972, twenty-six years before Spalding published her article. And she refers to Galdikas's second husband as Pak Bohap, unaware that Pak is an honorific similar to Mister and that the man's correct name is Bohap bin Jalan.)

Spalding sets out her goals early, and by doing so we start to learn a lot about Galdikas, and in passing we learn bit about the author:

> Galdikas had written in *Reflections of Eden* that "every trip into the field is also a journey into yourself."
> By following Galdikas, then, perhaps I could accomplish both journeys. Even if she is inscrutable, I thought, Galdikas might lead me to an understanding of how we Homo sapiens must look, in our exile, to the many eyes watching from the trees.
> —Linda Spalding. "The Jungle Took Her." *Outside*, May 1998.

Spalding goes to Galdikas's research center and discovers an unsettling scene, not quite a *Heart of Darkness* scenario but one certainly resembling a "Heart of Dim Light" situation. Spalding herself is ever-present, but she is not the focus of the story; Birutė Galdikas is.

∞

In a similar vein, but in a different voice, David Quammen wrote a profile of primatologist Russel Mittermeier. (In Quammen's piece, which ran about the same time as Spalding's, the editors of *Outside* repeat their mistake by annoyingly and incorrectly referring to the Indonesian capital as Djakarta.)

Quammen starts by asking a straightforward biographical question:

> "What makes a boy from the Bronx decide to be a jungle explorer?"

And then Quammen asks a more philosophical question:

> For Russel Mittermeier, "to see" is both a syntactical construct and a way of life, a means of exploring and keeping score on nature. Which raises a question: Where do ego and personal acquisitiveness belong when you're trying to save the world?
> —David Quammen. "And Lemurs Enough for Everybody." *Outside*, April 1998.

By the nature of the questions Quammen asks, we get a sense of him as well as his subject, as in the opening scene in which Quammen learns Mittermeier considers a kayak trip off the coast of Madagascar to be a race, a mano-a-mano test of will. The focus is on Mittermeier, as seen through Quammen's filter; we learn about both men.

Pro Tip

Prepare for Your Interview

> According to John M. Wilson, writing in Writer's Digest, "You can't 'plan' an interview – each conversation will be different, unpredictable and, if you're lucky, full of wonderful surprises. But you must prepare. Going into an interview cold is a shortcut to catastrophe ... The more you know, the more options you have in shaping and controlling the interview."

Sometimes I go on a trip and a profile subject will simply appear. This happened when I visited Komodo in eastern Indonesia. I was on a diving trip to explore Komodo National Park's spectacular coral reefs. In between dives I trekked in the savannah to see wild Komodo dragons, the world's largest, and arguably the most endangered, lizards. I was satisfied and well fed. I generally don't like souvenir shopping or tourist sites, but I had a few hours to kill in Komodo village one afternoon and saw in my guidebook that this was the home of a well-known carver. I passed half a dozen carving workshops, all producing similar-looking wooden Komodo dragons, before finding the house of the somewhat-famous artisan, a bit more substantial than those of his neighbors. I met Ishaka Mansur; his job, which he does very well, is carving wooden Komodo dragons.

If I had simply admired his lifelike hardwood reptiles, I might have wound up with a flat paragraph or two suitable for a travel guide. But I took the time to introduce myself, sit in his home, give his kids a quick English lesson, and learn more about the guy. I found out how much he earns and how he became famous. And most important, I got the story of his relationship with the Dragon Princess. Ishaka Mansur, like many people who enjoy telling stories, is frustratingly vague about details, time frames, and logical sequence. I had to ask him a dozen times to clarify one or another of his statements. As a result of my questioning, which eventually tried his patience, my final story made a bit more sense than it had on first hearing. There are huge gaps in logic, to be sure, but that's partly the nature of this particular type of tale. It's also indicative of the way his mind works, which is less concerned than mine about logic and story structure. Here's the profile that resulted.

It never hurts a wannabe businessman to have the support of the Dragon Princess.

Aside from several high-powered local businessmen who allegedly made their fortunes selling rare and illegally obtained reef fish and shark fins to Chinese middlemen, Ishaka Mansur is far and away the most prominent businessman in Komodo National Park.

Ishaka, 54, carves wooden sculptures of Komodo dragons, the world's largest lizard, which is only found in this area some 500 kilometers east of Bali.

I found his house easily – after all, his name is in the tourist guidebooks and Komodo village is a tiny place. He has enough business to sustain a workshop of some ten carvers, who whittle under his tutelage, much like the assembly-line studios of the great Renaissance painters. His statues sell for US$15 for a dragon not much bigger than my hand, up to more than US$250 for a full-size two-meter replica of a dragon, seemingly ready to pounce on an innocent deer, that would be an imposing decoration in most any home. That's good money in a region where poor fishermen are lucky to simply break into the cash economy.

And Ishaka owes it all to a special woman.

Like many romantic mysteries, the tale began on a tropical beach at night.

"It was in November, 1982, at the beginning of the rainy season," Ishaka remembers. "I was alone, and suddenly saw a beautiful woman come down from the mountains behind the village."

Ishaka's wife sits nearby and listens, with no obvious reaction. Undoubtedly, she's heard it before.

We sip cloyingly sweet coffee.

"This beautiful woman – much prettier than any movie star, suddenly said, 'Marry me,'" Ishaka said. "But I told her 'I have a wife.'"

"She isn't as strong as me," the beautiful stranger replied.

Suddenly, Ishaka says, his pressure lamp went out. The beach became dark. He heard a voice. "I'm original Komodo," the strange woman said, switching from the national language of Bahasa Indonesia into an archaic form of the local dialect.

According to Ishaka, she urged him to go with her to her home in the mountains, but he refused, not wanting to worry his family by not returning to the village.

Ishaka tells the story with relish, happy to have a captive audience. He is a slender man with a modest moustache, wearing tan shorts and a blue football shirt from the Bayern Munich team. I can't imagine him as an object of affection for any princess, Dragon or otherwise, but then I've never been privy to the sensual desires of female royalty.

Ishaka explains that he and the Dragon Princess made a date for the following night. She instructed Ishaka to come alone, and follow the river to the top of the mountain. She gave him an egg-shaped gray rock to show him the way.

"When I returned home that first night my wife was angry," Ishaka says. "She didn't believe my story. Then I took off my shirt and had *naga*, dragon, markings all over my neck and chest."

Ishaka explains this while sitting in his village home, more luxurious than most in this hamlet. His sitting room is decorated with a few antique Dutch plates, Muslim prayers in cheap plastic frames sit on side tables, and on the wall he has nailed photos and newspaper clips showing him with the American ambassador, taken during a cultural exhibition in the distant Indonesian capital of Jakarta. A small crowd has shuffled into his home to gawk at me, some perhaps hoping that later on they could sell me some of the off-white, oddly shaped pearls that Komodo fishermen collect. Outside, under a shade tree, Ishaka's carvers chatter softly while a radio plays Indonesian pop music. Their chisels and mallets produce a soft tympanic rhythm as they turn logs into souvenirs.

Ishaka explains that when he reached the summit a large stone suddenly turned into a palace. Then the woman appeared. "She told me to call her Ratu Puteri. Princess," Ishaka says. "She wore a fine silk sari, like an Indian, but she was a Komodo woman."

"It was strange and scary and I pleaded with her not to kill me," Ishaka recalls.

Instead, the Dragon Princess caused a door to open and Ishaka was ushered into a huge room with a table laden with all sorts of delicacies. "We sat on cushions on the floor while we ate. She explained that if I had a problem I should make an offering and she would appear to me as a Naga," he explained, referring to the Hindu dragon spirit based on the king cobra. "She said that if anyone in the village killed a dragon they would become crazy."

Then came the vocational advice.

"You must leave your job and start carving dragons," she instructed him.

And the rest, as they say, is history.

I examine his carvings. His statues are even sold in the United States through the assistance of The Nature Conservancy, which tries to develop income-generating activities in Komodo as a means to promote nature conservation.

I compliment him on the fluid nature of his sculptures, which are quite sophisticated compared to the clunky efforts of other Komodo carvers.

"All my wooden dragons are alive," Ishaka explains. "They have the Dragon Princess's essence."

—Paul Spencer Sochaczewski. "Want a Business Boost? Make Friends with the Dragon Princess." *The Sultan and the Mermaid Queen*. Singapore: Editions Didier Millet, 2008.

Rebecca Mead doesn't put herself in this profile, but I include it here because she does everything right – she trusts her elegant voice, writes in scenes, has a strong main character, uses telling details and dialogue, and incorporates plenty of Nancy Reagans.

Dressed in black, and carrying a frayed silver Kevlar and canvas shoulder bag, Anthony Roth Costanzo made his entrance at P.S. 37, in the Bronx, early one Monday morning just as first period was ending. "Getting kids engaged in what's emotional about opera – that's what I'm interested in," Costanzo said as he ascended to the second-floor auditorium entrance. Costanzo, who is thirty-one, is slight of build and vivacious of manner. He visits public schools as often as he can, as part of the Metropolitan Opera's education-outreach program. As a countertenor – he is appearing in "Die Fledermaus," at the Metropolitan Opera, in the role of Prince Orlofsky – he has what he calls "this built-in novelty factor."

Twenty-five fifth graders trooped in and seated themselves on benches on-stage. The school serves the Kingsbridge neighborhood, where seventy-eight percent of the students qualify for free lunch. "How many of you have heard of the Metropolitan Opera? Constanzo asked. Five or six wary hands went up. "How many of you have been to the Met?" Not a hand.

"I'm here to talk about singing," Costanzo continued. "When do you sing? Do you sing 'Happy Birthday' at birthday parties? Do you sing in the shower?"

"I sing Bruno Mars in the shower," one boy offered.

"Bruno Mars in the shower!" Costanzo said, with warm affirmation ...

[Costanzo] discovered his gift at an early age. "We had to play basketball, and I was really short, as well as really bad," he explained. "I would run up and down next to the ball, and, as I ran, I would sing really high and really loud. Do any of you have a really high voice, or a really loud voice?"

"My voice goes high when I'm lying," a boy said.

"That is so interesting!" Costanzo said. "Because my whole life is trying to make my voice sound more honest."

Costanzo asked the children to guess what his voice would sound like. "Really loud, and really high?" one of them offered. They had no idea. Costanzo launched into "Summertime," and, at his first note, several students reeled back physically. A few bars in, half the class looked utterly aghast. One girl scrunched up her face, as if she had something sour in her mouth. But, when the song ended, smiles and applause broke out all around.

"I got scared!" one boy said ...

Costanzo explained the difference between singing with chest voice, like a typical male baritone – the children placed their hands on their chests, and bellowed – and singing with head voice, like his, for which they put hands upon cheeks and sang out; they looked like a small army of Macaulay Culkins. Costanzo explained that the opera house has nearly four thousand seats, but that singers do not use artificial amplification. The students looked amazed. "So you have to use *yourself* like a microphone?" a boy asked. "Exactly!" Costanzo replied. "I couldn't have put it better myself."

He told the students that opera could convey an emotion, like sadness, even if the listener didn't know what the words meant. "What things might make you sad?" he asked. "A pet dying," one child offered. "A family member dying," another said, more quietly.

Costanzo asked the children to think of something sad that had happened to them in the past year, and to listen to him sing, even though they would not understand the words – which he explained, were in Italian. With Brian Wagorn, an assistant conductor at the Met, accompanying, Costanzo sang the aria "Pena tiranna," by Handel, filling the empty auditorium with his voice. The children were rapt. In the middle seat of the middle bench, a boy in a gray hooded sweatshirt leaned forward, his elbow resting on his knee and his chin resting in his palm, his eyes shining as if he bore all the sorrows of the world.

—Rebecca Mead. "Open Wide." *New Yorker*, January 20, 2014.

3. Event

"I can't help thinking there's a book in this."

If you find yourself participating (willfully or otherwise) in an unusual event, consider linking your story with the story of the incident.

State fairs. Religious celebrations. Political rallies. Hells Angels' conventions. Events are all around us.

Some thirty-two million people gather on the banks of the Ganges for a cleansing dip on a single day in January. Note how Anand uses the Story of One to represent the Story of Many (and I love the title).

323

The wealthiest pilgrims visiting India's Maha Kumbh Mela arrived in style, jetting in from London or New York. Others saved for months to buy tickets on crammed Indian buses and trains. But for Sahil Baba, a Hindu holy man or *sadhu*, the journey was far more tortuous.

"I crawled here on my hands and knees," says the ascetic, squatting by a fire of burning cow dung. "It took me three years. I did it to show my devotion to God."

—Anu Anand. "Kumbh All Ye Faithful." *CNN Traveller.*

One of my favorite event-oriented travel stories tells of a clash of giant egos as the Great Chefs of France visited the Great Chefs of Hong Kong. Here's the lead:

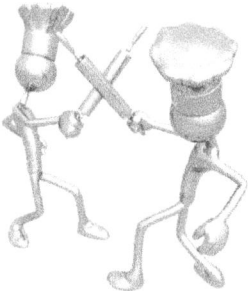

The Hong Kong Tourist Association went into battle mode. They had learned that several estimable French chefs were going on a dining tour of China – and they would not be stopping off at Hong Kong. Having just come out of their Cultural Revolution, where food was simple to nonexistent, China hardly had any interesting restaurants, whereas Hong Kong, a veddy proper British Crown Colony, had made damned certain that the food was top rate. With Chinese master gourmet William Mark, I was asked to help rectify matters. This is the story of that campaign.

1. Wherein a note of amity is conveyed from Versailles to an Asian colony; and wherein this note creates suspicion and confusion in the colonial power, giving rise to an undeclared war.

When Monsieur Claude Jolly, the most estimable gourmet journalist in that self-proclaimed centre of the world of gustatory delights, Paris, appraised a dish for his journal, *L'Express*, his culinary world swallowed. So when he decided, in his most Infinite Gallic wisdom, that it was appropriate that the master chefs of France pay a visit to the master chefs of the People's Republic of China, his declarations had all the weight of a Papal bull (Or a Versailles state banquet boeuf). M. Jolly prepared himself with the same finesse as he would prepare a Timbale de Poulet Rouen Voisin. First, he made diplomatic approaches to the Chinese Embassy, which were initially rejected since China recognized no cuisine save its own.

After a whisper in the ear of the Chinese Ambassador that the cuisine of France had a ... er, perhaps peripheral interest for barbarians, he reluctantly accepted receiving a quartet of French chefs for a two-week visit.

The chefs were truly les plus fameux of France. Alain Chapel of Chez La Mere Charles. Michel Guerard, founder of the Cuisine Minceur movement. Pierre Troisgros of le grand Troisgros Restaurant. And portly Alain Senderens, soon to be the cynosure of France, granted a third Michelin star ...

At this point, an informal note was sent to this writer (a notable gourmet journalist himself, specializing in popcorn avec beurre, pizza des fromages, and Trois Mousquetaires, the eminent chocolate bar). However, M. Jolly did not know my limitations, so he informed him (oh, hell, moi ... er, me) that he would be taking his entourage to China for some grand dining. And if I didn't mind, would I possibly prepare a light *repas* for the entourage on their route.

That is, if any decent food was available in this British colony.

The note was innocent enough, as are most diplomatic notes. The outcome, though, created the First (and only) French-Hong Kong War of the Twentieth Century.

Hong Kong, you see, took its chefs and restaurants almost as seriously as it took its accountants and banks. And when the Hong Kong Tourist Association learned of this informal note, they sized it up as an insult to the flag ...

"Do those frogs really think they're getting Chinese food in China? Ha! We'll give them food coming out of their damned ears by the time we're through."

—Harry Rolnick. "The French, Hong Kong, and Chinese Banquet Roadshow." *Spice Chronicles: Exotic Tales of a Hungry Traveler.* Santa Ana: Seven Locks Press, 2006.

The event: The second Mike Tyson-Evander Holyfield fight.

This is a feature to accompany the factual report of the fight itself (where Tyson bit off a small piece of Holyfield's right ear), and Reilly parodies Hunter S. Thompson and focuses on the attending celebrities and their wardrobes.

Twenty *hours to the fight*. There are two uniforms in a Tyson crowd: that of the Tyson Girl and that of the Tyson Guy.

The Tyson Girl is usually outfitted in a chartreuse stretch mini with matching stilt heels and a little purse. The heels are usually longer than the dress.

The Tyson Guy is right out of *Guys and Dolls*, which means his uniform is just the opposite of the Tyson Girl's: the more material the better. High-button vests go over silk shirts, and high-button jackets go over the high-button vests. Sometimes a lavish cape is added, and a bowler. All in various shades of neon. The Tyson Guy holds a cell phone in one hand and a bottle of Dom Pérignon ($200 per in the MGM's Betty Boop bar) in the other.

All of which makes Vegas clothiers very happy. "This fight," says a haberdasher at the Fashion Show Mall, "will save our June."

Six hours to the fight. J.J. Casper, 5' 10", blonde, blue-eyed, rose-lipped and only a little curvier than Vail Pass, is preparing to carry the round cards for the main event. We ask her to describe the perfect card-girl walk. "First of all, don't trip," Casper says. "Walk heel to toe, not toe to heel. No ankle movement. Arch your back and hold the card up high. Remember that the four-inch heels will get everything moving that needs to be moving. And the Number 1 rule is, Never make eye contact with the fighter. If you make eye contact with the fighter, it may break his concentration. I've seen it. They look up, and they're done for."

—Rick Reilly. "Fear and Clothing in Las Vegas." *Sports Illustrated*, July 7, 1997.

4 · Service

Most people appreciate helpful hints.

The service article is the most commercial (and often mindless) form of travel article, and if you want to collect bylines (and cash) this is the easiest way to start. You can still personalize a service article, but the focus is on providing useful information for the reader.

A popular offshoot of the service article is the numbered *list*, sometimes called a listicle: "Ten best pizza restaurants in Chicago." "Six cocktails created in Miami." "Five best websites to get global weather information." "Ten ways to deal with lost luggage." "24 hours in Phoenix."

∽

Here's a personalized service article that's a cut above the usual – the author is instructing the reader how to not be humiliated in fancy New York restaurants. She starts with first person, then continues with a mini-profile (and she comes back to M. Decré a few times during the course of the article, providing a useful framing structure.)

I wish to introduce M. Martin Decré. His face is pink. His hair is gray. His feet are flat. His cufflinks, by Cartier. He is the sentinel of La Seine Restaurant ... a *beau monde* cloister of drop-dead chic. Martin Decré stands between you and a good dinner in a great restaurant.

Martin is a warm, sympathetic, earthy good fellow. But that is the seven-eighths of the Decré iceberg *you* may never see. It is not that Martin is a born fascist. He does not eat ground glass for breakfast. He is simply a highly trained despot. A maître among the town's haughtiest maîtres d'. Let us not hack the tiniest chink in his armor of unshakable arrogance, thus tarnishing La Seine's snob cachet. If it were a snap to seduce Martin, would it be worth the effort? The canons of *haut snobisme* are perfectly clear: there are clients who adorn La Seine and clients who pollute its elegance. It is for Martin to court the former and discourage the latter.

—Gael Greene. "How Not to Be Humiliated in Snob Restaurants."
New York Magazine, April 13, 1970.

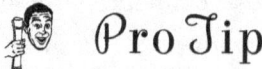

Pro Tip

Service Sidebars Help Sell Stories

Nick Foulkes wrote an article for HighLife, the in-flight magazine for British Airways, that has a simple premise: let's visit some of the exotic locations where the James Bond films were shot.

The article ends with a sidebar, written by travel expert Bruce Palling, that tells the reader where the stars stayed in the destinations mentioned in the text. No surprise, Roger Moore lodged at the Oriental in Bangkok during filming of The Man with the Golden Gun, and so can you.

. . .

You might write a personal essay about how you transformed yourself from a couch potato to a gym jock in six months following a heart attack scare. You could add a sidebar explaining five things to look for when choosing a gym.

. . .

You might be writing a family history about your grandparents who left Japan to labor in Hawaii's sugar fields; a sidebar could give statistics of the number of immigrants in similar situations and what happened to them.

WRITING TIP #10

Me / You

MAYBE YOU DON'T WANT TO READ THIS CHAPTER

Throughout the book I've been encouraging you to find your voice, to explore your own hero's journey, to write what you feel.

But this chapter, aimed at people who want to get paid for their personal travel stories, might bring you back to earth. It's all about understanding the needs of your reader.

VOICES IN YOUR HEAD?

Consider the durian.

Earlier I said that your voice is essential.

Well, so is the voice of your reader.

By this I mean you have to be aware of the background, life experiences, comfort zone, and sense of humor of the reader who opens the magazine where you want your article to appear.

Have you been to Bangkok?

Let's say I write:

We tread carefully along Silom, ate some durian, and then went to Chatuchak for some retail therapy.

A reader who lives in Bangkok would understand the references to the crowded, potholed sidewalk along Silom Road, the scene of vendors, food stalls, beggars, political demonstrations, and lots of sweaty pedestrians anxious to get to wherever they are going. A reader in Bangkok would understand the feel, heft, smell, and allure (or repulsion) of durian. A reader in Bangkok would understand that Chatuchak refers to one of world's biggest markets, open only on weekends.

But, a reader in Chicago probably does not have the same references and will need much more guidance about what I'm trying to tell her. So if these scene-setting details are important, I must write them.

The hard truth: few people really care about your story. They care about themselves.
The trick is to figure out a way to resonate with the reader.

Kids, Try This at Home

· · · · · · · · · Write the Scene · · · · · · · ·
from the Second Character's Point of View

It's too easy to get locked into the perceptions and voice of the point-of-view character (that's usually you).

As an exercise, pick a scene, preferably a dramatic scene full of conflict and passion, and write it from the other character's point of view – for example, from the point of view of the Caraibe Indian below. You don't have to use it, but it will force you to see complexity in the various Nancy Reagans that result. For example, George W. Bush's perception of 9/11 will be different from Osama bin Laden's.

Understand your reader's point of view.

Shift the Point of View (POV)

This is similar to Ping-Pong writing, bouncing from one perspective to another.

∾

Here's an example of how the dynamics change when you shift the POV:

> In *Forbidden Love*, a first-person account by lovers Mary Kay Letourneau, a thirty-six-year-old teacher, and her student Vili Fualaau, fifteen, Letourneau said of Fualaau: "He is a poet capable of lyricism, an artist full of spirit and talent." Fualaau said, "I was twelve years old and I had never fucked anyone ... I wanted to see what it was like."
>
> —The Editors. "The 1998 Dubious Achievement Awards." *Esquire*, January 1999.

∾

And another, documenting different viewpoints of a broom-closet tryst between tennis star Boris Becker and Russian model Angela Ermakova that resulted in a much-publicized paternity suit.

> Becker: "It was a mistake which will haunt me the rest of my life. The result is brutal for me, but also for my wife, my children, my mother."
>
> Ermakova: "Boris pulled me into the broom cupboard ... I felt like Cinderella in a beautiful dream. Boris was like a radiant German knight."
>
> —The Editors. "Notebook." *Time*, August 6, 2001.

Change the article's dynamics by changing your POV.

Who is your reader? The general rule is that the more desperately you want to get paid for an article, the better you have to target your reader and understand her desires and foibles. The rule of thumb is that when writing for a commercial publication, the "you" is perhaps more important than the "me."

Let's say you want to write an article about six ways to deal with a nasty divorce. Not sure whether to submit it to *Reader's Digest* or *Cosmopolitan*? Study the ads. They'll tell you about the target audience, and you can tailor your story accordingly. The *Reader's Digest* reader is older, more settled, buying cat food, home remedies for arthritis, taking a cruise. The *Cosmo* reader is ... well you know very well who she is. You can't write the same story for both.

Sometimes an article flounders because it has no target – it's written for the universe instead of a specific reader. Try this: at the top of your story write the name of the intended publication. (Hint: it's likely to be a publication you enjoy reading.) Then think of one reader of that publication. Write for her.

First, write to please yourself.
Second, think about whether you have anyone else to please.

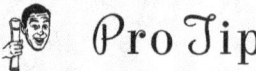 Pro Tip

The Homer Simpson Equal Opportunity Slander Principle

If you're going to praise/criticize/make fun of/belittle one person based on his race, gender, ethnic group, voting preferences, nationality or sexual orientation, you have a Homer Simpsonesque obligation to make fun of all the other races, genders, and suspicious behaviors in your story, including (especially) your own. Otherwise you will be perceived as a whiny zealot, and nobody likes those.

Treat your reader with respect.

DON'T TAKE YOURSELF TOO SERIOUSLY

A great way to endear yourself to the reader is by not taking yourself too seriously. Pop a hole in that balloon of self-inviolability. You don't want to make yourself look like too much of a jerk (unless it's true), but a bit of self-deprecation goes a long way.

Kids, Try This at Home

PUT YOURSELF IN THE SHOES
OF YOUR POTENTIAL READER

Ask yourself, "Why should I spend ten minutes reading this stuff? Will it amuse me? Teach me something? Give me some juicy gossip? Make my vacation more fun? Instruct me how to make a tuna fish casserole that will jumpstart my love life? Help me get an insight into my own neurotic behavior?" If you (the reader in this case) can't come up with a convincing "Yes it will, yes!" then you've just zapped your own writing. Start over.

It's risky to write something the audience isn't interested in.

MAKE 'EM LAUGH

If April is the cruelest month then humor is the toughest technique.

Most guys agree that the Three Stooges are the funniest human beings since the medieval popes; most girls beg to differ.

You might like politically incorrect jokes; your spouse thinks they're in bad taste.

If I tell a joke referring to Howdy Doody, Hopalong Cassidy, Doris Day, and Beaver Cleaver, some folks will understand the cultural references, some will not.

Few things separate or unite people as much as a sense of humor.

The reality is that if you can write cleverly, with humor and style, then editors and readers will love you.

Write in your comfort zone, but step outside once in a while and see how it feels.

FINISH IT AND GET IT PUBLISHED

Open a Vein

Nobody forces you to write. It's tough, often lonely, and your chances of making the big time are slim. Go bowling instead; nobody will blame you.

But if you insist on persisting, here are some thoughts on the "dangerous career."

It is only when you open your veins and bleed onto the page a little that you establish contact with your reader. If you do not believe in the characters or the story you are doing at that moment with all your mind, strength, and will, if you don't feel joy and excitement while writing it, then you're wasting good white paper.

—Paul Gallico. *Confessions of a Story Writer.* (the "open a vein ..." part of this quote is often attributed to sportswriter Red Smith, who used it three years after Gallico.)

The life of a writer is quite a dangerous career.

—John Cheever

What [writing] terrors are we talking about? Here are some. Can I pull it off? Do I have anything to say? Will I be exposed as a fraud who set out to write *War and Peace* and ended up with *Dick and Jane*? Will readers ridicule my pathetic efforts? Will they peer deep inside me and see nothing there? Will I look within and discover things about myself I'd rather not know? .. I'm afraid my publisher won't accept it. If my publisher does accept the manuscript, I'm worried that critics will hate it. If critics don't hate it, I'm sure no one will buy my book. And even if readers do buy my book, there's the danger that they won't like what they read. They might find it laughable. Worst of all, someone I care about may scorn my efforts.

—Ralph Keyes. "The Courage to Write." *Writer's Digest*, October 1995.

When you stiffen, you know that whatever you stiffen about is very important.

—Toni Morrison

A writer gives himself away all the time anyway. He has no important secrets.

—W.H. Auden

The best work that anybody ever writes is the work that is on the verge of embarrassing him, always.

—Arthur Miller

No one ever found wisdom without also being a fool. Writers, alas, have to be foolish in public, while the rest of the human race can cover its tracks.

—Erica Jong

"Sorry, old man. Because of the weak imagery, scanty plot, and pedestrian language in your latest, we've turned your table over to Joyce Carol Oates."

There are always risks.

IF YOU'RE BORED THE READER WILL BE AS WELL

You work for weeks or months on a report or article. You really slog away, staying up at night with a Quixotic-like drive to cram as much into it as possible, to cover all your bases, to make it fireproof and show how clever you are. I submitted a report like that in college; the professor wrote at the top, "Well typed."

I believe in energy. If you put positive energy into something (a relationship, a tennis game, an article) then the person on the receiving end will sense that energy. If you cringe at the thought of writing your article and feel a huge sigh of relief when it's done, then why should you expect the reader to be overjoyed to receive this compendium of pain? As James M. Cain said, "Writing that doesn't keep the writer up at night won't keep the reader up either."

WRITE YOUR PERSONAL ESSAY AS A SONG

Consider the architecture of a two-minute country and western song that has a distinct voice, big problems ("I lost my girl, my dog, and then my truck."), a quick lead, a quest, memorable characters, dialogue, conflicts (both physical and internal), a specific quest, a voice, a memorable message and, as in this example, a circular structure.

> My daddy left home when I was three
> And he didn't leave much to ma and me
> Just this old guitar and an empty bottle of booze.
> Now, I don't blame him cause he run and hid
> But the meanest thing that he ever did
> Was before he left, he went and named me "Sue."
>
> Well, he must o' thought it was quite a joke
> And it got a lot of laughs from a lot of folk,
> It seems I had to fight my whole life through.
> Some gal would giggle and I'd get red
> And some guy'd laugh and I'd bust his head,
> I tell ya, life ain't easy for a boy named "Sue."
>
> Well, I grew up quick and I grew up mean,
> My fist got hard and my wits got keen,
> I'd roam from town to town to hide my shame.
> But I made a vow to the moon and stars
> That I'd search the honky-tonks and bars
> And kill that man who gave me that awful name.
>
> Well, it was Gatlinburg in mid-July
> And I just hit town and my throat was dry,
> I thought I'd stop and have myself a brew.
> At an old saloon on a street of mud,
> There at a table, dealing stud,
> Sat the dirty, mangy dog that named me "Sue."

Well, I knew that snake was my own sweet dad
From a worn-out picture that my mother had,
And I knew that scar on his cheek and his evil eye.
He was big and bent and gray and old,
And I looked at him and my blood ran cold
And I said: "My name is 'Sue!' How do you do!
Now you're gonna die!"

Well, I hit him hard right between the eyes
And he went down, but to my surprise,
He come up with a knife and cut off a piece of my ear.
But I busted a chair right across his teeth
And we crashed through the wall and into the street
Kicking and a' gouging in the mud and the blood and the beer.

I tell ya, I've fought tougher men
But I really can't remember when,
He kicked like a mule and he bit like a crocodile.
I heard him laugh and then I heard him cuss,
He went for his gun and I pulled mine first,
He stood there lookin' at me and I saw him smile.

And he said: "Son, this world is rough
And if a man's gonna make it, he's gotta be tough
And I knew I wouldn't be there to help ya along.
So I give ya that name and I said goodbye
I knew you'd have to get tough or die
And it's the name that helped to make you strong."

He said: "Now you just fought one hell of a fight
And I know you hate me, and you got the right
To kill me now, and I wouldn't blame you if you do.
But ya ought to thank me, before I die,
For the gravel in ya guts and the spit in ya eye
Cause I'm the son-of-a-bitch that named you 'Sue.'"

I got all choked up and I threw down my gun

And I called him my pa, and he called me his son,

And I came away with a different point of view.

And I think about him, now and then,

Every time I try and every time I win,

And if I ever have a son, I think I'm gonna name him

Bill or George! Anything but Sue! I still hate that name!

—Johnny Cash. "A Boy Named Sue."

Useful Advice from Someone Who Wrote Pretty Well

1. Avoid fried meats, which angry up the blood.

2. If your stomach disputes you, lie down and pacify it with cool thoughts.

3. Keep the juices flowing by jangling around gently as you move.

4. Go very light on the vices, such as carrying on in society. The social ramble ain't restful.

5. Avoid running at all times.

6. Don't look back. Something might be gaining on you.

—Satchel Paige. "How to Keep Young." *Collier's*, June 1953.

THE EDITOR IS GOD, THE EDITOR IS A JERK

Both.

The magazine editor is god. She decides your fate. But not all editors are created equal.

A good magazine editor will recognize your unpolished genius and work with you to make your work shine.

But some magazine editors will break your heart. Not every editor is professional, punctual, efficient, or good-natured. And not all of them share your worldview.

I was raised that if someone asks you a question you reply, promptly and comprehensively. Jerky editors plead that they are busy, or they don't answer at all. They might schedule a story and then not run it. They might have to succumb to the whims of the advertising department, which is why an editor might reject your touching story of how, as a former alcoholic, you dealt with a wine tasting in Beaujolais, and instead ask for a service piece about cool B&Bs in the region. Editors might not pay and you have to chase them for a miserable sum. Worse, they might change your text without consulting you. They almost certainly will change your clever title. They are likely to introduce photo captions that are misleading or wrong (always offer to write photo captions).

If you have a good editor, cultivate her. Try to meet her face to face – it makes you harder to say no to. And remember that good editors, like gods, move on to greener pastures. They have shelf lives. If a good editor moves, maybe you should as well.

 Kids, Try This at Home

· · · · · · · · · RETYPE A GREAT STORY · · · · · · · ·

All writers have files of articles written by other writers they've kept simply because they are a pleasure to read. Find an article that makes you say, "I wish I had written that." Retype it – every word, every semicolon, every bit of dialogue and description. You will see how the author structured the piece, where he wrote in scenes and where he used narration.

This exercise is like attending a cooking class and following the instructions of the celebrity chef as you prepare the dish with him. After this exercise is over, you will want to evolve your own voice and style (just as you will adapt the chef's recipe to suit your tastes and abilities), but you will have in the back of your mind a feeling of one way to achieve excellence.

Pro Tip

Get a Mentor

Or a coach. Or whatever you want to call her.

Roger Federer has a coach. So does Tiger Woods, too many perhaps. So does virtually every athlete, singer, or dancer.

Find someone whose judgment you trust. You don't have to do everything she says. But you do have to try on her ideas like a new pair of shoes. If they fit, take them home.

 ## Kids, Try This at Home

· · · · · · · · · THINK LIKE A REPORTER · · · · · · · ·

All writers get asked career advice by folks who say, "what should I do to become a good writer?" Some mentors say, "write good stuff, bad stuff, just lots of stuff"; other people advise beginners to "read good writers." Baloney. The single best thing you can do, regardless of the kind of writing you want to produce, is to become infected with the principles of Journalism 101. Get journalistic stylistics into your bloodstream – like malaria, they'll be with you forever. Journalism will also teach you to write quickly, about anything.

"What about creativity?" you might whine. Well, you either are creative or you ain't, nothing anyone can do about it. Good communication means combining left-brained accuracy with right-brained emotional, heart-oriented human stories.

So learn to write a news story. Have your work ripped apart by an irritable, time-challenged sub-editor. You will hate that sub-editor, but he will be doing you a huge favor, goading you to figure out "what's this story about?", teaching you to write in inverted-pyramid style, forcing you to be accurate and check facts, insisting you write to a specific word count. He will enact ax murder on your work and you will be better for it.

Then you can take a deep breath, pour a single malt, and explore your creative side.

Be a reporter.
Get details, tell the story, and extrapolate with your view of trends and implications.

YOUR VOICE EVOLVES

Voice can be an elusive concept, and it is bound to change during your writing career. Look at how Picasso's artistic voice evolved.

Picasso, 1923, age 42   **Picasso, 1937, age 56**

Pro Tip

A Tense Moment

The default tense for most articles is simple past: "I drove to the store and bought cheap beer." "My wife threw a tantrum at the company dinner and I escaped with my secretary." "I said ... he said."

If you want to try something subtle and different, write the opening and end in present tense. This works best when the opening and ending form bookends of a single anecdote, with background and historical info written in simple past tense in the middle of the article.

COPY EDIT

Before you send a piece to an editor, print it out and check spellings, consistency, and punctuation.

Don't expect the editor to do this for you, at least not willingly.

If your submission has misspellings, grammatical errors, and poorly checked facts, it's like a painter dripping Extra-Bright Summer Golden Sunset emulsion on your Chippendale side table. Unprofessional, and done to excess, a deal breaker.

Useful Advice from Someone Who Wrote Pretty Well

You have to learn the rules of the game. And then you have to play better than anyone else.

—Albert Einstein

Kids, Try This at Home

······· GET A JOB AS A FACT CHECKER ·······

Fact checkers are first cousins to IRS tax auditors. In a vague corner of my mind, I know they are necessary, maybe even useful, but it's as hard to cozy up to one as it would be to kiss your second grade teacher on the lips - you remember, the one with the wart and breath like she had just eaten a rotten squirrel.

Still, working as one of these anal, "check it again - I told you I wanted two references" human beings will give you a discipline that will stick with you. If you ever sell a story to a major publication (one that pays big bucks) like Reader's Digest, Vanity Fair, or GQ, you will be introduced to a fact checker who will ask for your references for every statement she deems to be questionable.

Embrace her proclivity for accuracy. Stifle her by being accurate.

Your genius may not be instantly recognized.

GET PUBLISHED

Imagine you're a couch potato and you decide that in one month you will run a marathon. That's the situation a lot of early-in-their-career writers put themselves into

– they've been brainwashed by the "Yes I Can" mindset and send off an early-in-their-career manuscript to the *Atlantic* or *National Geographic*.

The rejection note comes quickly.

I look back on my early writings. My first pieces that I sold for money ($10!) when I was fifteen were about ancient Roman coins. Dull, dreary stuff. But I found coin magazines willing to publish the articles.

Then I moved up the ladder. I wrote dozens of pieces for my university newspaper (the George Washington University *Hatchet*, a great name). Better, but in retrospect my writing was embarrassingly sophomoric. I wrote articles for local Washington, DC newspapers. Eventually I moved up to more reputable publications, which paid better and were read by more people. I learned skills and built a portfolio. With each publication I learned more craft.

And along the way I schmoozed. Life is only partially a meritocracy. Life, and any career, is aided greatly by contacts, friends, and connections.

And along the way I got shot down. While at university I wrote a long investigative piece (this was the period of Woodward and Bernstein, and my pals and I wanted to be investigative reporters) about behind-the-scenes politicking in the Washington, DC theater community. I sent it to the *Washingtonian* magazine, one of the earliest city magazines. The editor liked it. They would publish it. This article would be my breakthrough story.

You can guess how this saga ended. They didn't publish it. They sent me a kill fee, but of course the money wasn't compensation for the disappointment of not having my name in lights.

So sure, you might be a genius and get lucky on the first attempt to break into the *New Yorker* or *Condé Nast Traveler*. That's a bit like sending a note to Aishwarya Rai/Angelina Jolie/Charlize Theron/Lady Gaga (choose one, it's your fantasy) and asking if she wants to go away with you for a romantic weekend at a love hotel in the Poconos. Possible, but unlikely.

Here's what happens when you send in an unsolicited book proposal or manuscript to a literary agent or editor.

It gets dumped on a staggeringly tall slush pile. The office cat pees on the manuscripts. The cleaning lady knocks over the pile. The senior editor sends down a mandate – clear out that rubbish. So the young ladies (they're almost all young ladies, often recently graduated from an Ivy League school with a degree in English literature, living in Brooklyn with four other young ladies in a tiny apartment and earning as much as a cook at a fast-food restaurant) decide "Thursday night is slush pile night." It's like a slumber party. They call in for pizza or Chinese food. They giggle and read opening sentences aloud to each other to gauge "degrees of badness." A very few manuscripts get put on a pile for the editor to look at. The vast majority of manuscripts get put on a pile marked "reject," and the next day the slightly hungover intern will send the writer a note that says, "Thank you for your submission. I'm afraid we're going to pass. Good luck with your writing."

So, I suggest you get published where and when you can. If it helps, remember this anecdote:

Joe Namath, the famous New York Jets quarterback who was as proficient at winning football games as he was at bedding starlets, owned, with two friends, a hot bar in Manhattan called Bachelor's Three. It was near closing time on one rainy Tuesday night and Joe was getting restless. It had been a slow night and just a few patrons were left. "Harry," Joe said to his friend. I'm going to talk with that brunette in the green dress and see if she wants to go home with me."

"Joe, she's kind of plain, don't you think?"

"Harry, it's two in the morning," Joe replied. "I'm horny and tired and a little bit drunk, and I have a feeling that Miss America isn't about to walk through the front door."

Put another way, by Crosby, Stills, Nash and Young: "If you can't be with the one you love, love the one you're with."

"Great news! Your novel is in a medium-size pile in the middle of the floor about four feet from the left side of Oprah's assistant's desk."

Avoid the tyranny of the intern.

How to Avoid This Tyranny of the Intern?

Go directly to a senior editor with one degree of separation. If you can say in your query letter to an agent or editor that "Our mutual friend Brenda kindly gave me your name," it opens a door, however slightly. Wouldn't you react the same way?

Don't have one degree of separation? Well, in a way you do. Find out who the agents/editors are for your favorite writers, the folks who write your kind of articles and books. Don't claim friendship if none exists. But you can claim resonance.

"Your book is a masterpiece, but, unfortunately, we're rather picky."

You're more likely to get a quick, straight answer if you go directly to the top.

If it's any consolation, Margaret Mitchell got thirty-eight rejection letters before finding a publisher for *Gone With the Wind*; Louis L'Amour, who has sold 330 million westerns, received two hundred rejections before Bantam took a chance on him. Robert M. Pirsig's *Zen & the Art of Motorcycle Maintenance* is in the Guinness Book of Records for one hundred twenty-one rejections, more than any other bestseller. Jack London's estate "House of Happy Walls" has a collection of six hundred rejection letters from his early years. And my favorite: To prove how hard it is for new writers to break in, Jerzy Kosinski used a pen name to submit a type-script of his bestseller *Steps* (it won the U.S. National Book Award for Fiction in 1969) to thirteen agents and fourteen publishers. All of them rejected it, including Random House, which had published it initially.

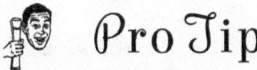 Pro Tip

Never Edit on the Screen

Print out your work – double-spaced, big margins. Turn off the TV and computer. Get out your favorite fountain pen, curl up in front of the fire with the cat, and edit, edit, edit. Rewrite on the computer. Repeat.

And never send anything out when you've just finished. A manuscript, like curry and sometimes pizza, is usually better the next day. Read it with a clear mind. Edit again.

Then stop fiddling. Send it out.

A MANUSCRIPT SHOULD NEVER SLEEP AT HOME

When you write something, give it air so it can ignite. If it's ready for publication, send it out into the cruel world. If it's still in draft, send it to your mentor. Be specific about what questions you'd like your mentor to answer – "Is the dialogue realistic?" "Are the conflicts sufficiently juicy?" "Does my voice come through?" "Is it appropriately hot or cold for my audience?"

SHOULD I BLOG?

Most blogs are egocentric and boring.

Most blogs are inflated tweets, with no storytelling.

Most blogs contain no nutritional value.

Observations: "Mary looks great today."

Comments: "A-Rod is laughing all the way to the bank."

Situations: "I'm eating pizza again. I will eat pizza tomorrow, but in a different restaurant."

But if you want your blog to sing, write it like a finished magazine article, using the suggestions in this book. Tell a story. Use dialogue and circular structure. Bring in conflicts. Go easy on the personal rants.

JOIN A WRITING GROUP

Maybe.

Note the chemistry. You have to like and trust these folks. You have to listen to what they say, but you don't have to agree.

Just as writing comes in a spectrum of cold to hot, so do writing workshops and support groups.

Cold groups will look mainly at the technical aspects of your work – story arc, dialogue, characters.

Hot groups, which often have names like Writing from the Soul, Heart Writing, Free-Writing, and Writing Without Limits can be enlightening. Most of these groups are loosely based on the principles of free-writing espoused by Nathalie Goldberg and Julia Cameron (and many other folks). You may find yourself writing stuff that surprises you, perhaps embarrasses you. You may scribble passages that open up new neural pathways and help you see your story in a different light. Choose your leader and group with care. If the chemistry is right, these hot groups can change your writing life.

You'll have no shortage of people keen to give you an opinion.
Listen politely to everyone, but at the end of the day it's your name
on the manuscript. Follow your own sense of what works.

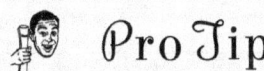 Pro Tip

Look Like a Pro

Kinky and creative might get you into the School of Performing Arts, but it'll get your manuscript rejected faster than you can say "unstandard typeface." Your manuscript has to be as conforming as an accountant's dress code. The editor should feel that your story "belongs." Follow the publication's guidelines, but if there are none, then Times Roman 12 point is fine. Double-space. Flush left, ragged right.

Know when to use numerals and when to write out numbers (in general, but not always: one to ten, then 11, 12...).

Know how and when to capitalize titles: Today, President Barack Obama said, "we're going to war against Texas." The president added, "and maybe Oklahoma. I'm thinking about it."

Know if the publication uses English measures (pounds, inches) or metric (kilograms, meters). How do they describe time: 4:45 P.M. or 16:45?

American or British spelling? Color or colour?

Do they capitalize animal names – Giant Panda or giant panda (as far as I'm concerned, it's always the latter)?

Are the readers American or European? Do they use the ghastly phrase "entrée" to describe what the rest of the English-speaking world calls a main course?

How do they treat titles of articles/books/movies/newspapers/songs/Broadway musicals? "Gone With The Wind" or Gone with the Wind?

You have to write their language.

Ask if the publication you're writing for has a style guide.

If not, follow the rules in one of these books: For American English: The Chicago Manual of Style or The Associated Press Stylebook; for British English: The Economist Style Guide or The Cambridge Handbook for Editors, Authors and Publishers.

A manuscript should never sleep at home.
But sometimes, like a lost dog, it finds its way back.

PRACTICE, PRACTICE, PRACTICE

That's the advice Yehudi Menuhin gave to a young man in Manhattan who stopped him in the street and asked; "How can I get to Carnegie Hall?"

But how much practice is enough?

In *Outliers: The Story of Success*, Malcolm Gladwell concludes (naïvely, I think) that the magic number to achieve greatness is ten thousand hours of practice, roughly ten years of intensive effort, and cites Bill Gates, the Beatles, even Mozart to support his contention. Gladwell quotes neurologist Daniel Levitin:

> In study after study, of composers, basketball players, fiction writers, ice skaters, concert pianists, chess players, master criminals, and what have you, this number comes up again and again. Of course, this doesn't address why some people get more out of their practice sessions than others do. But no one has yet found a case in which true world-class expertise was accomplished in less time. It seems that it takes the brain this long to assimilate all that it needs to know to achieve true mastery.

So, hit those keys.

Useful Advice from Someone Who Wrote Pretty Well

Writing is work. It's also gambling. You don't get a pension plan. Other people can help you a bit, but essentially you're on your own. Nobody is making you do this: you chose it, so don't whine.

—Margaret Atwood

LAW OF INVERSITY

The Law of Inversity proposes that the elegance of the writing is inversely proportional to the amount of action.

What does that mean?

In a story with little action (soppy love stories, meditations on nature, ruminations on Rumi) you have to write elegantly and intriguingly in order to keep the reader interested. For instance, if you are writing about two ladies of a certain age drinking Earl Gray, reminiscing about their long-dead husbands and debating whether to redecorate the dining room, you have to write like a prince because there is little physical action to keep us awake.

But in stories with lots of bang-bang (murder, mayhem, sex of the "earth just moved" type), you are well advised to write simpler, with less flourish, and let the action carry the day. When the grandmother steals the AK-47 from the hijacker and blasts her way to freedom, the writing (generally) will benefit by a sharp and quick tempo. Put another way, the hotter the action, the colder the writing.

HOW TO INCREASE MOVEMENT IN THE STORY?

What to do when the story drags?

Try these four techniques:

* Increase the conflict
* Introduce a new character
* Put the characters into a crucible
* Introduce a ticking clock

 Kids, Try This at Home

· · · · · · · · WRITE WITH TARGETED MUSIC · · · · · · · ·

I like to write with music. And different kinds of music can have an impact on the pace and tone of your writing. Have a look at Tune Your Brain by Elizabeth Miles. If you're writing a passage where a character undergoes a healing process, you might want to play Bach – one reason baroque music is so soothing is because the number of beats per minute in the music mimics the human resting heart rate. Creating a scene where kids are playing Cowboys and Indians in the backyard? Maybe Wagner. In need of a creative boost? She recommends John Coltrane.

Warning. Don't use music with words for your stimulus – too much distraction.

"A writer? Fantastic! I wish I had time to write."

Lots of wannabe writers say "I don't have the time." Life's full of choices, and the reality is that people always make time for what is most important to them. Nobody's forcing you to write. If you don't want to write (or exercise, or wash your clothes, or cook dinner) then don't. But it's not really a question of time. It's a question of desire.

KEEP THE READER CURIOUS

Your writing should trigger curiosity in the reader so he says, "what the heck is going on here?" as in this drawing by Maurits Cornelis Escher. Give the reader some work to do.

WRITER'S BLOCK?

There are countless bits of advice about what to do when writer's block strikes. Some coaches advise to write through it (like running through the pain.) Or they suggest you take the day off and go fishing.

Here are several techniques that work for me.

1. *Write something different.* If you're working on a personal travel story and get stuck, put it aside and write science fiction – I'm fond of giant, radioactive, flying squirrels invading Milwaukee.

2. *Write to one person.* It's a curious and impossible-to-explain fact that each person has one other person with whom we communicate well. We might equally love others in our entourage, but communications, whether it's an email, a phone conversation, or a face to face chat, with that one person flow particularly well.

   So my suggestion is that if you are stuck, write your story as an email to your special friend. That's the way Tom Wolfe wrote his breakout piece, "There Goes (Varoom! Varoom! That Kandy-Kolored (Thphhhhh!) Tangerine-Flake Streamline Baby ..." Wolfe's *Esquire* editor had sent him to Las Vegas to write about the car show; Wolfe took pages of notes but couldn't figure out a way to structure the story – a classic writer's block. The editor, in exasperation, said "send me your notes and I'll get a real writer to write the piece." Wolfe wrote up his notes as a memo to the editor and it was so good the editor published it with only minor edits.

3. *Talk, don't write.* Erle Stanley Gardner, who wrote approximately one hundred and forty books (no one seems quite sure of the number), including the Perry Mason series, used to have three secretaries – sisters named Jean, Peggy, and Honey – taking dictation for three novels at once. He would switch from one book to another by walking across the room, like a chess grandmaster might play several games at once.

   For some people the act of sitting at a computer is intimidating. So don't. Get a portable voice recorder. Or voice recognition software.

FOUR MORE WAYS TO GET UNSTUCK

Obviously in personal nonfiction – the theme of this book – you can't invent characters or situations, but you can nevertheless look for real situations that might change the dynamics of your story.

1. *Introduce another character.* You might be focusing too much on you. The result is an interior monologue, which is notoriously hard to write.

    But things get much easier when you add another character to play off. Don Quixote had Sancho Panza. John Steinbeck had Charley. Huck Finn had Tom Sawyer.

2. *Crucible.* Already have another character? Still dull? Put your characters in a crucible.

    This is an enclosed physical/emotional space from which the characters can't easily escape. Things heat up quickly. A long-distance bus stuck in a blizzard. The *Titanic*.

3. *Raise the stakes.* Let's say you have an injury at home. That's serious and important and inherently dramatic. But what if you get injured while you're at Disney World? More inconvenient, but they have doctors and hospitals in Orlando (and the story gets better if it was Minnie Mouse who punched you in the nose after you made a comment about her mini-skirt). Injured in Singapore? Yes, more problematic, but everyone speaks English and the medical care is superb. Kathmandu? Getting hotter. On a trek in the mountains of Nepal with a recognized trekking agency? That's getting hotter and more problematic, but you still have a support system. What if you're trekking by yourself, off the main trekking routes, two days walk from the nearest village, which itself is two days' walk from the nearest road? Now, you've got a story. You've got choices to make. You've got high stakes.

4. *Introduce more and bigger Nancy Reagans.* Or, less elegantly, put your character in the outhouse and keep piling it on.

You are not alone.

If you're frustrated, take five minutes from writing and enjoy Garrison Keillor's radio sketch about the travails of a budding novelist: "The Great American Office Novel." Sketch in "Beebopareebop Rhubarb Pie," in Prairie Home Companion. Broadcast Saturday, March 27, 1999.

SIX TIPS FOR PUBLISHING AN ARTICLE

Let's face reality: it's tough to get published. That shouldn't stop you from trying.

I wish I could say that excellent writing always finds an outlet and the publication of your excellent articles and books will make you rich and famous. Alas.

It's easier to start with publishing an article than it is to find a commercial publisher for a book, so let's start with that initial task: write and sell an article for publication in a (hopefully) paying newspaper, magazine, or website.

1. The most important element is to *write well.* Quality counts.

2. *Work your way up the ladder.* It's better to be published by the *Hometown Daily Planet* than it is to be rejected by the *New Yorker.*

3. *Understand the editor's needs.* Write well, with a style and subject that match the publication's style. You're not exclusively writing for yourself; you are writing for an editor who has specific needs. As they say, "read the publication before

submitting." If you want to send a pithy, funny, self-deprecating but insightful personal essay about what you learned about the meaning of life by buying your daughter a pet gerbil, you must first check that the magazine has a space for such literature.

4. *Connect.* Find one degree of separation with a real-life editor.

5. *Pay your dues.* Be prepared to start at the front of the magazine. Let's say you send a query to write a long feature article. If the editor doesn't know you (or your reputation), she might suggest you start by writing a shorter piece for one of the "front-of-the-book" sections. These are generally 200- to 400-word updates and news items. Less fun, less lucrative, less glory, but the editor is unlikely to give you a big assignment unless she knows she can trust you to write a professional-quality article.

6. *Query well.* Learn how to write a pitch letter (query letter). There are lots of books about how to do this.

SEVEN TIPS FOR PUBLISHING A BOOK

1. *Write well,* and have something to say.

2. *Get an agent.* Books are sold through agents. Not sure which agent to approach? Here's a tip. Look at the credits section of books by writers you admire, who write in your genre. Often the writer will acknowledge the help of her agent. If you can't find such a reference, here's what you do: ask the publisher which agent represented such and such a book. They'll tell you. That will give you a small, but nevertheless useful introduction to the agent – you can say, "I notice that you represent so and so, and I write for a similar audience ..."

   (Note: Agents handle books. They aren't interested in selling your magazine articles, unless you're Paul Theroux).

3. *Connect.* If no agent accepts you and you decide to go directly to a publisher, first find anyone who works in the publishing business and ask her advice.

Having a human contact is infinitely better than going blindly to a publisher and hoping your gem shines through the slush pile.

4. *Write a good book proposal.* Many books on this subject.

5. *Self-publish well.* If the traditional route – agent, commercial publisher, big advance – don't work out, then *self-publish, but self-publish well.* My logic is that you could be waiting for decades for Simon & Schuster or Doubleday to publish your book, but while you're waiting, your manuscript is gathering dusty bytes in your computer. How much more fun and satisfying to be able to give friends a copy of your book. These days there's no shame in having a self-published book.

   But, and this is a very big but, if you self-publish get a professional designer and tell him to make it look like a "real" bestseller. The reader has visual and emotional expectations about what a successful book looks like. I find that most self-published books, regardless of the quality of the contents, look amateurish. Find a few book covers for successful books that you admire and study what the graphic designer has done to make them look like the kind of bestsellers that one finds in the front of Borders (whoops, they've gone out of business. But you know what I mean).

6. *Create a buzz.* Don't expect any publisher to promote your book to your satisfaction. Here's where those magic words "social marketing" come into play. This can be intimidating (it is for me) but it's probably a necessity. The goal is to achieve a breakthrough in which your book rises above the chatter, like *Fifty Shades of Grey.*

7. *Study the business as well as the craft.* Read the books about the business of writing. *Writer's Market,* in the U.S., is the go-to-reference for lists of magazines, agents, and editors. Writer's Digest Books publishes dozens of useful volumes about every aspect of the business of writing, from writing a query letter to going on a book tour (you should be so lucky).

BOOTH

"I'll run through it again. First, the exhilaration of a work completed, followed by the excitement of approaching pub date. Reviews pouring in from everywhere while the bidding for the paperback rights soars to insane figures. An appearance on Merv Griffin or Dick Cavett, sandwiched in between like Engelbert Humperdinck and Juliet Prowse. Finally, a flood of letters from people to whom your name, yesterday unknown, now has the shimmer of national renown. Hit those keys!"

AND BE NICE TO YOURSELF

And after you hit those keys, pour yourself a glass of good wine and listen to music that makes you glad you're alive and able to create words that move people. My favorite: *Libiamo ne'lieti calici*, the drinking song from Act I of *La Traviata*, which basically says *carpe diem*, drink and make merry.

> *Godiamo, la tazza, la tazza e il cantico,*
> *la notte abbella e il riso;*
> *in questo, in questo paradiso ne scopra il nuovo dì.*
>
> Words: Francesco Maria Piave. Music: Giuseppe Verdi.

GLOSSARY

ANECDOTE. A shortened version of a **Scene**, sometimes only a few lines, that shows people doing something of importance to the longer story. An anecdote is an effective device to use in the **Lead**. See *Writing Tip #2: Tell the Story* and *Writing Tip #4: Start with a Bang*.

"AS YOU KNOW, JOHN." A clunky way of conveying background information through dialogue. See *Writing Tip #7: Cinema*.

AX MURDER. An editing technique in which you chop away fluff, sometimes ruthlessly. See **LIPOSUCTION** and **MICHELANGELO'S SECRET**. See *Writing Tip #6: E² = 0 – Chop Fluff Like Michelangelo*.

CINEMA. Cinema refers to the writer's obligation to show the reader what's going on and give the reader details that he would see in a movie. Does the main character wear hiking boots or Jimmy Choo? How is her hair done? Is her voice screechy or Southern syrup? Does she stride purposefully or limp on a prosthetic leg? Does she listen to Beyoncé or Bocelli? Is her bedroom filled with teddy bears or old pizza boxes? How many details are enough? Some writers paint the entire picture, others leave a lot to the imagination; there's no set recipe. See *Writing Tip #7: Cinema*.

CIRCULAR STRUCTURE. A writing device with two elements. First, the article revolves around a central theme. Second, the article always returns to a point near to where it began. The circular structure is often a more satisfying structure for the reader than a linear structure. See **STORY ARC**. See *Writing Tip #2: Tell the Story*.

COLD TO HOT. A way to remember that you always have a choice. Cold writing is intellectual, fact-based, and informative; Hot writing is emotional, sensual, and often personal. In general, the hotter your writing the more chance you have of creating intimacy with the reader. Cold writing is often the default positioning of many professional presentations and is a safe, but boring option. Hot writing infers bigger risks – some people will love you and want to take you out for a milkshake, but others will say "not for me." See *Writing Tip #1: You Have a Choice*.

CREATIVE INSPIRATION/CREATIVE WORK. For this book I've noted a difference between Creative Inspiration, which refers to the act of creation, and Creative Work, which is the editing, rewriting, and fine-tuning that inevitably follows. See *Getting Started: The Power of Your Voice*.

DIALOGUE. A conversation. Generally two types: Direct dialogue is a straightforward question/answer, while oblique dialogue veers off into an unexpected, and generally more interesting direction. The reason we love reading adventure stories is that they are perhaps half dialogue; dialogue is an essential technique for writing an effective scene. See *Writing Tip #7: Cinema*.

$E^2 = 0$. The concept that if you try to do everything squared (E^2), you wind up doing nothing (zero). In practical terms: don't cram too much into your article because the reader will get confused and fed up. See *Writing Tip #6: $E^2 = 0$ – Chop Fluff Like Michelangelo*.

ELEGANCE. *See* **MUSIC**.

EXPOSITORY LUMP. *See* **INFO DUMP**.

FIVE WS AND AN H. One of the basic tenets of journalism that recommends a news story should answer these questions: Who. What. Where. When. Why. How. See *Writing Tip #9: News*.

FRAME/FOCUS. Techniques to control your article or book by maintaining a single-mindedness to the main theme. The frame, according to Lee Gutkind, "represents a way of ordering or controlling a writer's narrative so that the elements ... are presented in an interesting and orderly fashion." Focus, he says, "is the overall theme, meaning, or intent of a nonfiction effort." Put another way, the frame is the story structure, the architecture, while focus is the recurring main idea and direction. See *Writing Tip #6: $E^2 = 0$ – Chop Fluff Like Michelangelo*.

HERO'S JOURNEY. Popularized by Joseph Campbell, the hero's journey reflects the archetypes and story arcs found in the classic myths of all cultures. Can be applied to an individual writer's journey. A hero's journey sometimes deals with big themes that resonate with readers.

The core of a hero's journey is the quest – the need or desire or obligation to do something specific in order to gain self-satisfaction/salvation/reward. During the quest the hero learns something about herself and often has to make an important choice. A quest is a strong way to structure a personal travel story – "I went to _____ looking for _____ and was surprised to find _____ which taught me _____ ."

HOOPTEDOODLE. A concept created by John Steinbeck; it describes a writer showing off writing skills that don't necessarily move the story. See *Writing Tip #6: E² = 0 – Chop Fluff Like Michelangelo.*

INFO DUMP. Irritating first cousin to **HOOPTEDOODLE,** *also see* **SHOW, DON'T TELL.** Throw-ing in a lot of information that the writer thinks the reader needs to know, often resulting in an indigestible lump. See *Writing Tip #6: E² = 0 – Chop Fluff Like Michelangelo.*

INTIMACY. Making contact with the reader by writing hotter. See *Writing Tip #1: You Have a Choice.*

"JUST SAY NO." *See* **NANCY REAGAN PRINCIPLE.**

LAW OF INVERSITY. The less bang-bang action that happens in a story, the better you have to write it. See *Finish It and Get It Published.*

LEAD. The opening of an article – generally a sentence or paragraph. The purpose of a lead is to hook the reader so she continues reading. Generally there are six types of leads you can use in a nonfiction article:

1. Ask a question

2. Anecdote/scene

3. Provocative statement

4. Dialogue

5. List

6. Current news, historical, celebrity or literary reference

See *Writing Tip #4: Start With a Bang.*

LIDGET. An invented word, "literary" + "widget"; a device to incorporate sometimes extraneous information (which otherwise might appear in a sidebar) into the body of a (usually longish) article. See *Writing Tip #6: E² = 0 – Chop Fluff Like Michelangelo*.

LIPOSUCTION. See **AX MURDER** and **MICHELANGELO'S SECRET**. An editing technique in which you scrape away the fat in a story. See *Writing Tip #6: E² = 0 – Chop Fluff Like Michelangelo*.

LITERATI INTERRUPTUS. See **SCHEHERAZADE SCENARIO**.

LITTLE RED RIDING HOOD STRATEGY. See **SCENE**. A mnemonic device that shows how important a scene is in a story, and how simple it can be. See *Writing Tip #2: Tell the Story*.

ME/YOU. The concept that, while it's fine to focus on yourself in the story, you should include information that is relevant and interesting to the reader. See *Writing Tip #10: Me/You*.

MICHELANGELO'S SECRET. Cutting away everything that doesn't move your story. See *Writing Tip #6: E² = 0 – Chop Fluff Like Michelangelo*.

MUSIC. Good writing has rhythm and elegance. See *Writing Tip #7: Cinema*.

NANCY REAGAN PRINCIPLE. The most important take-home message in this book. This is a mnemonic device based on the famous simplistic advice given by Nancy Reagan, wife of Ronald Reagan, as a solution to the United States drug problem. (When asked how the United States could solve its drug problem, she answered that people who are tempted by drugs should "Just Say No.") I use it as a way to remind writers that any article or book has to have a series of problems, challenges, disagreements, tensions, and frustrations, which can be described as Nancy Reagans. Without a Nancy Reagan (problem, conflict), there is no story. In general, the more, and the bigger the Nancy Reagans are, the more interesting the article. And bigger problems infer bigger stakes and more difficult decisions to be made. See *Writing Tip #3: The Nancy Reagan Principle – Conflict*.

NANCY REAGAN WORDS. These words force the writer to consider the opposing point of view and set up an inner tension in the article. The words: but, however, nevertheless, in spite of. See *Writing Tip #3: The Nancy Reagan Principle – Conflict*.

NUT PARAGRAPH. An often straightforward paragraph that summarizes the main point of an article. It often follows an anecdote lead. *See* **Tragedy/Disaster**. *See Writing Tip #4: Start With a Bang.*

POINT OF VIEW - POV. Observations made through a particular person's eyes, experiences, and voice. *See Writing Tip #10: Me/You.*

QUEST. *See* **HERO'S JOURNEY.**

QUESTION. The easiest way to create intimacy with the reader (or audience) is to ask a question. *See Writing Tip #5: The Easiest Way to Create Reader Intimacy?*

RULE OF THREE. *See* **TRIPLE WHAMMY.**

SCENE. The building block of all stories. Generally includes: characters, dialogue, problem/conflict, setting, movement in the story. *See Writing Tip #2: Tell the Story.*

SCHEHERAZADE SCENARIO. Based on *The Tale of 1001 Nights*, this refers to the technique of starting to tell a story early in the article but delaying giving the reader the conclusion until the end of the article. *See Writing Tip #2: Tell the Story.*

SHOW, DON'T TELL. Write action as a scene instead of as an **Info Dump**. Put another way – let the reader "see" what's going on, as if watching a film. *See Writing Tip #6: $E^2 = 0$ – Chop Fluff Like Michelangelo.*

SIDEBAR. A shortish piece of writing that accompanies a longer article; a sidebar provides additional (usually helpful) information. For example a travel story about lesser-known Roman ruins in Europe might include a sidebar about comfortable hotels near the sites mentioned in the main article. *See Writing Tip #9: News.*

STORY ARC. The structure in storytelling that keeps the reader turning the page. *See Writing Tip #7: Cinema.*

STORY OF ONE/STORY OF MANY. Relates to **Tragedy/Disaster**. The Story of One – an anecdote about an individual – is a useful device to get the reader's attention, after which you can introduce the bigger picture and its statistics as the Story of Many. The Story of One is generally hot, while the Story of Many, because it involves statistics, is colder and harder to comprehend because the numbers are so large and impersonal. For example: The story of 35-year-old Siti, wife of a fisherman and mother of two in Aceh, Sumatra, who was killed in the 2004 tsunami, is the Story of One that represents the 230,000 people – the Story of Many – who died in the event. See *Writing Tip #8: The Story of One.*

THREE-ACT STRUCTURE. A classic story structure for books, plays, and movies, generally comprised of the Setup, the Confrontation, and the Resolution. See *Writing Tip #7: Cinema.*

TRAGEDY/DISASTER. A tragedy happens to one person with a name, family, and pet beagle called Chester. Tragedy is when big trouble befalls one individual, also called the **Story of One**. A disaster affects a large number of people, called the **Story of Many**. It's more effective to lead with the focused individual tragedy than with the big picture disaster. See *Writing Tip #8: The Story of One.*

TRIPLE WHAMMY. The Rule of Three; the concept that readers are comfortable when examples and details are given in groups of three. See *Writing Tip #7: Cinema.*

VOICE. Usually used to describe a person's writing voice; generally as a writer's career develops a distinctive voice evolves, much like that of a composer or painter. See *Getting Started: The Power of Your Voice.*

Paul Spencer Sochaczewski has written *An Inordinate Fondness for Beetles*, *The Sultan and the Mermaid Queen*, the five-volume *Curious Encounters of the Human Kind* series, the eco-comic thriller *Redheads*, *Soul of the Tiger* (with Jeff McNeely), and other acclaimed books and some six hundred bylined articles in leading international publications. He has been invited to run his writing workshops in more than twenty countries, helping writers worldwide tell their personal stories.

www.ingramcontent.com/pod-product-compliance
Lightning Source LLC
Chambersburg PA
CBHW081652120626
46550CB00010B/2873